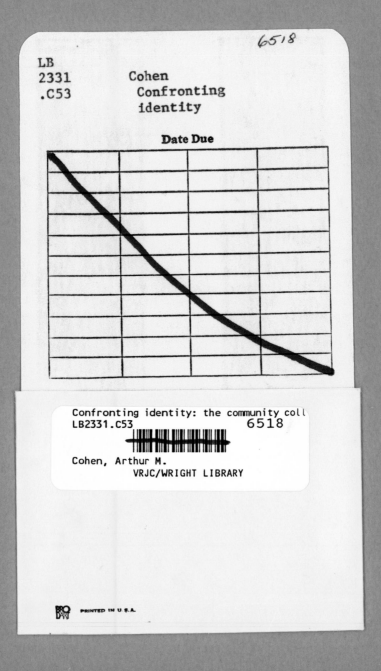

Confronting
Identity

Portions of this work were provided by the

EDUCATIONAL RESOURCES INFORMATION CENTER

ERIC Clearinghouse For Junior Colleges

UNIVERSITY OF CALIFORNIA, LOS ANGELES

The ERIC program is sponsored by the United States
Department of Health, Education, and Welfare,
Office of Education. The points of view expressed
here do not necessarily represent official Office of
Education position or policy.

Confronting Identity

The Community College Instructor

Arthur M. Cohen
Florence B. Brawer
University of California, Los Angeles

Prentice-Hall, Inc., Englewood Cliffs, New Jersey

ISBN: 0–13–167494–3
Library of Congress Catalog Card No.: 73–163401
Current printing (last digit):
10 9 8 7 6 5 4 3 2 1
Printed in the United States of America

Prentice-Hall International, Inc., London
Prentice-Hall of Australia, Pty. Ltd., Sydney
Prentice-Hall of Canada, Ltd., Toronto
Prentice-Hall of India Private Limited, New Delhi
Prentice-Hall of Japan, Inc., Tokyo

To the memory of two who taught
in their own special ways.

Harry Cohen   Henry Jacob Blum
1890–1971   *1891–1953*

Contents

Foreword

The era of student protest has taught us teachers something of how much we have relied on authoritarian structures and methods and on the submissiveness of students. This should remind us of an old but often neglected social–psychological principle: teachers and students, like doctors and patients, welfare workers and clients, parents and children, need each other. Each of these pairs constitutes a unity, a dynamic system in which actions to gratify the needs of one actor arouse and gratify some needs, and suppress other needs, of the other actor. The fate of the student, patient, client, or child depends on the kind of needs he satisfies in those responsible for his development or well-being. The psychiatric and clinical–psychological literature offers enough examples of the mutually harmful effects of some of these entanglements. There have been studies showing without doubt that back wards exist in mental hospitals, and that the blind are kept in a dependent state largely to satisfy the needs of care-givers for power and a sense of worth. To take it the other way 'round, sensitive psychotherapists have often reported that the patients they helped the most were the ones who helped them the most, that is, who aided self-discovery in an important way.

Does it not follow, then, that the development of students depends on the development of faculty? That faculty who would develop students will do best by taking actions that express and promote their own development? The authors of this book say "yes," and in organizing the evidence to support this major hypothesis and in showing its various implications, they make an important contribution toward opening up a neglected field of higher education.

Although "faculty development" is a familiar enough concept in the academic world, it has usually had reference to the upgrading of professors as representatives of their disciplines or specialties. If it were supposed that such "development" might improve teaching, it was on the assumption that undergraduate education consisted essentially in students learning the content of various subject areas. Almost nothing has heretofore been done, in research or in practice, about the development of the college teacher as a person. Indeed, in the extensive literature on teachers and teaching—most of which is fairly reviewed in this book—there is little to suggest that the teacher *is* a person, or is seen as such by the researcher or writer. Now at last we have a book that overcomes these glaring deficiencies.

Dr. Cohen and Dr. Brawer view the college teacher in the perspective of modern theory of personality development. This has provided a framework for their own significant researches as well as a basis for making sense of a wide range of other studies, most of which were narrowly focused. It is particularly gratifying to note that they use the term *identity*, which has been careening wildly through the educational literature in recent years, in a consistent and sophisticated way. They stick fairly closely to Erikson's original concept, and this serves them well. Since a stable sense of identity depends on performance in social roles and on the perceptions of others, the concept in the hands of these authors becomes the key to understanding the intimate interrelations of personal growth and professional growth. On the basis of this understanding they contribute a thoughtful and enlightening discussion of the crucial questions: what kind of professional should the community college teacher be? What kind of professional role best favors personal growth in teachers and students? And what kind is favored by professors who reach high levels of development?

The identity concept links the personal and the social; but Dr. Cohen and Dr. Brawer go further in their use of an integration of social theory and personality theory. This enables them to see how the teacher develops through interaction with various features of his social environment, most notably the students, role definitions and performances, the social structure of the community college. A particularly good theoretical idea is to speak of the identity of the college as well as that of the teacher. The authors stress the dependence of the former on the latter, but they do not neglect the mutuality of the relations between the two.

The fact that the community college is searching for identity presents a great opportunity for the advancement of developmental education. Since universities are organized with first attention to the production of knowledge and the training of professionals in the disciplines, and four-year colleges tend to follow the same pattern, it is difficult for the professor in these institutions to see himself as a teacher of students. Although he works hard at his teaching, he does not derive as much satisfaction from it as he should, his main trouble being that he has no suitable basis for gauging the effectiveness of his work. The way to evaluate teaching, as the present authors insist, is in terms of impact on students *and* on teachers. Truly significant impact will always have the form of developmental changes. It follows that a college which states its goals in developmental terms and guides its activities in accord with sound theory of development will have a basis for evaluating its educational programs. Community colleges, which as the authors say are still relatively open and flexible, still in search of a mission, can find identity and serve both their students and their teachers best by becoming true centers for developmental education.

What is to be done now? The authors offer many stimulating suggestions. Without neglecting the possibilities of structural change, they put the emphasis in the right place, which is on work with the community college faculty. They have, indeed, already rendered a service to the teachers by showing that they *can* change. The place for them to begin this process is with an examination of their own personal and professional purposes. This leads to self-awareness and, hence, to awareness of students. The teacher who reads this book will already have begun this rewarding activity.

Nevitt Sanford
The Wright Institute, Berkeley, California

Preface

This book is for the community college instructor who is making the transition from amateur to professional status—a transition that may be taking place in his first or his twenty-first year of teaching. The book concentrates on several psychological concepts, particularly "identity" and "maturity." To the beginning instructor who may well be thinking, "Never mind 'identity,' what do I do in class tomorrow?" we say, "Think beyond your very temporary groping for survival to a time when you will want to see yourself as a true professional person." In the long run, it really does not matter that one's lessons do not always exactly fill the allotted hour, that one's lectures do not always enthrall or one's discussions always strike sparks. What does matter are the overall effects on the students—effects that are not properly measured by one's feelings about the "goodness" of any single class or group of class meetings. In fact, if the beginning instructor heeds the message of this book—that his own identity and maturity are related to his tendency to judge himself by his effects—he will find his first days considerably less traumatic.

The book also has a message for the experienced instructor who long ago passed the first-term jitters but who still feels uneasy with his work. We hold that one hallmark of a mature, professional instructor is that he accepts responsibility for the effects of his efforts—that is, for the learning manifested by his students. This is certainly not the only distinguishing characteristic of the well-integrated person in the teaching profession, but it is the one on which we chose to structure this book.

Many studies of instructors at levels other than the community college have been cited. We point to such data on university professors and secondary school teachers not because we wish to draw comparisons between them and community college instructors, but simply because few studies of community college instructors have been made. Faced with a dearth of equivalents, we must fall back on analogues. Actually, although our book is addressed to the instructor in the two-year college, the concepts we discuss apply with equal validity to teachers in elementary and secondary schools, liberal arts colleges, universities—anywhere the teacher as "one who causes learning" may be found.

Several of the ideas treated here have been discussed previously in various publications of the ERIC Clearinghouse for Junior Colleges, particularly in the monographs entitled *Personality Characteristics of College and University Faculty: Implications for the Community College* (1968) and *Measuring Faculty Performance* (1969), and in the monograph *Focus on Learning: Preparing Teachers for the Two-Year College*, published in 1968 by the UCLA Junior College Leadership Program.

The entire manuscript was reviewed by several people. B. Lamar Johnson, Professor of Higher Education at UCLA, and John Lombardi, formerly Assistant Superintendent for Community Colleges, Los Angeles City School District, provided key critical comments, as did Leslie Purdy, teaching assistant in the UCLA Graduate School of Education. Charles Healy, Assistant Professor of Education at UCLA, reviewed the chapter on "Role." Our sincere appreciation to these valued colleagues.

The staff of the ERIC Clearinghouse for Junior Colleges provided much assistance. Ann Starkweather commented on an earlier version of the manuscript; she and Hazel Horn had the major responsibility for assembling the bibliography. Kay Carfagna and Katherine Gartin helped prepare the manuscript and Marcia Boyer was always ready to find a reference or correct a citation. Our thanks for their help.

Families have their own ways of contributing to long-term projects. Very much in our thoughts during the writing of this book were Barbara, William, Wendy, Andrew, and Nancy Cohen, and Sidney, Anne, and Michael Brawer.

Arthur M. Cohen
Florence B. Brawer
University of California, Los Angeles
February 1971

Introduction: A Question of Identity

The question of identity pertains both to people and to the institutions they create. Identity is the individual—person or agency. It underlies the beliefs "I am," "I exist." Without a clear sense of identity, a person or institution can have no sense of purpose. And without a sense of purpose, nothing can be considered relevant or esteemable. Identity is the unique experience of self with both continuity and sameness, a paradox of independence and dependence. The term *identity* is not used here in its literal sense of "absolute sameness," but as *awareness of self, of personality, and of individuality.*

Identity is a dynamic concept, a growing process, a moving forward simultaneously with an awareness of the past; it is never a fait accompli. Whether we think of identity in terms of an individual's own striving or whether we personify an institution by attributing "identity" to it, the process involves resynthesizing past experiences with those of the present and those yet to come. The roots are essential. So is the future. Identity is never given. It may be nurtured and aided but it is something each individual must attain for himself. Identity formation is typically considered to be a special function of adolescence—specifically, the transition from late adolescence to adulthood, when the person emerges as no longer someone's child but is recognized by others as a person in his own right. How-

1

ever, the process does not stop at post-adolescence; it continues throughout one's life.

Identity involves a drawing together, a crystallization of being. It allows the individual to preserve his sense of self "despite the vicissitudes of life that are yet to come" (Lidz 1968, p. 344). Thus, the process of formulating an independent identity encompasses both earlier stages of development and future processes, integrating all one's experiences into a holistic pattern.

Just as individuals strive for identity, social institutions attempt to attain a form of identity for themselves. Every hospital administrator wants his institution to be known as a helpful, efficient, friendly service agency. Every minister wants people to see his church as serving the needs of its congregation by providing a link to denominational traditions, succor to the needy, and a vision of ultimate values. But, although each institution has an ethos of its own, its real identity is inextricably interwoven with the people within it. A hospital may present a certain objective identity to the world at large, but the most important aspect of its identity is the way it is seen by its staff—doctors, nurses, technicians, administrators—and the patients it serves. A church's identity is also seen in terms of its members.

Similarly, schools maintain certain types of identity within the community at large. People who are proud of their neighborhood's good schools may be quick to cite them as one of the benefits of living in that neighborhood. Or they may abandon the city for the suburbs where "better schools" are supposedly to be found. In all cases, whether or not a person has children in the schools, he sees them as positive or negative elements in his community.

Here again, however, the institution's true identity is the way it is perceived by the people directly associated with it. The school cannot be understood as a functioning social force unless its people—faculty, staff, students, governing board members—are understood. Their perceptions, goals, needs, and values are the key to institutional identity. An individual's identity involves what he thinks of himself. A school's identity is what its people are. Individuals may have a strong sense of identity apart from a particular institution or organization but educational enterprises cannot have an identity apart from their people.

This book is about identity—the identity of the junior college and of its instructors, the people who play the key roles in institutional functioning. It covers a number of issues pertinent to identity formation, including images of the institution and its instructors, selection of appropriate roles, interactions between teacher and student, and evaluation of instructors. We see these and other issues as important not only to institutional and individual identity, but also as prerequisites for personal and professional maturity—a concept that we develop throughout the book. The term *maturity*, too, is used in a special way. It does not mean "age" or "ripeness" but *integrated functioning within a social context.*

This book, then, is not about education per se, but about people. It is addressed to—and talks about—the junior college instructor, viewing him as a person engaged in bringing about changes in other people. The book should be seen as a framework on which the instructor can hang his thoughts about his personal and professional situation. It should help him gain a sense of personal and professional integration, a way of assessing himself and his work that we see as a hallmark of the mature individual.

Two emphases are maintained throughout: the teacher as a person and the teacher as a practitioner in the discipline of instruction. We could give many reasons for emphasizing person and profession in a book addressed to college teachers. A major reason is that the instructor who better understands himself and his work can choose appropriate roles and can function with greater satisfaction, to the benefits of his students, his institution, and most important, himself. In addition, the process of junior college instruction is facilitated when all are aware of the various concomitants of the teacher's role: the individual can adopt the role for which he is best suited by temperament or training; the college can adopt the extrinsic evaluation scheme most likely to lead its instructors in the direction of its institutional goals; the university-based training program can develop models of individual and institutional functioning and help its students and the colleges in its area achieve professionalism in the teaching field. There is interaction among the three, but in every case, a perceptive view of the people and their professional situations is essential. Recognition of these elements is prerequisite to maturity for the person, the profession, and the institution.

Viewing the instructor as a practitioner in the discipline of instruction builds on what is known about instructional processes. The term *teaching* is used here primarily in its "success" sense; namely, *teaching as causing learning.* Teacher preparation programs, selection patterns, and evaluation schemes are all viewed as they tend to enhance—or detract from—student learning. In our view, student learning is the ultimate criterion for assessing the worth of any educational structure—particularly of the junior college, a self-styled "teaching institution."

Accordingly, studies of instructors, the teaching profession, the junior college, and particularly, instructional processes, are stressed. This emphasis is maintained in the belief that changed conceptualizations of teaching and of the teacher's role can help instructors to better understand themselves and the way they function within their profession. Personality studies, teacher typologies, and role differentiations all relate to the instructor as a person. Preparation and selection schemes, ratings of instructors, and interactions with students are extrinsics that bear on the instructor's role. These themes are maintained throughout, intertwining because it is impossible to separate the person of the instructor from the roles he plays and the tasks he performs.

Many particularized definitions and emphases—hence biases—are included in this book. We speak of the teaching role as it is deeply felt by the serious instructor, not as it is superficially perceived by the lay person or the casual school employee. We believe that if the two-year college is to succeed with the many difficult educational tasks it has taken on, it must have a professional, mature, self-aware faculty. As a *professional faculty* the group would operate autonomously, police its ranks, and set its own standards for employment. A *mature faculty* is one that is responsible for its actions and judges itself by its effects on its students' learning. As a *self-aware individual*, each instructor continually examines his own motives and modes of functioning. These are the premises on which the book is based.

What can we say about the teacher as person? We might relate anecdotes, record personal interviews, or review journals. But we choose to describe the instructor's role and personality patterns from the researcher's point of view because we feel that findings of educational and psychological studies have much to say to the instructor. The mature junior college instructor should be aware of studies about people and his profession because they can enhance his awareness of himself as a member of a professional community. Such awareness can also help him recognize that he does not work in isolation from the main currents of thought in the study of people and the instructional process. Also, the instructor deserves more than "Here's-the-way-we-do-it-at-our-place" or "So-you-want-to-be-a-teacher" literature frequently addressed to him. The profession will not be built by talking down to the people within it.

This book, then, is addressed to the instructor, but it is not a compilation of "teaching tips." Nowhere do we present "how to do it"—how to select audiovisual aids, how to use appropriate chalkboard technique, and the like. References to teaching methodologies do appear, but only peripherally and as they relate to the role of the person and the teaching profession. Other books provide information about the institutions and instructional practices in general. A book on the junior college and one on how to teach would complement—not compete with—this work.

Because this is a book about people, not about institutions, we do not address ourselves to the differences among the various types of institutions that fall within the category "junior college." Instead, we merge them all, including the publicly supported colleges—whether local, district, university branch, or state controlled—and the private institutions, both church-related and independent. We use the terms *junior, community*, and *two-year* interchangeably as qualifiers for these colleges. Nor do we differentiate among "academic," "vocational," and "remedial" instructors. The "junior college instructor" is someone who holds a position as faculty member in any of these types of institutions.

We feel that this book will aid each instructor in understanding present practices and provide him with clues to institutional values. He will be able to compare himself with others and to relate his own mode of approach to categories into which teachers may be classified—qualities that can further his efforts to contribute to the profession, to focus on the tasks of instruction, and to change institutional values in the direction of presumed institutional purpose. The result will be a faculty that focuses on student learning, one that enhances the effects—hence the worth—of the institution itself. And, above all, the instructor who accepts these premises, understanding the relationships between himself, his profession, and his institution, will become a mature, well-integrated, self-satisfied professional being.

This book is arranged in six sections. Part one reviews what we know about the junior college and the people within it, sketching person and institution in broad terms. Part two deals with the personality of the instructor, categorizing his traits and reviewing classification schemes that place him into typologies according to his mode of functioning within the profession. Part three relates the instructor as a person to the tasks of instruction. It discusses the teacher's work and postulates three original categories of instructional functioning. Part four introduces the students, the people with whom the instructor interacts, discussing not only his influence on them but also the way they affect his own orientations to— and satisfaction with—his work. Part five examines some of the other extrinsic influences on the instructor. Existing and projected preparation programs, patterns of professional associations, and teacher certification procedures are all seen as influences on the instructor's competence in, and awareness of, the modes of professional functioning. Part six discusses teacher evaluation as it relates to the purposes of the junior college, the roles played by the instructor, and the best ways of enhancing both. It proposes changed patterns of instructional evaluation.

It is nothing new to say that the instructor's effects on his students relate to the kind of person he is or that the instructor's personality in large measure determines what type of professional person he will become. Not only textbooks but entire teacher preparation programs have been constructed on that theme. However, the concepts surrounding an examination of the structor as person have rarely been extended into higher education. College teaching is most often described as an art form, although in some cases its "principal components" are discussed. But studies taking holistic views of the interactions between instructors, their students, and their institutions are rare.

If we occasionally seem harsh toward the colleges and the people within them, it is because we appreciate the many frustrations, problems, and conflicts that exist for all involved in the academic professions. We could have painted a bright picture by implying that all the people within community colleges are dedicated to aiding those institutions in fulfilling their glorious mission. However, it would serve no good purpose to gloss over the realities. No college is exclusively the home of dedicated students and scholars. The community college has assumed the particularly difficult task of mass education. We feel that by pointing out the negative and by presenting some of the pitfalls, we are encouraging the instructor to become aware of institutional realities so that he will be in a better position to approach his task with a mature, professional outlook.

Our intent is to build toward personal, professional, and institutional identity and maturity by stressing awareness of self and of the effects of one's efforts. The instructor who wants to be judged on the basis of his products and his effects is enhancing his own growth along with that of his students and his college. The two-year college needs this type of maturity.

part one

Who Am I?

Born at the turn of the century and now a vociferous adolescent among American educational structures, the two-year college is still seeking its own sense of identity. It has taken on numerous tasks of community education, offering transfer, vocational, technical, adult, and developmental education as well as guidance and community services. But a plethora of functions cannot be equated with a sense of being. A superficial perception of the college as a place where everyone has an opportunity to acquire an education is not a sufficient condition for identity.

Why does the junior college lack self-awareness? Because the institution has grown at such a rapid pace? Because it has been staffed in such a hurry? Because it has assumed the image and built on the structures of other educational levels? That the search for identity is not yet successful has frequently been alluded to and, nearly as often, lamented. But no one can determine the reasons for the lack.

We believe that if the junior college is to live in a truly viable sense, it must have a faculty that knows its own goals and directions. It needs a focus, and this focus must be closely related to the people who comprise its student population and its constituent community. Such a professional outlook is essential.

It's a two-way street. The institution must be fully aware of all its responsibilities to students, faculty, administration, community. Obversely, the people who staff the institution must have a sense of direction; they must be able to identify themselves as human beings and to define their position in terms of the educational system. This section—indeed, much of this book—deals with the identity of the people who give identity to the institution through their sense of professional being.

What does the quest for identity mean to the faculty in the community college? If identity for the college is to be found in the people who teach in it, how do these people, in turn, achieve their own sense of identity? While an institution can achieve identification through its physical structures and the numbers of people moving in and out of it, as well as through other extraneous measures, true identity cannot be achieved apart from the individuals who operate in the institution. Just as the students must be understood so that institutions can be shaped to serve them, the staff must also be understood. For the staff—especially the faculty—*are* the institution. If the college has being, identity, ethos, independent existence—then it must be seen in terms of the people who operate in it, contribute to it, draw satisfaction from it, and who, consequently, become the institution itself.

In this section, we focus on the twin themes of the instructor as an individual and the institution as a functioning entity. Chapter 1 is concerned with the instructor as person. Chapter 2 deals with the identity of the institution. Both chapters point up the basic question, "Who am I?"

The Person

Viewed from a perspective of time, the familiar adage, "The proper study of mankind is man," assumes diverse dimensions. Man's individuality was known but not substantiated in the 1600s when Pope paraphrased what Socrates had recognized long before. Until the late nineteenth and early twentieth centuries, however, few people were seriously concerned with the systematic study of individual characteristics and idiosyncratic behavior. The Cattells, Freuds, and Galtons were few in number, and consequently man's understanding of man was left to a limited number of curious students of human behavior.

In recent decades, the situation has almost reversed itself. People are concerned with themselves. They study their own motives, needs, desires, values, and behavior. The psychology of personality and the inevitable relationships between personal development and cognitive growth are now of widespread interest. Rather than being mere curiosities to a selected few looking out from laboratory or classroom perspectives—or from the legendary ivory towers—questions of human functioning lead to considerable soul-searching on the part of most individuals. The pursuit of self-understanding, of fairly recent origin, has become an accepted phenomenon.

This open concern with self has led to altered lines of inquiry. Whereas in earlier times people were viewed in terms of separate social, educational, or occupational dimensions, today they are seen as individuals comprised of many facets that all, more or less happily, mesh together. The person is an interesting entity for study. He is—ergo, it is important to understand him.

IDENTITY AND MATURITY

This book is concerned with the identity—the sense of awareness of self—of the junior college instructor. Having achieved a sense of certainty about his "Who-am-I-ness," he may already be launched into that period of development variously called actualization, individualization, becoming —terms used by Maslow, Jung, and Rogers respectively to describe what we call the mature human being. The mature instructor, in his search for identity, has successfully merged an awareness of self with a realistic relationship to his environment and to the demands posed by significant others in his academic-social-cultural milieu.

What does the mature instructor look like? How does he get that way? Answers to these questions are found throughout this book. The person with a strong ego, a firm sense of self, is able to cope with and to integrate both the intrinsic and extrinsic forces pressing upon him. He can accept the bureaucracy, the petty regulations, and the imprecise goals of the organizations; the different students; and the recurrent changes within his field, and still maintain a clear, consistent sense of his direction. The ability to withstand what are sometimes extremely demanding forces that tend to conflict with one's internal value system suggests a high level of ego development.

From the observer's point of view, maturity is indicated by the desire of an individual, of a profession, or of an institution to be judged on the basis of its products and effects. In the case of the college instructor, this means an integration of consciousness about self with a sense of professionalism. The truly mature person is open to his own experiences and free enough to focus on his profession. He can turn from a preoccupation with self to a concern for others; he views himself as effectual to the extent that he causes change in his students. This is not altruism in the usual sense; rather it is the ideal of man as one whose concern with self inevitably extends to others.

Identity is one of the many terms we use to describe the qualities of self-awareness, consciousness, sense of being—terms that we use interchangeably. It is an elusive quality, an intangible, yet very real dimension, whether its possessor is a person, a group of people, or a social institution. An individual's identity is interwoven with his perceptions of his role and with the different functions he performs. In fact, it is unlikely that one's self-identity can be separated from the identity achieved through one's role. Hence, for the individual, an integrated sense of identity is prerequisite to professional maturity.

The identity of the junior college depends on its people—students, administrators, counselors, members of the community in which it is located, and especially the faculty. Its identity is a conglomerate of the personalities associated with it. As Reynolds says, "... the self-image existing in any junior college is, in reality, the aggregate of the value systems of the three groups of personnel"—students, faculty, administrators (1969, p. 148). And Park's "institutional personality" (1971) relates to the same phenomenon. Before an institution can be called "mature," the people within it must know what it is about and the extent to which it is accomplishing its aims.

The college affects its people. Its identity both influences and reflects what the students become. It affects college administrators—their stature, outlook, and the way they serve their varied constituencies. But mostly, because it concerns the faculty in an institution that has no other valid reason for being except to teach, the faculty in fact *becomes* the institution. What they are is what the institution is; their collective goals are the institution's goals. The instructors are the key to institutional identity. Who they are, what they think, and the way they act make the college. Without instructors, the structure remains an empty shell of stones, brick, mortar, and statements of institutional philosophy tucked away in the pages of unread catalogues. But it has no viability.

There have been many attempts to study people who operate in educational institutions; however, individuals involved with schools are rarely considered as singular personalities. More often they are viewed as members of mass groups in impersonal organizations. Ideally, people must see themselves, and be seen by others, as individuals who function in a special kind of world but who also live in the much larger context of the total society.

The teacher does not function in isolation, dissociated from students, colleagues, and the educational milieu. He is tied to his own hierarchies of values and to the attitudes stemming from these values. He is a product of his personal and collective experiences. But he also interacts with the students he teaches, with his faculty colleagues, and with the organization with which he is affiliated. He may be his own man, autonomous, powerful, certain of himself and of his directions, but if he is functioning well, he cannot operate apart from either environmental or interpersonal forces. Thus, the teacher as person must be considered a unique and complex entity, tied to others in equally complex ways.

Our approach is holistic and phenomenological. We view people as integrated masses of diverse characteristics, traits, and functions. We attempt to examine junior college instructors from their own points of reference—in other words, to jump into their skins and to look at the world from their unique perspectives. Perhaps one can never really get into the framework of another person, but it is important that we try. The awareness of that difficulty and of different ways of approaching life's experiences may in itself provide us with insight.

There are distinct limitations in attempting to portray fully and accurately others whose experiences vary considerably, whose ways of looking at the world not only differ from, but may actually oppose, our own. However, our intent is to stimulate the junior college instructor to be open to his own experiences. When he has defined his own life style and is aware of his individual identity, he can empathize with his students and peers. He is then not only a conscious person but a mature professional.

THE JUNIOR COLLEGE INSTRUCTOR

What is the present status of the junior college and the people within it? We contend that the identity of the junior college is inchoate. Its instructors and, indeed, the teaching profession as a whole, have not yet attained professional maturity. This shortcoming is revealed in the lack of distinct identification, the ambiguity of direction, and the poorly articulated goals manifested by the people and their institutions. Over and over, whenever a policy decision must be made, one hears variations on the theme, "Just what is this place supposed to be doing? What is our real purpose?" These questions can reflect a healthy search or they can indicate a groping for identity. In either case they bespeak an incompletely developed sense of self.

Institutional and individual identity are inextricably linked. Just as the institution needs purpose, the instructor must know his own motives and goals. However, the junior college instructor, operating somewhere between the secondary school teacher and the university professor, is in a particularly ambivalent position. His uncertain professional stance both reflects and is reflected in a lack of clear-cut direction. He stands uneasily between two levels of education and has yet to carve out a defined place for himself.

One sign of immaturity is that so many junior college instructors attempt to identify with professors in higher education. Rather than seeking to create a unique niche for themselves and their own institutions, they prefer to see themselves as "college professors." In fact, nearly half the instructors queried in a national survey readily admitted that they would really rather teach in a four-year college or university (Cross 1969). Although where the junior college system is well established this figure drops (only 25 percent of the faculty in three California junior colleges gave this response [Park 1971], the university faculty continues to afford the reference group for many junior college people. The university—or more accurately, the junior college instructor's perception of it—still has a golden aura.

In some ways, this identification is appropriate. The increase of university-type academic senates in community colleges demonstrates the instructor's increasing voice in institutional operations. Research is becoming a more prominent factor in his life because, although he is not required to conduct investigations or to publish on his own, the junior college teacher is increasingly expected to participate in institutional studies. Faculty ranking systems patterned on those of the university are becoming more and more widespread. The severe reduction (in some states, the complete elimination) of credential requirements ties him even more closely to the university and four-year college than to the secondary school. These are some of the changes that strengthen the image of the instructor as college professor rather than as school teacher.

But no matter how many aspects of the university are discernible in the status and functioning of the junior college instructor, he must still be his own person. The nature of his responsibility is different for several reasons, all of which relate to the two-year college's commitment to teaching. Although the defined tasks of the university faculty member include teaching, that act is actually subordinate to several of his other functions. The main purpose of the junior college instructor, on the other hand, is to teach. The university professor is concerned with a narrow disciplinary range, a specific segment of an area of knowledge. The junior college teacher, however, must be committed both to a broad field of teaching and to a specialization in instruction. In the university, research is ostensibly for the purpose of gaining new knowledge. Junior college research, whether conducted by instructors or by others, is usually geared toward seeking better ways to help students learn. First and last, the junior college purports to be a teaching institution—student personnel and community service proponents notwithstanding. For the junior college instructor, then, the process of instruction is crucial to identity formation.

The individual searches for identity in many ways. He may compare his own behavior, appearance, and directions with peers; seek self-knowledge vicariously through literature; and otherwise attempt to learn more about himself. Or, refusing to undertake such introspection, he may choose to adopt a group identity, subscribing to the mores and ethos of a subculture that he hopes will indirectly provide him with a sense—albeit, an incomplete sense—of his own being.

One of the approaches to understanding self—and thus establishing one's identity—is through the eyes of others. How do different individuals typically view others? How are people in specialized occupational groups seen? How are teachers perceived and how do these perceptions relate to the teacher as a person? Postman and Weingartner wisely note that "Honest self-examination is seen as being essential as a basis for change" (1969, pp. 205–6). An understanding of others and an awareness of the ways people are perceived eventually lead the individual to discover that although he is a unique person, he also has many characteristics and problems in common with others. Knowledge of the ways people have been perceived can enhance the person's awareness of self; hence our emphasis on personality.

Information about the institution and the people within it is crucial to the instructor's identity formation. However, little is known about the junior college teacher, either as human being or as professional person. Certain gross data are available. In 1969–70, nearly 100,000 people were teaching in two-year colleges. Few (only 7 percent) had doctoral degrees; most (69 percent) had master's. Pay scales ranged widely, with the median for all ranks standing at just over $8,000 in private and nearly $11,000 in public institutions. Salaries were somewhat higher than in public schools and lower than in universities when the higher-paid professorships were averaged in (although there was considerable overlap). These instructors prepared courses, met classes, consulted with students, assigned marks, sat on committees—in short, did what instructors at all levels of education typically do.

Little more is known about the junior college instructor's professional activities. He is called on to teach many courses similar to those in the lower division of the university. He meets classes for 12 to 15 hours a week, serves on college committees, selects instructional materials, advises students, and engages in other activities that fall within the commonly held definition of "teaching." He is expected to be innovative, that is, to try various media and approaches to instruction. He must teach many students who have been classified as remedial, because the junior college is enrolling ever-increasing numbers of non-college level students. He must reconcile himself to a large drop-out rate that may either have a negative impact on his morale or lead him into questionable rationalizations. ("Sorry, fellow. You're just not college material.") He must handle large numbers of students, frequently meeting 150 to 200 per week, and he may feel as though he is being buried under a blizzard of paper work. He must also realize that the community itself keeps close watch on his manners and mores.

Beyond such general information, what do we know about the instructors themselves? Some studies of junior college faculty have been conducted; however, most deal with rather singular variables that are limited in their scope and in their implications. Hendrix (1964), for example, found that institutional policies regarding rank, tenure, and evaluation were related to such diverse—and possibly irrelevant—faculty life-record data as employment status, father's and mother's education, father's birthplace, varsity athletics, and debate participation. Brawer (1968) reviewed the literature on personality characteristics of college and university faculty members, relating it to junior college instructors. Other studies have focused on the characteristics of people in junior college teacher preparation programs (Cohen and Brawer 1968). Many publications of agencies such as the ERIC Clearinghouse for Junior Colleges and the American Association of Junior Colleges are concerned with patterns of faculty orientation (Kelly and Connolly 1970), the evaluation of instructors (Cohen and Brawer 1969), credentialing (American Association of Junior Colleges 1966), and related issues. Other particularized studies are cited throughout this book, and even though many of them deal with the instructor as functionary rather than as person, they are useful.

One of the most penetrating studies of the professional life of junior college faculty members was conducted by Garrison (1967), who visited instructors throughout the country. His study focused on their work, professional requirements, division and department relationships, professional affiliations, and matters related to guidance. Each instructor was asked such open-ended questions as, "Are you making junior college teaching a permanent thing?" "To what extent and in what way should faculty members counsel students?"

Responses to this line of inquiry suggested that the aims of the institutions in which junior college faculty members serve are so varied that the traditional criteria applied to college teachers are neither applicable nor accurate. The whole field of post–high school education has been expanding and changing so rapidly in the past few decades that previous academic customs and attitudes do not necessarily relate to, and indeed, are sometimes wholly irrelevant to, the junior college. Garrison's own impressions on this point were "that the junior college teacher is—or may be becoming—a new breed of instructor in higher education" (1967, p. 15). He saw teachers in the junior college as student-centered rather than subject-centered, as sincerely concerned with the problems of teaching students who represent an extraordinary range of abilities and motivations, and as attempting to serve their constituents through attention to the individual.

Other information has been gathered more recently. An in-depth study of faculty members in one geographical region that appears to have broad implications has been coordinated by staff members of the ERIC Clearinghouse for Junior Colleges (Brawer 1970, 1971; Park 1971). A group of reports about the career patterns of junior college instructors throughout the country is presently being compiled (M. F. Kelly 1971). And Medsker has updated his earlier study of junior college faculty members by collecting data on nearly 4,000 instructors in 57 colleges (Cross 1969).

Research studies and interpretations are the raw material on which the instructor can build his own set of perceptions. But can the instructor use such information to understand himself better? Can he use these data to bridge the gap between himself as an individual and the people with whom he interacts? Can he establish some degree of identity by studying reports about people in similar situations and professions? The answers to these questions must come from the individual himself.

The quest is not easy. It would be convenient if the instructor could sit back, read a few tips on teaching, accept or reject them as fit his fancy, pick up his textbooks, and go out and do a truly professional job. However, if teaching is ever to become a profession, serving those it purports to serve and satisfying the people within it, more is demanded of the instructor. A high degree of consciousness, awareness, and maturity is essential. No one can simply give it to the individual, nor can he gain it superficially. He must reconcile the tasks, learn the tools of the trade, and integrate them with his own personality. The job is not a weekend bagatelle. It demands constant effort and considerable thought and personal development.

2

The Institution

The instructor who would achieve personal and professional maturity must know something about the institution in which he works—its history, goals, apparent functions. He must also have a clear-cut picture of the profession to which he is committed. Finally, and perhaps foremost, he must know himself. This suggests a trilogy—person, institution, profession. Each possesses some degree of independence and autonomy. Each is dependent on the whole.

EDUCATION BEYOND THE TWELFTH YEAR

The two-year college can be understood only in the total context of post-secondary education in America. Arriving late (the earliest still-functioning junior colleges were founded at the beginning of this century) and growing rapidly, these institutions have yet to attain a distinct identity or a mature sense of purpose. They adopt new functions regularly; shift focus, direction, and intent sporadically. This statement, we hasten to add, is not necessarily disparaging. It simply describes the growing, oscillating institution that is the junior college, collectively and singly.

From the beginning, the American people have had an unquestioning faith in the value of education. Even though their faith wavers during times of stress—for example, during the student unrest of the late 1960s—the general trend in this country has always been in the direction of more and more formal schooling. The phrase "lifelong learning" adorns the masthead of university extension centers, adult education institutes, and a variety of other educational structures that dot the landscape. Young people are exhorted to "stay in school." Society increasingly closes off alternative settings where the individual may, with its approval, spend his time. This belief in Education with a capital "E" shows no sign of abating.

17

In the post–World War II era, the trend toward increased years of formal schooling moved great numbers of students past twelfth grade and into post-secondary institutions. Talk of "universal higher education" became common. In 1947, the President's Commission on Higher Education recommended that post-secondary instruction be made available to all individuals who could profit from such exposure. Ten years later, the Educational Policies Commission of the National Education Association echoed the Commission's recommendation. And in the 1960s, tangible evidence of the social response to those recommendations was demonstrated by the burgeoning of publicly supported colleges and universities.

Ubiquitous higher education is fed from many springs. More than 30 years ago, Sproul (1938) noted the growing tendency to accept the premise that every individual might profit by education and that the ultimate benefit to the state would far exceed the cost. The public was asked to support educational structures that would ostensibly provide vocational training, offer instruction in citizenship and basic skills, and allow young people a place to develop during a period of prolonged adolescence. It is not a great overstatement to say that by the 1960s a young person who had not gone to college began to be viewed as somewhat of a pariah.

The purposes of extended schooling were diffuse and indistinct. Although the comprehensive high school had evolved from its original function as a college preparatory institution into a vocational training and "education for citizenship" structure, the combination of a firm belief in the value of schooling and a lack of alternatives for youth mandated the creation of broadened opportunities for higher education. Actually, the philosophy that each individual should have the opportunity to develop to his society's ultimate benefit had become apparent with the founding of the land-grant colleges in the latter third of the nineteenth century. Its origins might even be traced to Jefferson's discourses in favor of founding the University of Virginia. Regardless of whether one believes that there are few occupational opportunities for the non–college trained youth or whether one takes a more positivistic view of the distinct value of higher education as a contributor to, or maximizer of, personal and social well-being, it is apparent that higher education has become a deeply ingrained American institution.

It is easy to document the scope of higher education in terms of numbers of institutions and of students, comprehensiveness of programs, expenditure of funds, and similar quantitative measures. More difficult, however, is the attempt to determine its purposes and effects. Various national associations and commissions, state agencies, and inter- and intramural committees frequently publish statements of higher education's purposes.

Beyond the traditional functions of transmitting the cultural heritage, training for an enlightened life, and preparing research scholars, these purposes include education for international understanding and for the administration of public affairs, the realization of individual potential and the enhancement of social mobility, and the preparation of workers for a technological or post-industrial society. These views reflect the belief that individuals and the social order are enhanced by post-secondary schooling of all types. Incidentally, they also demand from the institutions more than they can ever possibly deliver.

Higher education grows ever more inclusive. Professional schools fall within its framework and, as each occupation drives for status as a profession, college training for initiates becomes a requisite. Accordingly, in the twentieth century, the colleges have added journalism, business administration, nursing, and computer technology just as in the latter part of the nineteenth century they expanded to include agriculture, architecture, and various social services in their curricula. Occupational or professional training has intruded on higher education so much that most young people come to college with the intent of learning "to do something" or "to become somebody." The older functions—transmitter of the culture and medium of social class mores—have been all but squeezed out, much to the despair of the genteel professors and the alumni. The drive toward training members of a professional–vocational community is the most significant development in institutional purpose of the past generation.

Higher education has also been marked by the mental measurements emphasis of the post–World War I era. The attempt to categorize students and to sort them into programs or curricula presumed commensurate with their abilities, tendencies, and aspirations has become an institutional purpose. College admissions officers and intramural counselors assiduously categorize students, ostensibly for the purpose of better understanding human functioning but actually in order to enhance their predictions for student success within the institution or the profession for which they are being trained. By sorting, categorizing, and designating which students are able to do "college level" work; by assigning grades, granting degrees, and awarding honors, the college transmits to the larger community its assessment of each individual's value.

Colleges and universities are heavily involved in services to their local communities and to state and federal agencies. These services may take the form of research or they may be direct consulting activities performed by individual members of the institution. Formal agencies such as agricultural and engineering experiment stations conduct much of this public service; business and social research institutes engage in other activities that enhance local or national business and consumer industries. Also within the rubric of community services are the cultural activities brought to a region by a college or university cultural program, activities that might otherwise be unknown in the area. Whether community service assumes the form of extension courses for local residents or of professors who take leave to serve in the national government, it constitutes an ever-growing portion of college activities.

In the century following the American university's acceptance of the research function, the drive for new knowledge has, in some instances, become an institutional purpose of such magnitude that it has overshadowed student development activities. In fact, the view of the university as a bureaucratic, depersonalized research institute gave rise to much of the student unrest that began in the mid-1960s.

"General education," or the enhancement of individual development, is a thread that runs through all college and university programs and functions. Without students, the university would quickly become something else—a research institute or a public service agency. Yet general education is itself much maligned. Apologists for the colleges' professional schools insist that one's personal development depends on his attainment of marketable skills. Those who speak for the research function suggest similarly that an apprenticeship to a research scholar is the most effective route to individual growth. And the proponents of general education argue that personal growth is probably affected more by one's student peers than by anything the institution does overtly (Jacob 1957; Newcomb 1962).

Even though the actual effects of the institution may be difficult to discern, general education is recognized as a major institutional function, if only because in the latter half of the twentieth century, the college is one of the few places where young people congregate. Therefore, if they are to grow and develop and learn from each other, they are more likely to do so on a college campus. Dunham sees the students engaged in "a revolt against professionalism divorced from the realities of life as students see them," and concludes, "At no time in our history has there been a greater need for a general education movement that has relevance for the hordes of young people pouring into our colleges" (1969, p. 163). Sanford (1962, 1967, 1968) builds a strong case for developing the "whole individual," arguing that the so-called cognitive functions cannot be separated from the affective functions and that educational institutions must encourage total individual growth. He alludes to a process that, if it achieves its purpose, must inevitably be tied to identity formation. As adolescents and young adults attempt to establish their identities in ever more diverse (and frequently, socially disapproved) ways, colleges and universities must direct themselves to these total development programs. That is the general setting of higher education today.

THE TWO-YEAR COLLEGE

The same phenomena that enhanced the development of four-year institutions—the demands for post-secondary education for greater numbers and increasingly diverse groups of young people, and broadened institutional purposes in general—in the twentieth century spawned what is frequently called a junior college "movement." Beginning as private finishing schools, expanded public high schools, university branches, or new institutions organized under state plans, the junior colleges expanded in numbers and in size so that by 1970 they enrolled 2,400,000 students.

Evolving from their beginning as post-secondary schools, many junior colleges have become comprehensive community institutions that offer diverse occupational, lower division college, and community service programs. The community junior college—the name applied to the publicly controlled and supported institution—is in the forefront of the move toward expanded educational opportunity. The steady push for mass public education—especially for the young person from the family that, in an earlier era, would have been considered "non-college-going"—is a major and continuing force for junior college development.

But although the two-year college has resulted from the same forces that stimulated expanded scope and diversity in the universities, certain differences between the two institutions are apparent. The curricula of both organizations may be comprehensive, but the junior college* rarely pursues specialties to the extent that is typical of senior institutions. Also, its treatment of subject matter is not as intensive as that pursued in a university—particularly one that includes a graduate division.

The two-year college prides itself on being community-centered, adapting its offerings to the changing needs of the area in which it is located. Local citizens are frequently involved in planning and developing curricula—especially trades programs—and community advisory boards influence junior college programs to a much greater extent than they do programs offered in the university. Although in the 1960s universities came under attack for their selective admissions criteria, the community colleges suffered less from these criticisms because they were more likely to be "open-door colleges" admitting all high school graduates and, frequently, students who had not graduated from high school but who might be presumed to profit from the junior college experience. Other differences might be mentioned, but in most cases, the types of curricula offered, the extent of local control, and the non-selective admissions policies are the hallmarks that differentiate the two-year college from its four-year counterpart.

*We use the terms *junior college, community college,* and *two-year college* interchangeably throughout this book.

The heterogeneity of purposes, students, programs, and personnel is reflected in the many different junior college institutional structures. Junior colleges are organized as segments of public school districts, as single-campus colleges, or as multi-campus colleges within independent districts. Some are privately supported, while others operate as two-year branch campuses of universities. As these institutions move toward full partnership in the higher education enterprise, the publicly supported institution coordinated at the state level becomes increasingly common. The phenomenon of a junior college organized as a "tacked on" portion of a school district or as a private liberal arts college becomes rare.

What Is It?

For the institution as well as the person, identity cannot be built on comparisons alone. Phenomenal growth and a variety of functions have marked the development of the community college, now the most common form of two-year institution. In terms of sheer numbers, it has grown with unprecedented speed. In terms of general development, it has evolved in a variety of ways unparalleled by any previous American educational enterprise. Other forms of education have provided some direction but because of the unique tasks assumed by this structure, it has had no set patterns on which to build.

For many years, few people bothered to ask the "why" of this new structure; it was simply there. Now, decades later, this branch of education is coming under close scrutiny. Seeking independence and recognition, it is sincerely attempting to attain its own identity (its advocates realizing suddenly, perhaps, that mere growth in size and numbers is hardly justification for existence). It is gradually but steadily becoming aware that it must have a reason for existence and that its goals need to be defined. As Cohen notes,

> Despite its size, growth rate, and multiplicity of functions, the junior college has not yet succeeded in gaining a position as a genuinely respected force in American education. A sense of self is lacking, an unease reflected in the defensive character of much of the writing by leaders in the field. . . . Can the movement achieve direction, focus, emphasis, and withal the identity so long desired but so futilely sought? (1969, p. xvii)

There have been some tentative attempts to define the junior college in terms of its multifarious functions; for example, Johnson (1960), Blocker et al. (1965). The two-year college is called an open-door institution when it welcomes all high school graduates and individuals over 18, whether or not they have high school diplomas. It is characterized as a melting pot for the inner city and as a path to higher status for vast numbers of otherwise "socially deprived" students. It is also called "democracy's college," "opportunity college," and the "last chance" institution—all reflections of the American dream of unlimited access. Gleazer (1968) suggests that in many cases the community college symbolizes what the community wants to become. And every community wants to be known as an area of boundless opportunity for success.

This type of nomenclature is adequate only to a point. It serves to *identify* the institution, but because it fails to confront certain basic issues of institutional existence, it does not afford it an *identity*. Institutional amorphism is exposed when college purposes and modes of functioning are examined together. Some of these patterns seem tied to a mythological ideology. Others appear to serve the function of wish fulfillment, the realization of dreams of status or stature. Whatever these patterns may be, however, they must be viewed in terms of both the institution and the people within it. The directions discussed here are but a few of the many that may be evoked.

In those states where master plans for higher education have been developed (for example, California, Illinois), respective functions are specified for two-year, four-year, and graduate institutions. The implication is that the public junior college will do the preliminary sorting and screening of students, allowing all young people in the state to enroll but passing on to the university only those who have demonstrated competence in "college level" studies. Often spelled out in the plans is the expectation that many of the other students will be shunted into occupational curricula—a form of segregation against which numerous educational theorists have spoken, but one that is increasingly seen as a "proper" junior college function.

That development bespeaks further evolution of its institutional role. Mayhew has predicted that by 1980 the two-year colleges will not be the source of lower-division education for those who receive bachelor's degrees, but will provide general and vocational education for those who do not. Jencks and Riesman state that this has already occurred, noting that the community colleges' "failure to produce a significant increase in the overall proportions earning B.A.'s" suggests that although "a cheap and academically accessible path to a B.A." is available, few students take that route (1968, p. 490).

Is the institution to achieve identity as a non-college college?

Recently there have been some serious efforts to help the junior college build an objective reality on a teaching–learning model. Implementation of the teaching–learning paradigm demands adherence to a strict definition of *teaching* as *causing learning*. Unless learning—changed capability for, or tendency toward, acting in particular ways—occurs, by definition there has been no teaching. Simply *calling* the junior college a teaching institution is not enough.

Cohen (1967, 1969) suggests that if the junior college is conceptualized as a teaching institution, it must collect evidence of the learning it effects. His defined-outcomes approach offers a model for structuring courses and programs to such ends. He sees the concept of defined learning both as a structure for the college and as a goal toward which the institution might strive. More recent calls for "accountability" stress similar premises (*Educational Technology,* January 1971).

Identity as a "teaching institution"?

Another input to the concept of institutional identity is the notion of innovation. Many writers in the junior college field speak with pride about the institution's abilities to adopt new curricular, instructional, and organizational forms. As a result of his visits to junior colleges in 22 states, and of subsequent correspondence, conferences, and meetings with representatives of many other junior colleges, Johnson (1969) compiled a massive list of innovative practices. His theme is that junior colleges readily adopt new techniques and that this tendency is a significant strength of the institution, one that differentiates it from other educational structures. Many others in the field similarly strive to gain for the junior college a reputation as a flexible organization, as the one most likely to adopt new practices. And in fact, the institutions frequently do generate different curriculum patterns, adopt new admissions procedures, and accept the very latest instructional techniques.

The junior college as chameleon?

Yet another perception of the community college comes from those who equate comprehensiveness with identity. In the twentieth century the structure has taken on a great number of educational tasks. Within any single institution, the range of functions is broad—lower-division university courses, vocational–technical programs, guidance and counseling operations, community services, adult education, custodial care for the community's youth, and a number of other activities, both overt and implied. Each of these has become a part of the community college ethos; each has its own adherents. Taken together, the functions reveal a picture of comprehensiveness that is perceived by many to be a hallmark of the two-year college, one that is readily attested to by the fact that some educators tend "to measure the progressiveness of any given public junior college by the extent to which it has instituted and implemented a comprehensive educational program" (Friedman 1966, p. 418).

Identity through attempting everything?

A switching station, a teaching institution, innovation exemplified, and something for everyone—these are but a few of the characterizations that have been applied to the two-year college in attempts to define it. Can such perceptions provide it with a sense of self? Does it have a singular identity? Should it? What is it now? What will it become?

Several possibilities are immediately apparent. The community college will surely continue to evolve; presently in a state of flux, it shows few signs of solidifying. However, it is also likely that if it continues its efforts to accomplish everything, it will undoubtedly disappoint its constituency. Promising more than can possibly be delivered must eventually lead to disillusionment.

More than anything else, the junior college needs clear-cut direction and purpose, finite and feasible goals. The goals of an institution not only give it internal direction, but also mark it as a particular kind of social structure. Much of education is, in fact, an effort to help people define goals for themselves. An institution with its own goals clearly stated is likely to enhance this form of development within and among the people it serves and, more to the point, is likely to have a distinct sense of self. Distinct goals are inputs to institutional identity—necessary, albeit not sufficient, conditions. But no matter how crucial the establishment of institutional goals may be, goals cannot be seen as new buildings, parking lots, and IBM forms. Goals are set by people. And in order to set goals— for self and for social organizations—people must be aware of their own beings, of who they themselves are.

We see faculty identity as the key to institutional identity. The instructors personify institutional goals. It is they who most frequently associate with the institution's clientele, the students. A student may see a counselor once or twice a year for a few minutes; he may never see the college administrators. To him, his peers and his instructors are the reality of the college. And in the community college, a commuting institution, peer influence is minimal. Perhaps more than in any other post-secondary institution, the opportunity is present in the community college for the faculty to exert an influence on their students. As James Allen said in one of his last speeches as United States Commissioner of Education,

> Education should fundamentally concern only two people: the student and the teacher. Anyone else whose presence is considered necessary to make the university work is subordinate to these two and must remain so. The power working between the student and the teacher is the only power that can exist in a university, the *only* power that can define the university and hold it together. (1970, mimeo)

Read "community college" for "university" and the statement is even more apropos. Instructors are the central force in the junior college. Without them, there is nothing but buildings and grounds—no product, no process, no purpose, and no identity.

The thesis of this book is that the college will achieve its own identity only when—and only to the extent that—its faculty attain their own sense of professional—and personal—self. We call this merger *maturity*.

part two

Traits
and
Typologies

Identity—that elusive, ambiguous, essential concept—is both a process and a product. As a person experiences each period of development, he achieves some degree of certainty about himself. Moving on to greater maturity, he carries with him this awareness and integrates it with other phases of the life cycle. The search for identity continues simultaneously as effort and attainment, input and output, avenue and destination.

One of the inputs to a sense of identity is examination of others. Comparisons between self and others are valuable tools—not for purposes of competing, but rather for attaining more comprehensive views of self. Implicitly, one's understanding of self is prerequisite to his understanding of others. Similarly, understanding of others leads to a deeper awareness of self.

Reference groups provide a filter through which the person can look at himself and the people with whom he interacts—friends, authority figures, peers, professional colleagues. The person who seeks a more definite orientation to his work may well look to the various ways he and his colleagues are viewed. If a teacher, new or experienced, can see how other people have classified and typed instructors, he is better able to understand how he himself is perceived. This can help him answer his immediate questions about self and allow him to develop a more integrated sense of being.

This section relates primarily to views of the instructor as a person. It is not presented for the purpose of making value judgments about people, nor does it tie into the attempts to assess and evaluate teaching effectiveness that are brought out in part six. Rather, it provides a basis for awareness by pointing up some of the ways in which people view teachers.

No section on teacher types can be complete without noting the ways in which teachers are portrayed in the popular media. Novels, films, and television series all play major roles in building images. Barr's *Purely Academic* (1958) and Malamud's *The New Life* (1961) are but two examples of novels about college teaching. "The Halls of Ivy" was a popular radio show. "Mr. Novak" ran for several seasons on television. The pipe-smoking, tweed-coated college professor has been the hero of numberless plays, and the harassed but loved, bloody but unbowed, high school teacher has been seen on television, in novels, on film.

How influential are the media? Images lead to choices. A teacher may have chosen to enter the profession primarily because he wanted to play the role made familiar by books and films. His own sense of self is shaped accordingly. "All I had to go on at the onset of this year," said a new instructor, "were such experiences as are described in the popular literature; e.g., *To Sir, With Love, Up the Down Staircase,* and *The Blackboard Jungle*" (Ryan 1970, p. 83). And what instructor has not engaged in the fantasies described by the heroine of *Up the Down Staircase*:

> What is it that I wanted? A good question. . . . I wanted to make a permanent difference to at least one child. . . .
>
> . . . I wanted to share my enthusiasm with them; I wanted them to respond. To love me? Yes. I wanted to know their minds, shape souls, guide my flock through English and beyond. To be a lady-God? That's close.
>
> I wanted to fight the unequal battle against all that stands in the way of teaching. To blaze a trail? Indeed. (Kaufman 1964, pp. 313–14)

Such teacher characterizations are saccharine, but they can be inhibiting, too. As Lieberman points out,

> . . . even the favorable ones do not portray the teacher as a genuine professional. The characterizations of teachers in the mass media . . . often emphasize some of the best personal qualities of teachers, but they are qualities designed to win affection rather than to win respect for professional attainments. (1956, p. 473)

One may also look at the people in his profession by reading the literature that classifies people according to categories developed by social scientists. This section deals with some of the formalized systems for categorizing teachers.

No review can possibly reflect the magnitude of the effort to define "the good teacher"; thousands of investigations have been conducted. Much research attempts to assess the relationships between the instructor's personality and his effects on students. Specific personality characteristics have been isolated and then plotted against estimates of future teaching success. It has been suggested that traits such as belongingness, empathic potential (Dixon and Morse 1961), and organization (Coffman 1954) discriminate among individuals who adjust to new situational demands with varying degrees of success. Both specific and global judgments of personality have also been used to predict success (Brawer and Cohen 1966; Zamansky and Goldman 1960).

The many quantitative studies that attempt to measure and predict teaching success and the various testimonies reporting classroom observations suggest that the teacher's personality is an important influence on the behavior of his students. Although it has not been specifically demonstrated that teacher personality has an appreciable effect on achievement, there are strong indications that it markedly influences pupil adjustment. Nevertheless, this type of research has been criticized because it lacks independent criteria on which to base appraisal and because the studies are conducted in a "theoretical vacuum." Getzels and Jackson point out that

> Despite the critical importance of the problem and a half-century of prodigious research effort, very little is known for certain about the nature and measurement of teacher personality, or about the relation between teacher personality and teaching effectiveness. The regrettable fact is that many of the studies so far have not produced significant results. Many others have produced only pedestrian findings. For example, it is said after the usual inventory tabulation that good teachers are friendly, cheerful, sympathetic, and morally virtuous rather than cruel, depressed, unsympathetic, and morally depraved. But when this has been said, not very much that is especially useful has been revealed. For what conceivable human interaction—and teaching implies first and foremost a human interaction—is not the better if the people involved are friendly, cheerful, sympathetic, and virtuous rather than the opposite? (1963, p. 574)

3

Creativity, Flexibility, Authoritarianism

Man has long sought to know himself by examining dimensions of his personality and cognitive functioning. His attempts have come down through the ages in the form of written documents—philosophical essays, novels—and through verbal reports of folklore and mythology. In recent years, psychologically oriented approaches have found an ever increasing audience. The reason is simple: more than ever we want to know what makes us "tick."

No attempt is made in this chapter to discuss all the variables used to describe the individual. Instead, we have selected three global conceptualizations that relate directly to the instructor as person. They deal with dimensions of his personality, and especially with the way these dimensions are revealed in his approach to his work. These three concepts—*creativity*, *flexibility*, and *authoritarianism*—are as important to the administrators who employ and supervise instructors and to the people who prepare them for teaching as they are to the instructors themselves.

CREATIVITY

Who is the creative person? Can dimensions of creativity be isolated? How do they relate to teachers and to teaching? Simply defining creativity is a major task; volumes have been devoted to little more than sorting out appropriate definitions—for example, Kneller's *The Art and Science of Creativity* (1965). Many discussions of creative people in education founder on the rocks of inadequate conceptualizations; hence, assessments of creativity are by definition—or by the lack of it—equivocal.

Creativity is important in a teacher for at least two reasons. First, for the sake of creative students; studies that attempt to trace the ways in which creativity is nurtured among students often conclude, "It takes one to make one." Second, the creative person is presumed likely to generate innovative instructional techniques. Thus, he becomes particularly important in schools that strive for a contemporary view.

Much of the published material on the creative instructor is conjecture. Related to the problem of inconsistent definition is the lack of any consistent pattern that can be isolated as a prototype of the highly creative individual. Instead, the profiles that are drawn exhibit many incongruities. The numerous studies of the highly creative person suggest that he is as complex as the creative process itself. It is therefore wrong to assume that only one kind of characteristic can be considered when studying creativity.

Variant characteristics seem to estrange creative students from their peers and teachers and to isolate creative instructors from their colleagues and supervisors. Highly creative individuals are frequently seen as subject to "occasional regression," and as emotional, critical of others, stubborn, negativistic, and domineering, especially when they are creating ideas. Creative people also are described as having an unusual talent for disturbing the organization wherever they find it.

However, it is not altogether certain that interpersonal problems are universal among creative people. A number of studies suggest that the creative person is just as likely to act in a cooperative, social, and friendly manner. In fact, his needs for conformity and human relationships may be so great that he tends to squelch his creative potential. His environment apparently plays a large part in determining his stance. Foster concludes,

> If the role we ask the creative individual to play is that of a withdrawn isolate, or an aggressive, rebellious deviant, he is likely to play it that way. If, on the other hand, we acknowledge that this is what society has caused creative individuals to be in order to preserve their autonomy and sense of self [we will recognize] that this is not the true description of every creative person. . . . (1968, p. 116)

Individual instructors are often admonished to allow creativity to flourish. But most assessments of schools, colleges, and classrooms suggest an environment that militates against the creative process. Indeed, an unfortunately large number of teachers find it difficult to understand students who demonstrate creativity. When instructors are asked to rate the qualities they deem most desirable in students, they too often pick traits that explicitly are *not* marks of creative people. The needle-nosed pedant lives on!

Supportive contentions come from the students. The creative college and university students studied by Heist and Wilson reported that the faculty tended to be insensitive to their needs and interests as individuals. As a result, these students "found it difficult to involve themselves or commit themselves to their work" (1968, p. 192). Other major complaints voiced by creative students were the lack of quality and stimulation in faculty teaching. Their major concerns related to what

> . . . faculty members do or fail to do, both directly in their interactions with students in and out of the classroom and indirectly in their roles as formulators of policy and structure. The effects of the latter roles are manifested in instructional goals, curriculum content, standards of excellence, and methods of evaluation and grading. (Heist and Wilson, p. 194)

Heist and Wilson continue,

> . . . most college faculty members, while they may be professionals in their subject fields, are amateurs in their capacity as teachers. The term "amateur" describes a number of aspects of their role as teachers. They have, first of all, a limited understanding of their "clientele." Most, in fact, have only a small awareness and appreciation of the great diversity in abilities and motivations existing among their students. Many see no need to become concerned about individual aspirations, interests, and problems [but] in the teaching of creative students such personalization is . . . important. (Ibid., p. 194)

If creativity is to be fostered among students, the creative instructor seems to be needed. However, he is seldom found in the schools. Do his colleagues really want him there? From an institutional viewpoint, he doesn't fit well. On the one hand, the administrator may insist that he values creative individuals who tend to challenge the bright students. On the other hand, the administrator finds that the creative instructor is often difficult to deal with, and consequently he does not allow him his "transgressions." Student or instructor, the typical structured school situation presents dry and rocky ground to the seeds of creativity.

If creativity has a value, then teachers need to recognize and develop creativity among students and to be creative themselves. If teachers are to encourage these processes, they need freedom to experiment with the involved concepts and the diversions of thinking that appear to be related to creativity. They must be open to a variety of experiences. This is a large order for the teacher and for the administrator who must select these types of people.

Notice that the person usually tagged as the "creative teacher" is not the one of whom we speak. The administrator who points with pride to his "most creative" instructor is invariably identifying the one who introduces one fad after another, giving the impression of constant effort. These "innovative" instructors have picked up the appropriate cues: "Make it look as though you are willing to try every new gimmick that the dean hears about and he will think you are great!" In education, rewards tend to be associated with the apparent desire to enhance learning by frequent altering of instructional patterns; they are not contingent on the effects of the effort.

Even—perhaps especially—if the creative instructor is simply "one who generates different instructional techniques," environmental constraints cannot be ignored because of their large effect on his behavior. As Evans and Leppman (1967) point out, extrinsic pressures—the presence or absence of tenure, for example—seem to affect the instructor's tendency to adopt new instructional forms. Support from administrators or colleagues usually enhances the process.

There is some indication that creative teachers do show certain characteristic reaction patterns toward the world and that they affect their pupils in particular ways (Yamamoto 1965). However, these issues require further study. Whatever the conditions that foster creativity, if the environment encourages—or better still, promotes—flexible behavior, and if individuals can be encouraged in their uniqueness and allowed to exercise their own strengths, new ideas may be tried out and creativity stimulated.

FLEXIBILITY

Many difficulties in identifying, measuring, and developing creativity stem from a lack of consensus about the concept itself and about its cognitive and affective dimensions. Perhaps one way to understand creativity is in terms of ego strength. While individuals who demonstrate strong ego functioning may not necessarily be creative, many creative people possess high ego strength. This suggests a relationship between certain properties of ego strength—for example, flexibility, ability to "regress in the service of the ego" (Kris 1952)—and creativity.

Like other dimensions of personality, flexibility is present in varying degrees in different people. Within the person, it shifts according to the dynamic forces impinging on him. When these forces—the interaction of internal and external pressures—are normal, the person performs according to his usual style; when new situations arise, his mode adjusts accordingly. The person might, for example, demonstrate flexibility at certain times, while at others his behavior might be fairly rigid.

Some degree of fluctuation is to be expected. In social situations one behaves differently from the way one acts in academic or occupational roles. Most people are able to adjust with the situation; in fact, the very ability to adapt indicates flexibility. Different conditions stimulate different degrees of flexibility just as they foster such traits as authoritarianism, withdrawal, and the ability to delay gratification.

When degrees of flexibility/rigidity—or any other personality characteristics—are being discussed, the exact conditions under which the individual is behaving must be known. Accurate assessment of an individual's behavior demands that he be observed under different conditions and as he interacts with various others. One indicator of the reality-oriented, flexible person is the appropriateness of his behavior to the situation. However, when behavior is consistently rigid or extremely labile, then tendencies toward the pathological might be inferred, regardless of external conditions.

Making the Transition

Although flexibility is important to all people who must vary their behavior according to changing conditions, it is especially pertinent to the person involved in a transition from student to professional. In the context of education, this person is the teacher-in-training, who is changing his role from student to teacher. The many new demands, both internal and external, with which he is confronted require degrees of flexibility. Since people vary in flexibility, they differ in how well they handle the transition. Some find the role change difficult; others make it smoothly. The new instructor's perceived goodness or effectiveness on the job may depend on his ability to shift focus when appropriate—hence, on the degree of flexibility he manifests in particular situations.

Is it possible to determine in advance of actual placement what types of people possess the ability to adapt to new situations, especially as these are typified in junior college teaching? That is, do certain personality dimensions—such as flexibility—relate to the "success" of neophyte teachers? If flexibility is a necessary quality of the beginning instructor, assessment of flexibility among new instructors should relate to supervisors' ratings. The more flexible person should be judged the "better" teacher.

Several studies have been conducted in an effort to relate these dimensions. Sprinthall *et al.* (1966), for example, used the *Rorschach* (Rorschach 1922) to assess variables evolving from Rokeach's (1954) focus on the openness or closedness of belief systems. He established a positive relationship between cognitive flexibility and effective teaching.

In an effort to test this contention further, a group of studies using the *Rorschach Technique*, the *Myers–Briggs Type Indicator* (1962), and the *Adaptive-Flexibility Inventory* (Brawer 1967) were conducted under the auspices of a junior college teacher preparation program (Cohen and Brawer 1967; Brawer and Cohen 1966). Teaching interns were the subjects of these studies, which attempted to determine (1) whether there were, indeed, particular types of individuals who would be considered "good" and "poor" teachers; (2) their general "adjustability" and their abilities to endure the transition from one situation to another; (3) the degree of adaptive flexibility required by the "good" intern, as compared with that demonstrated by interns who were judged less effective in their subsequent teaching positions. Point three was of special concern in these investigations.

For two groups of junior college teaching interns who were assessed at the beginning on their first year of teaching, the dimension of flexibility was found to have a definite relation to the rating assigned to them by their deans at the end of the school term. And, although the question of whether instructors exhibit variety in their teaching was not investigated as part of this study, such flexibility might be inferred if we assume that these measured characteristics are reliable indicators of underlying traits.

A difficulty in extrapolating from these types of studies is that supervisor ratings, the dependent variable, are unreliable and subject to a "halo" effect. Unless supervisors have evidence of extreme deviation, they tend to rate all instructors as "good" or "doing a fine job." Therefore, no matter how precisely the instruments discriminate, the possibility of predicting which instructors will "do well" on the job is reduced.

Flexibility
and Innovation

Flexibility is also important because of the need for changes in the schools. Education has a long heritage of rigidity. The gap between what is and what could be is wide. However, recognition of systemic inflexibility has in some cases resulted in people's going to the opposite extreme. Attempting to counteract what unfortunately exists, they have adopted "innovation" as a watchword, using it simultaneously as an excuse for instituting untested changes, as a respectable reason for spending money, and as a device for appeasing those who exhibit their disenchantment with old systems by demanding new ones. Heedless of reason or potential effect but with high expectations of finding answers to everything, these "innovators" plunge blindly into any new approach. This tendency has been called "neophilia"—the belief that novelty is inherently good. Inferred is the confidence that newness can compensate for lack of direction. However, novelty for novelty's sake does not indicate flexibility among people or institutions.

Despite the prevalent interest in innovation, few investigations deal with the "innovative teacher" in the junior college. In one of the few efforts to isolate characteristics consistent with the change-minded person, 52 junior college teachers rated either as "innovators" or as "traditionalists" were surveyed by Wygal (1966). He found that innovators see themselves as being deviant from the innovativeness norms of their schools, while traditionalists do not perceive themselves as deviant. Nevertheless, a teacher's self-perception of his own degree of innovativeness proved to be of little value; no significant difference was found between the innovators and the traditionalists on that trait. The only personal characteristic found to differentiate between the two was age; innovators are younger than traditionalists.

One of the requisites for successfully incorporating innovation into existing school systems is knowledge of who will accept or reject change. The major responsibility for accepting new instructional media, for example, lies with the faculty, who must make the ultimate decisions regarding the extent of their use. This seems self-evident, yet most media research is concerned with hardware and software rather than with the people involved. Hundreds of studies have shown that students learn as well—or as poorly—with instruction from a professor on television as they do in a live classroom situation. Yet television is still far from having significant impact in the classroom. Therefore, this is not a problem for hardware research but for psychological and sociological research. The crucial questions are: What is the role of the professor if the subject is presented from an automated data file instead of by the professor? Who will accept change and who will reject it? Dimensions of flexibility relate directly to both these queries.

Authoritarianism

Authoritarianism is another personality dimension that is extremely important to the junior college instructor, both in his quest for professional identity and in his adaptation to the school situation. According to the group of psychologists and political scientists who, in the 1930s and 1940s, addressed themselves to the potential effects of ultra–right wing political movements on American ideology, authoritarianism is a basic dimension of personality. In *The Authoritarian Personality* (1950), Adorno, Frenkel-Brunswik, Levinson, and Sanford postulate nine components of this syndrome of organized beliefs and symptoms. Developed from Freudian concepts, these nine dimensions are conventionalism, authoritarian aggression, authoritarian submission, power and "toughness," anti-introception, superstition and stereotype, destructiveness and cynicism, projectivity, and overconcern with sex. These researchers, along with others, have described authoritarian and dogmatic individuals who employ stereotyped and conventional thinking, lack original responses to projective techniques, use crude generalizations, and are compulsive, critical, and emotionally inhibited.

It is important that the junior college instructor understand authoritarianism because it is so directly related to interaction among students, faculty members, and administrators. In one of the few studies relating this concept to people in the junior college, Pratt (1966) ranked 16 presidents and 395 faculty members according to their scores on the *California F Scale,* a test of authoritarianism developed by Adorno et al. No significant difference was found between the actual degree of authoritarianism shown by the presidents and the authoritarianism of the total faculty. However, when time considerations were explored, a negative relationship was found between the presidents' scores and the mean scores of faculty who were in their first and third years of employment in the schools. Pratt concluded that presidents tend to *hire* those instructors who, as a group, are like themselves in authoritative personality. But they *retain* those who are different from them in their degree of authoritarianism or flexibility.

The relationship between dogmatism, a dimension of authoritarianism, and the teaching experiences of school counselor trainees has also been examined. Using Rokeach's (1960) scale to assess the degree of dogmatism (expressed in terms of a closed belief system), Wittmer and Webster (1969) reported that counselor trainees who had had teaching experience made significantly higher dogmatism scores than did trainees without such experience. Dogmatism tended to increase with age and with teaching experience, although not to a statistically significant degree.

Indeed, it may be that teaching as a profession attracts and holds people with authoritarian tendencies. Who, from his own student career, cannot recall a number of rigid, dogmatic instructors? Is it a function of age alone? Of the perceived role? Axen sees authoritarianism as a general trait among instructors: "Scratch the surface of the collective faculty and it would appear you reach a substratum of authoritarianism only slightly disguised in moments of noncrisis by a thin patina of liberalism and intellectualism" (1968, p. 111). Apparently the trait develops early in the career of many instructors who, unsure of their stance, are "persuaded to test out the role of that old standard: The authoritarian, aloof teacher" (Ryan 1970, p. 173)—the role with which the students are most familiar.

Authoritarianism is characteristic of the interactions between teachers and students. Waller describes this relationship as

> . . . a special form of dominance and subordination, a very unstable relationship and in quivering equilibrium, not much supported by sanction and the strong arm of authority, but depending largely upon purely personal ascendancy. Every teacher is a taskmaster and every taskmaster is a hard man; if he is naturally kindly, he is hard from duty, but if he is naturally unkind, he is hard because he loves it. (1960, p. 334)

Just as the creative instructor may foster creativity among his students, the authoritarian instructor has his own effect, encouraging either countervailing authoritarianism or subordination. Each type of person employs different types of controls in the classroom. The controls, as a major determinant of classroom climate, probably have a greater effect on the students than does the content covered in the course. The undemocratic classroom stimulates students' subsequently accepting authoritarianism as a socially sanctioned mode of approach to interpersonal relationships.

Subordination is the other side of the coin. When one person acts authoritatively and the other submits, fragmentation of personality results. "Subordination is possible only because the subordinated one is a subordinate with a mere fragment of his personality, while the dominant one participates completely . . . [The] subordinated ones attempt to protect themselves by withdrawing from the relationship, to suck the juice from the orange of conformity before rendering it to the teacher" (Waller 1960, p. 334). Both authoritarianism on the part of the teacher and the resultant fractionated submissiveness on the part of the student are humanistically undesirable.

According to Biddle and Ellena (1964), dominating behavior on the part of teachers also tends to create unhappiness and frustration. As a direct consequence of a teacher's dominance, some students move to the extremes either of resistance or of conformity and are less spontaneous than those who have been exposed to less authoritarian teachers. Other studies have found that authoritarianism penalizes the bright students. While less intelligent students may do better in group problem-solving situations conducted in an authoritarian manner than in groups conducted in a permissive manner, these achievement differences are not true of the more intelligent students (Darley and McNamara 1961).

What are the implications of these findings—for the students, the school as a social system, and the individual instructor? Is this what teaching is all about? Is it not a sign of maturity and self-integration to be able to say genuinely to a student, "I don't know," or "You have pointed up a relationship that I, an expert in this field, had not seen"? How unfortunate, then, that most practicing instructors cannot make such admissions, and by their humility indicate their own maturity. The perceived role demands take their toll.

PERSONALITY DIMENSIONS
AND EDUCATIONAL GOALS

The concepts of creativity, flexibility, and authoritarianism are pertinent to the identity of the person, the profession, and the institution. They also relate directly to educational goals and purposes. If educational experiences are to foster the students' cognitive and emotional development, school personnel should attend to Sanford's statement that

> . . . ego development is hampered both by authoritarian or overprotective regimes and by permissive-chaotic ones. The former do not give the synthesizing functions of the ego a chance for exercise; the latter, through too much stimulation of impulse with consequent anxiety, may put too heavy a strain upon the developing ego. (1966, p. 288)

Rather, development of the ego seems to be facilitated when the person experiences situations that free him from the necessity of erecting defense mechanisms. Difficult and anxiety-provoking situations often force the student to fall back on primitive or archaic maneuvers that deter him from actually facing the situation. They thus prevent the further strengthening of ego-related functions. Conversely, when in increasingly difficult situations the person finds his actions meeting with success, his ego gains strength.

The college experience offers many opportunities for acquiring skills that simultaneously build self-confidence and augment ego development. In *Self and Society*, Sanford notes that

> Teaching can make a contribution by giving the student a glimpse of the variety and complexity of the social world, by showing how people feel and what it means to be human, by forcing self-awareness through empathy with many kinds of people, real and fictional, by confronting the student with some of the deficiencies of his old, automatically adopted values and thus inducing conflict and requiring decision. . . . But college is not always a perfect culture for the ego. There may be authoritarianism in teaching, with rewards for doing precisely what one is told, or authoritarianism in the regime—perhaps in the student government—with its invitation to substitute external control for inner direction. (*Ibid.*, pp. 288–89)

Although the individual teacher must see that his students comply with certain administrative regulations, he can still be wary of any temptation to adopt an authoritarian posture. He can also help himself and his own development by not falling prey to the inflexible and dogmatic sides of his own personality. Each person needs a certain amount of authority and structure. However, it is important that he be able to distinguish between authority and authoritarianism, to realize that he will function better if he is not subject to mere dogma, and concomitantly, to understand that human growth demands opportunities to explore and to engage in trial and error experiences. He must realize that issues cannot be isolated as absolutes but rather that they have many nuances. The flexible person knows this; he knows who he is and can allow others to be themselves.

The creative, the flexible, the authoritarian teacher—all are found in the schools. What makes them that way? Can they change? What conditions foster one or another pattern of development? These questions cannot be answered definitively. We do know, however, that the role of teacher traditionally has tended to bring out the authoritarian in the individuals who have played it, and that each instructor must consciously resist these tendencies in himself.

4

Profs,
Clock Punchers,
and Such

Bleeding Heart	Facilitator	Extrovert
Pedant	Mr. Chips	Stimulator
Ham	Scholar	Clock Puncher
Guide		Poseur

How many labels can be applied to instructors? Dozens could be added to this list. People have always categorized their associates as a way of understanding their many points of similarity. Call it pigeonholing or stereotyping, nearly everyone does it.

It is one thing to assign labels, but quite another to systematize the categories. Schemes have been devised for ordering people on the basis of any number of dimensions—physical traits, personality characteristics, cognitive styles, and vocational orientations, to name a few. Creativity, flexibility, and authoritarianism represent but some of the many concepts that have been identified for purposes of ordering people into various groups.

Other typologies are presented in this chapter. Stemming more directly from sociological and social–psychological theories, they deal with the person in relation to the groups within which he functions. Whereas, for example, the individual may be creative by himself, the typologies reported here view him according to his orientations in the context of his group.

Theoretical divisions of people into separate categories have been proposed by investigators in many fields—psychology, sociology, anthropology, education. These systems have a long history. Following Galen's approach to ordering people, Jung (1923), Kretschmer (1945), and Sheldon et al. (1940) all developed theoretical frameworks for their own classification schemes—introversion and extroversion; the asthenic, athletic, and pyknic biological type; and the somatotypes of endomorphy, mesomorphy, and ectomorphy.

Horney's (1937) examination of "neurotic" populations in terms of their movements toward, away from, and against others also has implications for categorizing so-called "normals," as does Riesman et al's (1950) description of traditional-, inner-, or outer-directed people. Anthropological orders of entire cultures—based on such dimensions as subsistence patterns, extent of aggressive activities, and degree of acculturation—are fairly common.

From a plethora of systems we have selected a few typologies that were constructed to categorize people in higher education. These appear especially relevant to the junior college instructor and, accordingly, are outlined in this chapter. Included are Gusfield and Riesman's pioneer settlers, pioneer adventurers, and job holders; Friedman's high schoolers, profs, and grad students; Jung's taxonomy of psychological types; Clark's teachers, scholar-researchers, demonstrators, and consultants; Cohen's hierarchy of disciplinarianism; and Brawer's end of the roaders, ladder climbers, clock punchers, and defined purpose routers.

What bearing do such typologies have on perceptions of faculty roles? Can these classification schemes help the individual better understand his colleagues and himself?

Any of these typologies has some interest for the person who would search for identity through comparisons. Certainly classifications can help him organize his thinking about others in the profession and, concomitantly, help him define his own role. The instructor may decide to identify with a particular academic field, with the more pervasive role of the instructor, or with some group or type not yet defined. For some people, clear-cut identification may be a step toward clarity of direction. For others, the critical questions may well be, not "Who am I?" or "What am I?" but "How do I conduct myself in the role I play?" or "What are the results of the activities in which I engage?—and upon whom?" In any case, typologies can be helpful in understanding individuals in groups.

Despite their potential value, classification schemes have certain disadvantages. Type-casting, emphasis on weaknesses to the exclusion of strengths, static stereotypes—all may emerge as a result of the grouping or pigeonholing effort itself. In such cases, the very classifications that were developed for increasing understanding hinder the process. In addition, if they are realistic and representative of their populations, subcategories in any typology cannot ever be completely discrete; inevitably, they overlap. One additional caveat: none of these schemes is sufficiently well developed to be called a "system." Instead, each is a tentative postulation. Yet, as long as the instructor is aware of the shortcomings inherent in all classifications, he may use such typologies to understand his associates better and, by extension, to gain awareness of his own identity.

PIONEER SETTLERS,
PIONEER ADVENTURERS, AND JOB HOLDERS

Gusfield and Riesman (1968) devised a classification scheme based on the career orientations of instructors at two proximate colleges. Both schools were affiliated with universities in a large midwestern state. Both were developed under the auspices of the state university, but openly attempted to depart from the mode of higher education exemplified by their parent institution. Both were explicitly dedicated to "average" state university students who were, for the most part, the first members of their families to go to college and who would normally have pursued rigidly narrow vocational aims at the large universities. Obviously, these colleges had much in common with the open-door community college.

The faculty were categorized into three groups: *pioneer settlers*, *pioneer adventurers*, and *job holders*. The pioneer settlers were seen as career-oriented planners in the image of the Caplow and McGee (1958) models. Embedded in firm professional orientations, these instructors were considered conservative, career-oriented "young fogies" despite their having elected to teach in experimental colleges. They were further described either as "growth stock professionals" who viewed the new college as a potentially permanent abode, or as "transient professionals" who saw their new college positions as way stations toward more settled careers. In either case, the pioneer settlers looked on their appointments as the chance to put their ideas into effect, or as one of them put it, "to decide what I would teach and to have a say in the department" (Gusfield and Riesman 1968, p. 280). As a group they emphasized efficiency, insisted on teaching material that was closely related to their research and writing interests, and "tended to judge their colleges and themselves in terms of their ability to prepare undergraduate students for graduate schools" (Ibid., p. 282).

The pioneer adventurers expressed a dissident attitude toward the more conventional professional career orientations espoused by the settlers. Focusing on what they were escaping in their former school positions or on what they were moving toward in the future, they were attracted to their new roles because of the colleges' innovative posture rather than for the general career advantages accruing from the move. Perhaps because of their essential attraction to contemporary and novel approaches to education, the adventurers appeared less committed than the settlers to the values and standards of professional disciplines. While they might be—and indeed, many were—competent scholars in their own special subject fields, they did not visualize their academic lives in the same manner as did the settlers. Rather, their roles appeared less to reflect a measure of dedication toward their fields than an orientation toward an interdisciplinary, more broadly defined occupation. The men in the sample who were over 50 years old had a strong involvement in innovative aspects of the new colleges; their pioneering efforts represented decided breaks from their previously established commitment to their disciplines.

The job holder was the third type of teacher classified according to Gusfield and Riesman's system. These people differed from both settlers and adventurers in that their academic positions did not represent the central dimension of their lives but were seen, rather, as means to other ends. Numbering relatively few of the faculty in the two colleges, the job holders were motivated by neither the ". . . academic marketplace nor the ideologies of missionary commitment to the experiment. . . . [This instructor] stands outside the diversities represented in the orientations of settlers and adventurers, getting his 'kicks' perhaps in the enjoyment of family, in the context of leisure time or in some other occupation" (*Ibid.*, p. 278).

While their attempt to appraise faculty in terms of discrete groups presents a fairly clear-cut picture emphasizing decided traits, Gusfield and Riesman caution that most of their respondents embodied a little of each type. Thus, faculty members might be simultaneously settlers, adventurers, and job holders. This may well be true of other classification schemes. Because a person rarely fits one group exclusively, the categories point only to tendencies.

HIGH SCHOOLERS,
PROFS, AND GRAD STUDENTS

Instructors in four midwestern community colleges were described as high schoolers, profs, and grad students by Friedman (1965; 1967a). This typology reflects the teachers' prior institutional affiliations and suggests their orientations as "subject matterists" or "disciplinarians"—two other categories created by Friedman.

Of the former high school teachers in Friedman's population, the majority had taught in the secondary school for five years or more, had earned the master's degree in a given academic field of specialization, and were over 35 years of age when they assumed their new careers as junior college instructors. These high schoolers emphasized their subject matter and prided themselves on their lack of identification with teaching methods. They frequently deprecated methods courses and professors of education—in spite of the fact that at one time they had earned 20 hours or so in education courses to meet certification requirements and that much of their conversation contained words typically described as "educationese" —"motivation," "units," "supervised study."

According to Friedman, the high schooler overtly rejects certain roles and identifications that he unconsciously projects because they are, in fact, a part of him. He frequently expresses a "subject matterist anti-educational viewpoint." This dualism "promotes something of a rivalry between the subject-matterist teacher and the professor of education who often holds a position of leadership and power in junior college planning with the teacher refusing to listen to any advice emanating from an 'ed school'" (1967b, p. 13).

At least in their early years at the college, the grad students are in a transition phase. They come to junior college teaching directly from their graduate degree programs, usually with no prior teaching experience. From then on, they spend much time scaling down their expectations of acceptable student performance and filling in gaps in their own knowledge —particularly the differences between their own academic specialties and the content necessary to build and teach freshman, sophomore, and "remedial" courses. They tend to be less committed to teaching as an occupation than either the high schoolers or the profs and regard junior college teaching as an interim position to hold until they get other jobs or go on to further study.

The profs—former four-year college professors—adjust more readily to teaching lower division courses because they come from institutions where they had previously taught large numbers of freshmen and sopho-mores. In the junior college setting, they typically continue to deal with similar course content. They consider the role switch to the junior college as permanent but interpret the move as a step downward—a failure or demotion.

On the other hand, the high schoolers consider their switch from high school to the junior college as a definite step upward in organizational mobility. One individual in this group suggested that his main reason for preferring the junior college to the high school was the fact that "the emphasis is on teaching" rather than on "maintaining classroom order." Classroom interaction is the chief source of work gratification for these instructors, who enter the junior college with the hopes and expectations that their move will be permanent. They thus tend to be rooted in their decisions.

Friedman further differentiated instructors by placing them into "subject matterist" and "disciplinarian" categories. The subject matterist identifies with his local colleagues rather than with a national disciplinary group. He "teaches students" and does not typically concern himself with the discovery of knowledge in his field. Conversely, the disciplinarian sees research as his major purpose, and identifies with an academic field association; for example, the American Psychological Association, the American Sociological Association. For the subject matterist, the sense of colleagueship is local, centered in the employing organization; for the disciplinarian, it is a cosmopolitan or nationwide association.

Regardless of their former organizational affiliation, most of the instructors in Friedman's population were subject matterists, seeing their professional purpose as the transmission of information about their subject fields. This differentiated them from many elementary and secondary school teachers, who view the teaching process as a professional orientation toward the general area of education. Friedman found few disciplinarians and concluded that the prototype of the subject matterist is the high schooler in the public junior college, whereas the university professor in a graduate school of arts or sciences is the prototype of the disciplinarian.

If identity for the institution is seen in terms of its faculty members' orientations, according to Friedman's schema, the junior colleges are extended high schools. However, other approaches to classification do not suggest the same distinctions that are posed by Friedman's models. Rather, they point to a diversity of types that transcends institutional boundaries.

JUNGIAN TYPOLOGY

To be relevant, systematic approaches to understanding people do not have to be contemporary. A typology developed by Jung in the early 1900s is still pertinent. According to Jung's scheme, every individual is considered to possess the attitudes of both introversion and extraversion, his particular type being determined by the relative dominance of one attitude over the other. The bipolar distribution thus postulated is further enhanced by the four functions of thinking, feeling, sensation, and intuition, the preponderance of one function over the other three adding a further distinction to the basic attitude. Further, the theory holds that what is consciously dominant finds its opposite expressed in the unconscious.

The fact that Jungian typology depends on underlying process as well as on conscious posture suggests its applicability to dimensions of teaching. For just as individual attitudes and functions may shift with age and situational press, so portions of the teacher's role—counselor, classroom manager, test maker—bring manifold aspects of his personality to the fore. If the various functions a teacher must assume do, indeed, have a consistent underlying feature, it is then conceivable that teaching may best be handled by special types of people. But which types?

In a study based on Jung's conceptual scheme, Cohen and Brawer (1968) described certain personality dimensions of beginning junior college teachers. Fifty-six candidates for junior college faculty positions were examined in order to test the hypotheses that (1) individuals identified as "intuitive-feeling" types would be rated higher as teachers than would those identified as "sensation-thinking" types, and (2) "extraverted-feeling" subjects would be more likely to be hired for first-time teaching positions than would "introverted-thinking" types.

On the basis of his responses to the *Myers–Briggs Type Indicator,* an objective technique built on Jung's typology, each of the teaching candidates was placed in a type category. Correlations were found to be in the predicted directions. Subjects who indicated preferences high in the "feeling" dimensions were more likely to be employed in first-time teaching positions than candidates with different orientations and, after several months as junior college instructors, they were given higher ratings by their supervisors than were those candidates who had been classified as "thinking" types. The results corroborated the statement in the *Myers–Briggs* manual that "intuitive-feeling" people "... may excel in teaching (particularly college and high school) [and] ... their best chance of success and satisfaction lies in work which involves the unfolding of possibilities ... for people" (1963, p. 55).

Although this study was limited in both numbers of subjects and geographical representation, it does have implications for the junior college field as a whole. Perhaps the broadest of these implications is that, although the "feeling" type predominated, no single type of person is employed as a first-time teacher in the junior college to the exclusion of other types. That there was no evidence of clustering in any one group suggests that what is typically described as a heterogeneous junior college student population is matched by the heterogeneity of first-time teachers and teaching applicants—at least in the group examined in this study.

CLARK'S SCHEMA

The conception of his work role plays an important part in the life of the academic man, but just how the instructor perceives his role has not been systematically determined. Expanded research on college faculty members in the 1960s led Clark (1963) to concentrate on their work orientations, definitions of task, and work identities.

Clark proposed a four-cornered typology of faculty subcultural orientations, based on two general variables: (1) whether the teacher identifies himself with his college; that is, a local versus a cosmopolitan orientation; and (2) whether he is committed to, or interested in, pure work or study—liberal arts or academic orientation versus vocational, applied, or professional orientations. When these two dimensions are combined, four types of faculty subcultures result: the *teacher,* the *scholar researcher,* the *demonstrator,* and the *consultant.*

The teacher is identified with his college, committed to students and to their liberal education, and impatient with researchers. Conversely, the scholar researcher is not particularly identified with his college, is interested in pure study but not in its application, has a cosmopolitan interest in his discipline, and holds a liberal arts orientation.

The demonstrator is identified with his college, is embedded in the local community, and is not particularly committed to pure study. He is "... often a local professional technician who comes to the college or university on a part-time basis to show apprentices how to do it"; for example, he might be the "local dentist serving on the staff of the dental school, going from chair to chair in a dental school clinic, checking the work" (*Ibid.*, pp.44–45). The consultant neither identifies with his college nor commits himself to pure disinterested study. Instead, he is a "big-time" professional man with a national reputation who is primarily concerned with the application of knowledge.

Clark's categories fit the university more closely, but they become pertinent to the individual community college as it grows in size and program scope. As this occurs, consultants—college faculty members with national reputations and reference groups—emerge, and demonstrators—part-time professional technicians—become more prevalent. The metropolitan community colleges, frequently larger than many universities, can be compared organizationally to them; accordingly, the staff members in such colleges may find Clark's schema relevant.

A HIERARCHY
OF DISCIPLINARIANISM

Another way of viewing junior college teachers is to classify them according to their own behavior as disciplinarians within the field of instruction and within the academic field they represent—for example, biology, anthropology, history. A person may work in an academic discipline on any of several levels of involvement. He may be *discoverer, synthesizer, translator, practitioner,* or *commuter* (Cohen 1970a).

The discoverer (or researcher) stands in the vanguard of the discipline. He develops theory and designs and conducts original studies. Frequently, he invents tools or techniques of investigation in his field.

The synthesizer draws on the findings of the discoverer, combining them into new knowledge suitable for use by others in the discipline. He is the writer of original textbooks, the one who repackages information and concepts and sometimes injects a few ideas of his own. Both the synthesizer and the discoverer contribute to the first-line journals in the field. More importantly, they take the discipline itself into uncharted areas by merging and reforming knowledge within the field.

The translator defines areas of work by reviewing the publications and ideas transmitted by the synthesizer. He transforms these ideas into modes of practice both for himself and for others in his institution by selecting useful portions from the synthesized knowledge. Although he may occasionally read the leading journals in his field, he is a contributor to second-line journals only.

The practitioner uses the tools of the discipline as his own. He accepts ideas from others at more involved levels but rarely, if ever, contributes his own ideas to the field at large. He stands as the mediator between his area and the layman. Accordingly, the practitioner has considerable contact with students.

The commuter is affiliated with the discipline only by ascription. He reads popularized information readily understandable to any layman. He may belong to a professional association but he does not take an active role in it; in fact, his involvement often stops with his payment of dues. He operates within the boundaries of his discipline as it was taught to him at whatever point in time he completed his formal learning in the field.

The nature of his position dictates that the junior college instructor holds a dual disciplinary membership. He is affiliated both with his subject field and with the discipline of instruction, but his levels of involvement may well differ. The biology instructor, for instance, may only be a commuter in biology, whereas he is a translator in instruction. For example, he may have taken a leading part in building a new audio-tutorial laboratory for the teaching of biology, but he may have done little or nothing to keep up with current developments in the field of biology itself. On the other hand, the English instructor may be conversant with the most recent developments in linguistics but may address instruction as a commuter—that is, he may still be delivering lectures on the use of the comma rather than using even the most rudimentary techniques of imaginative instruction.

Viewing instructors in terms of an allegiance to two disciplines might be particularly useful as a way of predicting the extent to which they will change methods or adopt innovations either in their subject fields or in the discipline of instruction. It is unlikely that a person can operate at a level higher than that of translator in more than one discipline at the same time. The imaginative researcher may be a plodding pedant when it comes to teaching; the creative instructor may well be the person who has drifted so far from his academic field that he has nearly lost contact with it.

This mode of viewing instructors may also help to explain why certain people are working in two-year rather than four-year colleges. By definition, the junior college is a teaching institution. Accordingly, it is unlikely that an instructor involved with his academic field at a level higher than that of translator will find much support in the junior college. If he wants time to conduct theoretical research and to write for first-line journals in his field, he must go to the university. Conversely, the university professor who works in an academic field at a level below translator is not likely to be supported at his institution. If he does not act as a discoverer or synthesizer at least part of the time, he may well find advancement in rank and concomitant reward difficult to obtain.

A FOUR-PRONGED TYPOLOGY

We have described several approaches to classifying people. This particular scheme, developed especially for the junior college, is outlined on the basis of the roles typically assumed by faculty members. Instructors are placed into one of four groups: the *end-of-the-roaders*, the *ladder climbers*, the *clock punchers*, and the *defined purpose routers* (Brawer 1968).

The end-of-the-roaders group is an amalgamation of Gusfield and Riesman's settlers and Friedman's high schoolers and profs. In this case, the designation is based on the teacher's actual behavior rather than on his background. The type of person falling into this category might come to the junior college from a high school or university teaching position, directly from graduate school, or from a non-academic position. These people perceive teaching in the junior college to be simultaneously a means and an end. They seek a field they can call their permanent home; for better or for worse, they settle in a particular school. This does not always imply an elective choice, for while many end-of-the-roaders consider the junior college the epitome of success, others come to it as a last resort. For the second group, any of several reasons may explain the move: they have been unable to hold former positions; they had wanted to teach in a university but did not complete the doctorate; the community college paid more than the liberal arts college where they would rather be working. This is consistent with Medsker's finding that 44 percent of junior college faculty members would really rather be in a four-year college or university (Cross 1969).

The end-of-the-roader is neither satisfied nor dissatisfied, neither a good nor a poor teacher. The name of the category should not imply such a judgment. Many people are able to make peace with their previous lack of success; in fact, the very failure to find satisfaction in former positions can be an incentive to subsequent accomplishment. The end-of-the-roader who comes from the high school is devoted to his subject matter. His idealization of the junior college as the goal toward which he has been working suggests that he will, indeed, make the most of his opportunity to teach. Those who have other backgrounds may similarly serve the institution, their students, and themselves well.

Ladder climbers are closest to Gusfield and Riesman's pioneer adventurers, more like "transient" professionals than "growth stock" professionals. They see the junior college as a place to stay for a limited period of time, and whether or not they give their all to their professional roles, they hold themselves aloof from those who view the junior college as the terminal point in their careers. They may still be working toward advanced degrees, or they may plan to spend a few years at a junior college until something better comes along. Since only a small percent of junior college faculty members hold doctorates, some ladder climbers hope they will go on to other organizations—in higher education or in another profession—after obtaining their degrees. Of the four groups of people described in this scheme, the ladder climbers are probably the most unstable in the sense of their devotion to the junior college. They might, of course, be "stable" individuals (if "stable" means having emotional balance), but they view their junior college positions as transitory steps toward selected goals. In many instances, these "transitory steps" may last for decades.

The reasons for the clock puncher's interest in education vary. Whatever they may be, he has chosen to work in an educational institution and the junior college presents him with as good an occupational opportunity as any. His true devotion, however, is to another field or avocation. For example, he may be an artist who teaches in the junior college for bread and butter but is primarily interested in furthering his own professional image outside the school. He may be a staunch citizen of his local community, considering his job merely an eight-to-four occupation while he remains primarily interested in other personal pursuits. He is at the opposite pole from the person who takes his profession home with him.

Again, interpretations are tenuous. The attitude of the clock puncher is not necessarily one of disinterest. He may be completely involved in his teaching role for the time he spends in school, and indeed, he may be a good teacher in any sense of the words. The essential difference between him and other instructors is that he views his job only as a way to earn a certain wage or to be in a certain place at a particular time—not as an opportunity to further himself or his profession.

The defined purpose routers are closest to what we would hope most junior college teachers—in fact, teachers at all levels of education—might become. They are like Heath's (1964) "reasonable adventurers"—people who have found a reason for being, who have dedicated themselves to the integration of self and to the meeting of their goals. They see the junior college as a teaching institution, a place where diverse types of students come to seek satisfaction for many different needs. They are involved in their subject matter and can define it in terms of specific behavioral objectives. Although our classification system is tentative, the defined purpose routers are considered to be teachers who bring their students to goal-oriented, specified behavior, and personality integration (Brawer 1968). They have found their sense of identity and they project this identity into a professional image.

Questions about faculty typologies all relate to the broader question of identity. One of the greatest hindrances to identity for the junior college instructor results from his straddling his role as he would balance a teeter-totter. He rocks between the high school teacher on one end and the college professor on the other. He may consider himself a disciplinarian— an anthropologist, a historian, or a psychologist—yet feel separate from his university compatriots. Nevertheless, he frequently identifies with his own subject matter rather than with instructors of similar ages or of comparable orientation to the discipline of instruction.

This parochialism was evidenced when, in the course of gathering material for this book, a large group of faculty members representing several junior colleges and all teaching similar courses were asked if they would like to read about other community college instructors. Their reply was that they would be interested only in knowing what other teachers do or say *if* they represented a similar field—nursing instructors were interested in the daily activities of other nursing instructors, physical education instructors with other physical education instructors, and so forth. By seeking identity through subject matter affiliation, the instructor isolates himself from instructors in different subject fields. Further, he tends to remove himself from the discipline of instruction itself, in essence acting like the commuter rather than the professionally involved person he might better be.

Grouping people into categories on the basis of certain characteristics is one way of viewing the people within a profession. The traits (creativity, flexibility, and authoritarianism) described in chapter 3, along with the typologies outlined in this chapter, can help the instructor to cement an identity of his own through comparing himself with others. They may also allow him to realize that he frequently holds orientations in common with both high school and college instructors. In this way he may be able to affiliate temporarily with both groups, taking inputs to his own identity from each. Eventually, by merging the teaching orientation of the ideal high school teacher with the professional orientation of the prototype university professor, the integrated junior college instructor will evolve.

part three

Roles and Images

Some conceptions of schooling assume that there exists a finite body of subject matter, the mastery of which constitutes an education. Educational programs, selection of instructors, methods of teaching, and erection of institutions are all based on the belief that knowledge of subject matter is the desired end product of formal education. If facts are learned and skills are acquired (as measured by examination), the teacher and the school are judged successful.

An alternative view conceives of education as a process whereby the individual realizes his potential, cognitively and affectively. This premise builds on the uniqueness of each individual. The task of the school and of the instructors is to release creative talents and to allow the flow of natural abilities. According to this conceptualization, learning practical skills is only a means to an end, not an educational end in itself.

Those are the extreme positions. No single type of instructor, no one kind of institution, no one approach to teaching invariably stems from either a product or a process orientation. Similarly, neither conception invariably has either positive or negative impact on students and neither leads unswervingly to the instructor's adopting unique functions. Nevertheless, understanding these conceptualizations is basic to understanding the many dimensions of the instructor's role.

Each instructor in today's college actually engages in several functions including service to the school and to the community, student guidance, and teaching activities. The teaching role itself may be sub-divided into many areas—dispensing information, arranging a classroom climate, serving as model, facilitating student development, managing a total instructional environment.

To some degree, every instructor is involved in all these operations. But very few people can perform with equal facility in every area. Instead, they tend to emphasize certain functions and minimize others, their emphasis depending on many intrinsic and extrinsic factors. The in-structor's personality, his own purposes, and his perceptions of the teaching role are intrinsic determinants. Extrinsics include the students and colleagues with whom he interacts and the general climate of the college.

All functions within the teaching role are important and all must be performed. However, the individual must eventually choose to perform in the area that best fits his own capabilities and orientations and the demands of the institution in which he works. A person must be well integrated in order to make appropriate choices of role, of function, and of response to internal and external stimuli. Reconciliation of demands and emphasis on the appropriate functions suggest a synthesis of the personal and the situational. The very "whole," well-integrated person may also be able to compartmentalize his operations; in fact, such a merger may suggest that the individual is operating at the highest order of development to which he might aspire, that he is an integrated person, aware of his own identity.

In the previous section we noted various ways that people have been categorized—in terms of personality traits and of typologies built by various social scientists. In this section, we classify instructors in terms of the global functions subsumed in the teaching role. Chapter 5 discusses role conceptualizations and various writers' interpretations of the role of the instructor. Chapters 6, 7, and 8 apply the concept to an original three-way classification of faculty functions. The instructor is viewed in terms of the facets of teaching that he chooses to emphasize and the images he projects. Our three categories are the instructor as *model*, as *mediator*, and as *manager*.

In common with other ways of looking at instructors, the categories presented in this section are not mutually exclusive. The instructor is never solely a model, a mediator between the student and the knowledge to be gained, or the manager of a total learning environment. However, most instructors tend to adopt specialized styles of functioning and may actually become identified with one of these styles. Because our newly formulated classification scheme relates particularly to the *teaching* function, it may be useful for the instructor not only as a way of clarifying his role, but also as a structure into which he can incorporate many of the subordinate teaching acts that he routinely performs.

5

Role

The concept of role is inextricably tied to the individual's concept of self and of identity. The individual, with his own traits and orientations, cannot readily be perceived apart from the roles he plays or the functions he performs. The role must certainly reflect the person, just as the person reflects the role.

No one goes through life playing a single role. The child is son or daughter but also playmate, student, grandchild, and so forth. As he develops, his range of roles widens. Earlier roles may be maintained or altered, and others are acquired. For both the person and the people with whom he associates, the necessary adoption of new roles is sometimes difficult to accept. The parent who has known his child as a dependent youth may be unable to see him as an independent adult. Such perceptions markedly influence one's own self-image, since roles are invariably tied to the expectations of others.

At any point in time, the person can be playing many roles. The adult is simultaneously spouse, parent, professional person, and tennis player or gardener. When a physician injects an antibiotic into a patient, he is performing a particular act incorporated in the healing role. When he tells the patient not to smoke, he is acting in the teaching role. Both are part of his overall role of physician. Similarly, a portion of the parent role involves teaching. When a parent cuddles his child, he may be simply a father, but when he tells the child not to play in the traffic, he becomes a teacher.

Each person plays his many roles concurrently. In each he assumes a particular stance, often displaying characteristics in one situation that do not appear in others. This is why it is often distressing to see a person we know in one context playing a different role in another situation—for example, the teacher acting as administrator, the colleague as judge. The person must reconcile his many roles, despite the conflicts often inherent among them.

ROLE CONCEPTUALIZATIONS

Role is a pervasive concept, frequently referred to but rarely described with precision. It can be seen in many ways: in terms of the reference group defining the roles, of the personality characteristics and perceptions of individuals who perform in different roles, or of the actual functions performed within a specific role. And, although different theorists describe the term *role* in different ways, the variation is one of degree rather than of content.

Murphy (1947) views the role as a more or less fixed way of behaving, forced on the individual by his culture. In particular, he emphasizes the importance of the individual's role as it relates to his interactions with significant others in his entire environmental context. On the other hand, Kelly holds that role is a psychological process leading to "an ongoing pattern of behavior that follows from a person's understanding of how the others who are associated in his task think. In idiomatic language, a role is a position that one can play on a certain team without even waiting for the signals" (1963, pp. 97–98). While this definition ties the concept of role to the individual's personal construct system and anchors it to his perceptive framework, Kelly also points out that seeing oneself as playing a role is *not* equivalent to identifying oneself as a "static entity." Rather, role refers to a process that is carried on in relation to other people— appropriate to the psychological system of the individual but also dependent on the cognitive developments within a group. Here too role is conceptualized as being dependent on a social process or an interaction between the individual and the group.

Cottrell further emphasizes the social-interactional aspect, defining role as an

> . . . internally consistent series of conditioned responses by one member of a social situation which represents the stimulus pattern for a similarly internally consistent series of conditioned responses of the other(s) in that situation. Dealing with human behavior in terms of roles, therefore, requires that any item of behavior must always be placed in some self–other context. (1942, p. 617)

When applied to the schools, then, the concept of role would be viewed in terms of the relationships between teacher and students, teacher and colleagues, and teacher and administrators.

Like other behavioral scientists—for example, McClelland (1951), Newcomb (1950), Parsons (1951), and Waller (1960)—Sarbin (1954) emphasizes both the synthetic and the interactional nature of self and role. However, a more important contribution to understanding individual functioning lies in Sarbin's analysis of role conflicts. Several conditions may foster self–role conflicts that call into play various personal adjustment techniques or defense mechanisms; for example, rationalization, repression, and negativism are sometimes used to reconcile the disturbances stimulated by the broader system.

In the schools, conflicts between administrators and faculty members frequently stem from their incongruent perceptions of role demands and role performance. In an academic context, role demands are what the teacher is supposed to do to carry out the formal educational program; they arise from certain traditions, ideologies, and social organizations of the college, and from the entire cultural climate. Role performance is what the instructor actually does, and although performance is generally determined by role demands, it is not always consistent with these demands. A major determinant of role performance is the teacher's perception of role demands. He may—and frequently does—see them very differently from the administrator and those who write the regulations.

Basic to the conceptualizations of role demands and role performance are the assumptions that (1) interpersonal/environmental contexts determine role—that is, other people's anticipations of how a person playing a certain role will act are, in fact, the determinants of "proper" role behavior; (2) each individual plays a number of roles; (3) the role expectations held by individuals or defined by other members of a group are related to the individual's position in a given social system; (4) the individual's position in the social system affects the nature of his social relationships as well as his role expectations; and (5) role expectations emanate both from the broader society—that is, from the individual's reference group—and from his own perception of the situation.

CLASSIFYING TEACHERS' ROLES

We have described role as the pattern of behavior an individual exhibits according to the expectations of others and to his own interpretation of appropriate attitude and action. One's behavior is thus a function of the positions he occupies. By assuming the position of teacher, he may immediately become a classroom lecturer because he feels that others expect him to. Or he may act as judge and distributor of fines (transmitted as poor or failing course grades) because he perceives his role as one of a manipulator of destiny, a punisher of behavior that falls short of expectation, and an overall judge. In all cases, his role depends on the interplay between the group and the person himself. The role of the teacher depends on students, colleagues, community, and administrators. It varies with the situation and with the people who interpret it. Differences in interpretation are reflected not only in the many ways faculty members act but also in the many definitions of "proper" faculty role that have been sketched by different authors.

The academic role has been described by Buxton (1956) as a composite of all the functions a person fills in his department or institution. Because there is evidently much specialization of function by staff members, roles need to be described as explicitly as possible. Any or all functions may help define role: the courses the instructor teaches, the research area in which he functions, his special skills. Other teacher functions include activities such as lecturing, dealing with non-academic groups, curriculum development, directing and stimulating undergraduate research, tutorial advising of students, administration of inter-department programs, and lecturing at colloquies. Again it becomes apparent that the words "teacher" and "professor" include a variety of functions that both complement and conflict with each other. Accordingly, they may add to the stress and complexity of the actual teaching performance.

The teaching role may also be viewed in relation to the instructor's actions with adults in the community as well as with students in the school. Adult-relationship roles of the teacher are delineated by Symonds (1949; 1954) as those of the employee who is subordinate to his supervisor but is simultaneously an advisor to superiors and colleagues—the follower and the leader. On the other hand, student-relationship roles of the teacher are seen in terms of learning mediator, disciplinarian, parent substitute, confidant, and paragon of middle-class morality. These types of relationships give rise to the categorizations of particular functions within the teaching role that are explored in chapters 6, 7, and 8.

The many roles assumed by the American college professor, classified by Knapp according to a historical perspective, are designated in terms of three "focal functions": *research, information,* and *character-developing.* The primary purpose of the research function is to coordinate and extend human knowledge in both scientific and humanistic areas; it is a sort of reconnaissance function wherein the teacher must move "intellectually into unexplored domains, obtain new information, and then return and report it with his interpretations, to the main host of society" (Knapp 1962, p. 291). The informational function is performed when formal knowledge is transmitted to students, community, and colleagues. The third function is concerned with the development of character and values. In each case, the manner in which an instructor conducts his teaching depends on which function he sees as most important.

Several areas in which the teacher must have special competence were identified by Bush (1954), who then listed six distinct teaching functions: director of learning in groups; counselor and guidance worker for individual pupils; member of the school community; link between adult society and the future members of that society; link with the community in helping to formulate goals; and member of the profession. Kinney (1952) assumed that the good teacher would function in all these roles, while Fishburn (1955), believing that a person strong in one area may not necessarily be strong in another, saw the functions as requiring distinctive roles, not readily assumable by all.

Role classification is another potentially important approach for understanding teacher behavior. Sorenson, Husek, and Yu (1963) present a design to assess teacher role expectations in terms of six dimensions: information giver, disciplinarian, advisor, counselor, motivator, and referrer. A three-dimensional process relating a teacher's behavior to other adults in the school system and to the students has also been posited in terms of the concept of role (Havighurst and Neugarten 1967).

These interpretations of role appear especially relevant to understanding the teacher in the community college. Although he performs many functions, he may be able to differentiate his own role by viewing its functions separately. Since it is difficult—perhaps impossible—for anyone to perform consistently in all areas and to meet every demand equally well, it may also help him to consider how he is most effective and most comfortable.

THE ROLE AND ITS PARTS

The teaching role has been characterized in many ways. What is being described, however, is one general role that combines many specialized sub-roles, or functions, and relationships. The failure to recognize that the role is composed of separate functions explains some of the dissonance in interpretations of "teaching" and "the teacher."

Like instructors at every other level of education, the junior college instructor is subject to many demands. He is expected to be a combination of high school teacher, chaperon, model person, instructional leader, college instructor, and personal and public relations counselor. This often creates conflict as he is torn between what he has to do, what he would like to do, and what is interpreted as rewarding by his colleagues and administration. The consensus perception of role largely determines both how people are prepared to fulfill roles and the type of person who seems best suited for it. However, perceptions vary—ask any psychologist!

Further confounding the instructor's perception of his own role are the popular images of "teaching" and "the teacher." In *Up the Down Staircase*, the high school teacher is characterized as "many things at the same time: actor, policeman, scholar, jailor, parent, inspector, referee, friend, psychiatrist, accountant, judge and jury, guide and mentor, wielder of minds, keeper of records . . ." (Kaufman 1964, p. 169). Hence, to the layman—and to many professional educators as well—"teaching" is usually defined as "doing that which a teacher typically does." This view of teaching as an activity rather than as the process of causing learning leads to many difficulties in understanding the role. Almost any activity can be subsumed under the teaching role.

Imprecise use of the terms *teacher* and *teaching* influences role expectations. Significant others—parents, students, administrators, colleagues—expect the instructor to play each of his roles and perform each of his functions at the most propitious time. Conflict obviously occurs when one set of expectations is not matched by corresponding behavior— for example, the teacher who plays policeman when the student expects him to be a friend is acting out of character. The lecturer who fails to gather evidence of student learning may be "teaching," but one would never know.

The varying demands take their toll. The opposing forces on the university faculty member are frequently seen in terms of the false dichotomy, teaching versus research. While research does not have the same priority for community college instructors that it does for university faculty, other situational presses demand attention, often disproportionally so. It will certainly not surprise anyone that general managerial tasks— filling out grade reports, serving on committees—can be overwhelmingly demanding, and that the unsuspecting (frequently the new) instructor may easily take on more than he has time to handle.

Commitments to time dispersion also conflict with one's personal desires. For example, the teacher who feels deeply involved with every student may find this involvement most rewarding, but such intense concern can soon become overly demanding and may pose a dilemma. Can he devote all his time and energy to individual students and still fulfill his commitments to his profession? Is he also able to handle community responsibilities? If an instructor prefers to emphasize one function when he is expected to perform all, can he maintain a proper balance? Must he oscillate among several functions? These questions can be answered only by the person himself—or by the institution that mandates particular directions.

The variety of roles the instructor is called on to play and the number of functions he must perform lead to other difficulties. Instructors frequently become inflexible as a result of the demands their profession makes on them. Sometimes this happens early in one's career: "Craving dignity, elegance, and beauty, I had become base and vulgar and thus could see only the base and vulgar wherever I looked" (Ryan 1970, p. 113). Sometimes, when the beginning teacher has a firm sense of his own identity, his corruption takes longer.

The role has an insidious effect. Waller, a sociologist, explains the phenomenon as follows: a teacher must move in and out of roles, on one occasion saying, "I am your teacher. Do as I say!" and on the other, "But I am also a human being and a good fellow. We have some good times together, don't we?" If the teacher tarries too long in the second role, he loses his authority and must revert to the first. This change of posture occurs a hundred times a day and is equivalent to a rhythmic contraction and expansion of the instructor's personality (Waller 1960, p. 336). "To a great extent, then, I found my first year of teaching to be a period during which I gradually became accustomed to the problem of pedagogical schizophrenia—the phenomenon of reconciling two personalities: the human being and the disciplinarian. . . . Constantly I felt the tension of an internal conflict between the way I knew I had to act as a teacher and the way I really wanted to act as a person (Ryan 1970, pp. 4, 15).

The result of these fluctuations can be marked: "In the life of every teacher there is a significant long-term change in the psychic weight of these roles, a not unusual result being that role number one, the authority role, eats up the friendly role, or absorbs so much of the personality that nothing is left for friendliness to fatten upon" (Waller 1960, p. 336). Or, as Emerson put it, ". . . the gentle teacher, who wishes to be a Providence to youth, is grown a martinet, sore with suspicions . . ." (Silberman 1970, p. 144).

The impact of the teacher's role has led to calls for structural changes that would mitigate its effect on the teacher's personality. Rogers suggests that the constraints presently surrounding the role be reduced in order to "rescue the professor from the intolerable double bind in which he currently lives—on the one hand his desire to be a helpful human being to his students, and on the other hand the continuing necessity of being a judge and executioner at the same time" (1969, p. 202).

The Role in Transition

Perceived in different ways by psychologists, educators, and sociologists, faculty roles and functions are greatly in need of redefinition. As Axen says, "When it comes to the crux of the matter, reformed higher education will require a radically changed faculty role—a role more open, less status-bound, less authoritative, and less self-centered—but such a redefinition of role we shun like the plague" (1968, p. 111).

The growth of both faculty and student activism suggests clearly that the teacher's role has moved away from one of authority and is undergoing an important transition. Perhaps a definition of the special functions played by teachers would facilitate better understanding of their many roles. Just as courses are classified on the basis of content and curriculum, so it might be appropriate to consider separately the teacher's various functions in terms of lecturing, test building, engaging in tutorial exchanges with students, counseling, and so on. Such an approach holds several possibilities. By understanding that personalities vary and that characteristics of effective teachers may, indeed, be quite different, we may be in a better position to discover the kinds of teachers who best perform specific functions. This, of course, is a recommendation in favor of specialization on the basis of function rather than according to academic discipline.

The literature disseminated by many colleges seems to imply that good teachers are born and that the roles thrust upon them are consistent and constant. Although all colleges tend to boast about their "good" teachers, the "good" teacher is seldom described and no hint is given about how he became that way. There is seldom any recognition of personality differences, different conceptions of role demands, different ways in which the various teaching functions will be performed. Perhaps some elements of role theory can be used by the instructor to develop a better understanding of the way he and his colleagues function.

Understanding and classifying his functions, differentiating dominant and auxiliary acts, separating the "teacher" from the "teaching process," may all provide the person with a better view of his roles, lead to specialization within the profession, and enhance the identity of the instructor. If the teacher sees himself—and is seen as—a master performer of all functions, he must then be a flexible, adaptable kind of person who can jump from one type of activity to another. Perhaps he can best be likened to the actor who dons many masks and is able to play various roles with some degree of abandon. However, while flexibility is an essential trait in the well-functioning personality, unrelated, non-integrative adaption to all roles appears undesirable.

Accepting a variety of roles must be built on a core of self-knowledge. The new instructor often struggles to find simultaneously self and appropriate role. "But I did not know myself," said the insightful teacher at the end of her first year, "and I did not know the role I haphazardly tried to play.... Perhaps the lesson hardest to learn during the first year of teaching was that I could not be the same kind of teacher as someone else.... I could not seem to gain from imitating those whom I thought successful teachers. Teaching, I finally decided, is somehow too closely knit into the basic fabric of one's character and personality to be copied" (Ryan 1970, pp. 105, 119).

Unless the individual operates within his own framework, he is doomed to frustration of intent. The most consistently unsuccessful instructor (in terms of lasting effect on students) we have ever encountered was a professor whose own life style was authoritarian in the extreme, but who "knew" that "good teachers must be permissive." For years, in his determination to manage his classes on a "Well, what do *you* think?" basis, he condemned himself to violent headaches and his students to anxious bewilderment. Putting it in the idiom of the seventies, you must do your own thing.

6

The Model

Some men . . . [write] books, others build institutions, others teach, still others are. (Arrowsmith 1970, p. 50)

The model of our behavior, not our radical arguments, is what is most persuasive. (L. Friedman et al. 1970, p. 12)

The teacher has been idealized as a model person, as an all-powerful, ever-righteous image to which the subservient person must attach himself, or at which he must at least gaze reverently. Indeed, it is frequently implied that students achieve their maturity by introjecting the strength and wisdom of their teachers. Even the redoubtable Dr. Spock emphasizes that students pick up a teacher's basic attitudes through identification more than by attending his explications (1969, p. 195).

Almost every book on education refers to the idea of the teacher as model. Yet there is no one theory of modeling, no one generally accepted definition of the term. We actually know little about the archetype of the teacher, the perceptions held by students of their teachers, or the long-term effects of teachers on students—all elements of modeling. As Adelson so perceptively points out, theories of education often include views of modeling that are "implicit, unacknowledged, unexamined" (1962, p. 397).

The concept might be better understood in terms of its parts. We can conceive of model *elements* rather than model *wholes*. Further, we think of some model elements as positive and others as negative. Each component is able to affect the other, and thereby to mandate the general impression gained by observers. Accordingly, a model can have either a positive or a negative effect—students can assume the weaknesses and ignorances of a teacher model just as they can gain strength and wisdom from him. When the positive side of a person dominates, the model is presumed to have a "good" effect. When negative elements stand out, the model is perceived as a debilitating force.

How the instructor is seen by significant others relates to how he perceives his role and thus to the way he functions as a model. The teacher who is aware of the many features he may project as model may also become more aware of his own many facets. He can then become conscious of those dimensions that he would want to incorporate—and to project to others—and of those that he would reject.

THE PROFESSOR
IN PERSPECTIVE

Many ties bind the community college instructor and the four-year college professor, not the least of which are the images he presents to others. The college professor has been seen in several lights. He has been esteemed and respected and has also become the subject of both casual and derogatory remarks by administrators, students, and the popular press. Views shift with the times.

A survey of American periodicals from the turn of the century to 1938 produced many articles alluding to the professional college teacher; it found him described in terms of "unselfishness, humanness, practicality, love of knowledge, competency, social inadequacy, inpracticality and dispassion" (Bowman 1938). Farley (1964) updated this survey and found that the image had changed somewhat. According to the popular literature, the professor had become "more practical and less theoretical, more humane and less aloof, more a 'man of the world' and less a recluse." The popular press also expressed concern over burning issues of the time— academic freedom, for example, during the period from 1946 to 1955 (Hakanson 1967). All the summaries made prior to the student uprisings of the late 1960s found the professor generally well treated—often considered misguided and ineffectual but nonetheless well meaning.

In their investigation of the occupational stereotypes held by students, Beardslee and O'Dowd (1959) found college professors rated highest of all professions in intelligence, thoughtfulness, personal satisfaction; and wisdom. As the professional whom the students would most prefer to be like, he received the highest ratings. On the other hand, the professor was assessed low in conservatism, absence of emotional problems, and wealth.

Study upon study has ranked characteristics of the "ideal teacher." As long ago as 1930, Clinton found that students attributed to the ideal college professor such qualities as interest in students, fairness, pleasing personality, keenness of intellect, and range of information. A similar approach to defining the image of the ideal professor was employed by Bousfield (1940), who discovered the same attributes but in different order: fairness, mastery of subject, presentation, organization of material, clear exposition, keenness of intellect, interest in students, and helpfulness.

When several hundred college presidents were asked to list the most valued characteristics of college instructors, their ideal qualifications—or model elements—for faculty in liberal arts colleges were encouragement of individual thoughts, emotional stability, tolerance, and sympathy (Trabue 1950). The college presidents also preferred the kind of instructor who identified himself primarily as a college teacher rather than as a specialist in a subject area.

Several other investigations have been concerned with the attributes of teachers of known or acknowledged distinction. An early study of instructors in 187 church-affiliated colleges found the highest ratings given to those individuals who were characterized chiefly by their interest in students, sympathy, helpfulness, and enthusiasm; mastery of subject matter and industry were rated the least desirable qualities. Social skills and organizational competency ranked ahead of intellectual distinction, while an emphasis on a "teaching" rather than a disciplinary orientation was noted (Kelly 1929).

Certain predominant characteristics of college instructors cited by Gustad (1960) suggest that, as a group, college professors would score very high on measures of intellectual ability. Since this dimension does not differentiate people in academic life from members of other occupational groups where a high degree of intelligence is mandatory, however, it is a necessary but hardly a sufficient characteristic.

These are but a few of the studies that have described various perceptions of the college instructor. If the investigations were repeated now, the views might shift. The extreme pressures on institutions of higher education in the late 1960s would probably be revealed in changed perceptions of instructors, especially as held by particular groups both within and without the college community.

The Model
in Transition

The campus unrest of the late 1960s called into question the concept of the instructor as a positive model. Whereas he was still seen as a model of rational being, his image was less secure. At his best, the instructor exemplified the fruits of scholarship, thought, and logical dialogue. He was still the image of man thinking, using his talents to build a good life, functioning as "witness to the satisfactions of scholarship, sensibility, and expertise." He was also the "model of a learner" who reflected the values implicit in the ideal of humanistic scholarship (Schwab 1969). The ideal instructor—model had integrated his profession and his personal self and become a figure worthy of emulation.

However, the number of these positive models and their suitability to the times became issues of concern. Was "man thinking" the most appropriate model? Many students thought otherwise. And how many models are there that truly fit this description? Schwab deplores the scarcity of these types of people on the college campuses, arguing that although many disciplinarians may be found, few use their thinking ability to build a comprehensive stature. According to Schwab, in many colleges there is

> ... a literal poverty ... of models as such. The faculty have no professional lives apart from their teaching. They make no music. They write no books. They uncover no new knowledge. They forge no policies. They are not conspicuously engaged in honorable public service. They administer little apart from their homes and classrooms. They teach, to be sure, but their teaching is the full-time service they perform, not a flowering or sharing of expertise or scholarship. (Schwab 1969, p. 18)

And only by accident, Schwab continues, "... are students witnesses to the satisfactions of developed competences and cultivated tastes, of lives of research and scholarship, artistic and institutional creation, thoughtful public service and administration" (Ibid., p. 39).

Taylor echoes these remarks, saying that a student "judges a man by what he does with his life, and he finds few among his professors whose lives reflect the values implicit in the ideal of humanist scholarship" (1969, p. 85). Unless the instructor has used his professional activities to build a style of life that stands in contrast to what Schwab calls the "convention-bound, competition-directed, indulgent, tasteless, or vacant styles, one or more of which is likely to characterize most students' homes" (1969, p. 50), his effect may not be positive at all. And for students who are in college principally because of the draft or because they choose to postpone making a vocational commitment, the faculty member is no longer the seductive model that he was for undergraduates in the small liberal arts college of fond memory.

The image is valid but the sentiment is hardly new. More than 40 years earlier, Bode questioned the implications that study and research were the only ways of exhibiting intelligence. He saw the academician as "just a person with a highly specialized type of interest," as one who "should not be permitted to set up his personal idiosyncrasy as a model to be copied by everyone else" (1927, p. 296). And he found repugnant "the view that academic specialization ... is somehow superior to other forms of specialization" stemming as it does from nothing except "an aristocratic tradition" (Ibid., p. 307).

The very idea of a model adult—reflecting, musing, spending time in an academic discipline, reading, thinking, not acting—may be invalid for students who will be spending a portion of their adult lives in the twenty-first century. Taylor expresses it well: "That the academic mind at its best ... is usually a good one for general intellectual use is not at issue. But the academic mind is one which is trained to do particular things very well, and is not necessarily the model for the mind and character of the liberally educated person ..." (1969, p. 142). It is a limiting, uni-dimensional model developed originally by the Greek philosophers who saw it as the highest order of humanity, a pattern that set them apart from those who performed tangibly productive labor.

The model of "reflective" man is opposed to "man in action." It perpetuates the popular belief in a dichotomy between those who think and those who do—between the leisure and the labor classes. However, as society progresses toward technological automation, that dichotomy is proving false. It is even more than false—it is potentially debilitating, because all the young people in college do not desire, and cannot be expected to lead, "the reflective life"—even if there were such a thing.

The very idea of a life of reflection is anathema to the more socially committed students, and it has stimulated charges of faculty irrelevance. " 'What is the relevance of this pedantry?' " students cried out at the end of one of Goodman's lectures on history, philosophy, and science. " 'It's detached scholarship! ... Who gives you the right to lecture at *us*? ... How can you talk about *that*, when people are being killed in Vietnam?' " (1970, p. 45). Similar cries have been heard throughout the land.

Some instructors have reacted to such charges by becoming political activists. Others have attempted to minimize their reflective or rational orientations, choosing instead to use their own "feelings, thoughts and behavior ... as the prime content to be weighed, analyzed, commented upon" (Cahn 1968). These individuals feel that it is their responsibility to be models of good group members. However, even though they have changed the model from "reflective man" to "man revealing himself to others," they still serve as models; instead of "man thinking" they have become "man feeling." By rejecting one element—rationality—because "it is no longer relevant," they have gone to the opposite extreme. However, they may soon find the students' reactions against this new style just as intense as they were against isolated disciplinarianism. Whether a total commitment to "feelingness" is well suited to the times remains a moot point.

THE NEGATIVE MODEL

Comprised of many dimensions, the person does not always project a positive image. Indeed, when all elements are considered, some models emerge as negative archetypes. The teacher who uses a ruler to control his class, the instructor who waves failing grades as his banner of frustration and revenge, the person who masks bigotry with unsubtle selection devices—all convey impressions of negativism that prevail long after formal schooling has been terminated.

Teachers project positive images *and* negative images. Consider these types:

The Defender:	"I like the way I teach. My methods and my old shoes both feel good. Why are you critical of my comfort?"
The Actor:	"Laugh and applaud when I expound and posit— or else."
The Swashbuckler:	"En garde! Take that! I'll teach you to turn in papers like this! Ha! Watch the red ink (blood) drip down your page."
The Jokester:	"I've got a secret. I know something you don't know. Guess what you have to do to pass the course. All right, I'll tell you. The final exam will cover the first 14 shelves to the left as you enter the library. Ha ha."
The Raconteur:	"Today, the first day of class, reminds me of something that happened to me in the first year of my marriage. . . . Tomorrow, I'll have a story about the second year."
The Self-Deceiver:	"I know I'm a success. My students tell me so. Why, just last week, a student called and said. . . ."
The Voyeur:	"How *is* your psyche these days? *Do* tell me more about it."

Although these categories are somewhat overstated, at least one of these types is encountered at every level of education. Other negative models include the unrealistically strict and frustrated pedants who tell serious junior college students, "I don't give 'A's because if you deserve an 'A', you should be in the university." Or teachers who toss into the classroom irrelevant, insidious, and wholly unnecessary personal remarks about students' long hair or short skirts or shabby moccasins. There are many examples of bigoted racists who use their positions as a cover and a license for prejudice, and of instructors who blithely encourage a selected few students while consistently denigrating the others.

The negative model may also be a pseudo-therapist—the English instructor, for example, who attempts to teach symbolic recognition by means of mathematical formulas, accusing students who contend they want to study literature, not algebra, of having a "psychological block against numbers." They do, and under this sort of treatment they quickly develop "psychological blocks" against teachers who so obviously operate well out of their own provinces. Such people use public classrooms, supposedly dedicated to learning and individual rights, as amateur treatment centers or as soapboxes from which to express their own hatreds.

It has been said that hate makes haters of its victims. Is this what "education" is all about?

Rogers talks about an approach/avoidance stance adopted by many instructors: "In some instances faculty members put the student in a real 'double bind' situation by giving him a contradictory message. It is as if the faculty member said: 'I welcome you to a warm and close interpersonal relationship—and when you come close I will clobber you with my evaluation'" (1969, p. 184). More than negative models, these teachers are sadists. And although we might charitably assume that all sadistic teachers are unconsciously so unless they are psychopathic, the effect on the student is the same.

Where do such teachers come from? Why do they act as they do? To be sure, Silberman notes, teaching has its share of sadists and clods, of insecure and angry men and women who hate their students for their openness, their exuberance, their color, their affluence, or their youth. However, they may not have been that way at the start of their careers. The teaching role demands a high price. Persuading young people to perform according to an impersonal schedule can be debilitating, and the teacher's interest in students "can quickly degenerate into being harsh for the student's own good or hating him as an incorrigible animal" (Goodman 1970, p. 77).

It is difficult to identify all the effects of these negative models, but we may readily speculate on their *own* problems. Menninger suggests that

> ... a significant proportion of teachers are either mentally ill or suffering from serious emotional maladjustments.... Many others have so meager a background of experience in life that they lack adequate grasp of reality or any possibilities for either insight or genuine affection. To the extent that they attain any influence with their students, they often foster prejudice, superstition, emotionalized attitudes, and, worst of all, fears and withdrawal.... [They live] drab, colorless, empty lives, ... lacking in esthetic sensitivity or cultural background ... [and] reveal their emotional pathology in the form of moodiness, sulkiness, sarcasm, hypercriticalness, bullying, and domination.... [They] suffer from such neurotic conflicts [as] inferiority feelings, racial prejudices, depression, feelings of being discriminated against, ... [using] the teaching situation as a means of obtaining relief. (1959, pp. 58–59)

These are severe indictments. Menninger is not castigating the entire profession—yet, the maladjusted person certainly is to be found in the schools. According to Brenton, "In almost every district one finds pure and simple time servers and, worse, teachers who can't control themselves and who make school a cruel, unbearable experience.... Who are they? Teachers know—because they talk about it among themselves—which of their colleagues are sadists, or voyeurs or too hysterical to contain themselves or their classes" (1970, pp. 250–51). Why, then, are they not cast out? Because they are protected by the rules of a system that makes dismissal an onerous procedure, by administrators who don't want to stick out their necks, by professional associations that will not take responsibility for policing their own ranks, and by their own knowledge that their effects cannot be readily assessed. All this makes them dangerous. Our present procedures of teacher selection, promotion, and evaluation are too crude to identify such individuals with much accuracy or reliability. We can but speculate on the extent of the problem.

Setting aside clear-cut cases of pathology, there is much that can be said about the vast majority of instructors, most of whom are "normal." These teachers may still serve as negative models, but in fairness to them it must be noted that their rationalizations are frequently so ingrained that they do not realize what they are doing. This type of instructor may condemn a student to a vocational program ("for his own good—it will help him earn a living") because the instructor does not know how to structure the concepts in his field so that they appear meaningful. Or he may firmly believe he is aiding his students' learning by making essay exams esoteric and by constructing quick-score items with triple negatives because he "has to get them ready for difficult work."

However, his colleagues must share the blame for his attitudes and actions. The instructor may fail a large proportion of his class under the guise of "college standards," never really knowing that his own "standards" shift at his whim. With Rogers, we ask why this person is frequently considered "a better (because more 'tough-minded') instructor than his colleague who fails none" (1969, p. 184). In many institutions, the faculty and administration not only condone, they even support this form of rejection.

The unaware person who is unconsciously negative rather than pathologically sadistic needs understanding, not condemnation. Let his colleagues question the instructor who "maintains high standards," who refuses to set specific objectives because "they inhibit the students' learning of higher order concepts," who maintains an air of secrecy regarding course content and examination procedures "to keep them on their toes." Let them wonder why he needs his students' deference or why he refuses to change his methods, regardless of the evidence of their ineffectiveness that may be brought to bear. But they should try to be sensitive to the pattern of the entire person before attempting to deal with his manifestations of unease. The profession can impose sanctions, but in all these matters there is no substitute for self-awareness. If the teacher who exemplifies a negative model is to change, it must be he who effects the change.

MIRROR IMAGES

The case of the negative model is not one-sided. The person—student or teacher—often sees his own positive and negative images mirrored in others. Accordingly, much of the acceptance or rejection of the teacher is independent of the instructor himself; instead, it actually reflects the students' own projections.

People react to models in different ways. A particularly tenuous position is that of the student who looks to models of authority but, unaware of his own inner processes, is correspondingly blind to the trap of identification in which he might be caught. Other students resist the identity of the teacher just because it *is* too tempting. These students affect a guise of distance or aloofness because they are, in Erikson's words (1963), in a kind of "moratorium," thinking, waiting for the proper time to pledge commitment, but not yet ready for a personal ideal. Still other students shop around for models, not merely aping a teacher's mannerisms and tricks, not assuming the irrelevant qualities of the professor role, and not abandoning their own resources to incorporate those qualities.

All these mechanisms, of course, depend on the student's own percepts and needs as well as the percepts and needs of the professor. It is therefore no wonder that discussions of the "good" teacher, as Adelson suggests,

> . . . are likely to leave us more uplifted than enlightened. [Since they] . . . generally amount to little more than an assemblage of virtues; we miss in them a sense of the complexity and ambiguity that we know to characterize the teacher's work. Here are some paradoxes . . . : a teacher may be a good teacher yet not serve as a model to any of his students; he may inspire his students and yet fail to influence them; he may influence them without inspiring them; he may be a model for them and yet not be an effective teacher; and so on. (1962, pp. 405–6)

The model—positive or negative—is one function that the instructor assumes, but even this function is in transition. The idea of a single-faceted individual does not apply to the 1970s—if, indeed, it was ever appropriate. It is possible for an instructor to be seen as a total person without stripping himself naked. One can be "visible as a *man*, visible as one who could be helpful, who probably would help if asked, who *does not want* to help—a man of penetrable reserve" (Schwab 1969, p. 292). But this is the integrated man, the total person exemplifying a full life, the individual Sanford (1968) sees as continually learning, increasing his understanding of situation and of self, and revealing his humanity. This is the man with a sense of purpose, who is aware of the many facets of his personality—both positive and negative—and who knows what he is about. This is the mature professional instructor.

7

The Mediator

Because a major tendency among American youth is toward functional equality, the concept of the teacher as authority figure is gathering cobwebs. In fact, the archetypal notion is on its way to becoming as obsolete as the caricature of the old maid schoolmarm or the punitive wielder of the hickory stick. The concept of the "model person" suggests someone to emulate, a superior figure—the person of whom one can say, "I want to be like him." It also suggests an individual from whom one would recoil—"He is just about the last human being I would want to be like!" Both reactions, however, imply a figure whose authority derives from his age and status. It is this concept that has gradually eroded. The implication of a figure apart from and, indeed, greater (or lesser) than, the perceiver is not as viable as it was to earlier generations.

A growing number of young adults choose to emphasize the unity of relationships. They see a wider assortment of people as peers and they prefer to look on their teachers as coequals. This view has led to a breakdown in the idea of authority as being ascribed to a select few. Many students would rather not see their instructor as "Professor Blank" who stands aloof, but as "Bill" who involves himself actively as one of the group. This attitude is not confined to the students alone. Many instructors prefer to step out from behind the lectern, to erase the image of model, and to interact closely with their students. A more humanistic element creeps in, a sharing rather than a superior–inferior relationship.

The concept of functional equality implies a sense of relatedness. It refers to basic attitudes, to the way people honestly see themselves, not to the physical arrangements of a classroom or lecture hall. A person can be alone, indifferent, or closely connected in a crowd or in a tête-à-tête. There may be rapport between the instructor and the 500 students to whom he is lecturing; there may be aloofness and alienation in a one-to-one situation. It is not the structure that gives rise to interactions, but the feelings, the sense of openness, and the desires that exist within the people who are involved. The *mediator* builds on these feelings.

The mediator sees his primary function—and indeed, often his exclusive function—as one of intervention with his students. Consciously or not, he focuses directly on the processes of human development. Conceptually, the very existence of the mediator depends on the element of interaction itself. Although the model may be perceived separately—apart from the audience—the mediator must actually intervene with others. He is within and a part of his students' lives, and he feels they are equally a part of his.

This chapter describes the way the mediator functions. It points up his feelings of closeness to his students, as exemplified by his reactions to automated instructional processes. Finally, it considers him in three of the forms in which he may appear: the mediator as indispensable man, as therapist, and as mystic.

MEDIA AND THE MEDIATOR

Certain controversies arise when different perceptions of the same role are held by different people—especially when those who do not share the perceptions misunderstand the motives of those who do. The continuing questions of how, when, and why to introduce reproducible media into the schools is a case in point. Concomitantly, and more directly related to our purposes here, it helps to present a picture of the mediator.

A popular position holds that most instructors typically overemphasize the transmission of data—their information-dispensing function. Many writers who insist that the teacher should lecture less suggest that he spend more time selecting and using reproducible media—Richmond (1969), for example. They are, in fact, opting for the teacher's acting less as a medium of information transmission and more as an organizer.

Others reject the information dispenser on different grounds. They contend that students should be exposed to the "scholarly model, counselor, facilitator, and friend" rather than the "information-giver" (Heist and Wilson 1968); accordingly, they advocate that the instructor present an image of a model person rather than of a medium of instruction. Thus, for differing reasons, the conception of the instructor as a medium—one who inserts himself between the student and the knowledge—is attacked.

Why are criticisms of the instructor as intermediary so frequent? The most commonly extended reason relates to the instructor who, in his capacity as medium, acts as a mere dispenser of information. The position holds that that activity is obsolete because information in the form of raw data, analytic treatments, and syntheses is available from myriad sources other than the teacher himself. Because reproducible media, from the printed book to the computer-assisted tutorial, may be readily found, the teacher should engage in other types of activities.

In addition, these critics present a picture of the instructor standing between the student and a pool of knowledge, ladling out dippers at will, and sprinkling drops on the student. Some go as far as to suggest that he sprays data as with a fire hose—and heaven help the slow drinkers! It follows, then, that the student should be allowed to drink at his own pace—as in programmed instruction, pick his own sequence—as in independent study, and not be forced to endure the frequent impatience, ineptitude, and the irrelevant comments of the live instructor.

Although the vision of students being led to knowledge through carefully designed reproducible media seems attractive, it has gained meager support among college teachers. Usually, views on the teaching–learning process are presented to the faculty by programmers, media specialists, certain administrators, and other educators. These "outsiders" prepare the media, arrange the sequences, and introduce their materials. However, as the instructors resist both passively and overtly, the media specialists are inevitably foiled. Despite broad promises, as Oettinger (1969) notes, at no level of the educational enterprise have reproducible media made significant inroads into the teacher's domain. Frequently, instructors have subverted them, contending as an excuse that they are "mechanistic" or "dehumanizing." Thus, the media often remain in locked closets, not doing what they were supposed to do, not "releasing the teacher for creative work with the students," not living up to the claims of the media specialists.

An attempt to understand why reproducible media have failed to change the schools would take many pages. Part of the problem is that the media specialist (tapes in hand) and the instructor (clinging to his classrooms full of students) are arguing at cross purposes. In their soi-disant capacity as "systems analysts," the media specialists speak of "feedback loops," "control functions," and "process constraints." To them, instructors are part of the school environment, to be cajoled, coerced, or shunted aside.

But the instructors put themselves at the center of the enterprise, feeling genuinely that what the students need most of all is "contact with *me*." In their view, the school is a housing whose major purpose is to bring students into proximity with teachers (Cohen 1970c). Hardware and programmed lessons, computers and audio tapes are only devices that foil this aim.

It is rather easy to demonstrate the superior efficiency of a printed, taped, filmed, or computerized medium of data transmission as compared to a live lecturer or discussion leader. But the mediator who refuses to move away from his apparent function as information dispenser does not actually see himself as a data transmitter at all. He sees the data as unimportant. Whereas the media specialist views the instructor as an information dispenser of minimal efficacy, and accordingly seeks to move him out of the way, the mediator sees himself as actually intervening for the students' benefit—data be damned!

The instructor as mediator may grant that certain reproducible media present certain course content better—in fact, he may even use a variety of media forms in his own teaching activities. But it is conceptually impossible for him to remove himself from the role that places him between the students and their learning—not necessarily because he fancies that he knows and can explain better than anyone else what is in the pool of knowledge, but because he does not perceive a pool at all. His conception of the teacher's role lies elsewhere.

The mediator's goal is the process of student learning. To him the purpose of college—and, concomitantly, his own purpose—is involvement with the students, becoming a party to their development. No extrinsic pool of knowledge for him! Learning is perceived as being primarily self-generated, and he, the teacher, must project himself into each student's mind and being to facilitate the process. Whether the mediator is actively transmitting information, overtly offering support by creating a sympathetic climate, or serving somewhere between those two positions, he feels that he must personally be involved with his students. Therefore, he rejects what he sees as mechanistic, ends-oriented media. And there the controversy rests.

THE INDISPENSABLE MAN

For the mediator intent on process, assessment of effects seldom enters the picture. If he appraises anything, it is usually his own functioning. In his conviction that he is indispensable, he is especially open to self-deception.

The point warrants elaboration. Instructor self-deception appears frequently in the form of instruction known as the "discussion section." The real purpose of discussion should be to lead students to think independently by allowing them to participate, to share ideas, to discern whether arguments have merits or weaknesses—in short, to practice the role of "the rational being in dialogue with his fellows." This is the presumed product of discussion. Yet the instructor functioning as mediator tends to focus primarily on self; thus he can most easily mistake his own progress for the progress of the group. This happens especially when students become more and more susceptible to the climate of the discussion sessions. They begin to participate, to speak when they have something to say, and to share their inmost ideas and feelings. At that point the instructor feels that the sessions are contributing to student change, while actually, the students have only learned to conduct themselves the way he wants them to—they volunteer or speak when spoken to, address themselves to the topic, or, being divergent, bring in new ideas or parody old ones. They do whatever pleases their leader. In two different discussion groups with two different instructors, the same student, wittingly or unwittingly, may so adopt the posture chosen by each instructor that he acts two distinct roles, each of which is accepted as evidence of his learning to think for himself. He has learned something, but it may be quite different from that which the instructor thought he was teaching.

As an instructional form, the primary purpose of the discussion session is to lead students to think independently. It is commonplace to say that it is only what students can do *without* the instructor's help that distinguishes their competence from his. However, a discussion section—or indeed, any instructional situation—where the students are truly acting and thinking independently tends to arouse the anxiety of the mediator because it indicates that he is not indispensable. Therefore, he is tempted to "intervene nervously, to describe, to explain, to organize the knowledge for the student, leaving the student with little to do of his own" (Taylor 1969, pp. 182–83). As Holt says,

> Anyone who makes it his life work to help other people may come to believe that they cannot get along without him, and may not want to heed evidence that they can, all too often, stand on their own feet. Many people seem to have built their lives around the notion that they are in some way indispensable to children, and to question this is to attack the very center of their being. (Holt 1967, p. 71)

Whether leading a discussion session, participating in an encounter group, or otherwise mediating in the educational milieu, the teacher–mediator who focuses primarily on self imagines that his efforts will have positive effects on his students' psyches. He supposes that, as a result of his arranging a situation or climate, an environment or mood, something of value will accrue to the student. He sees himself as the manager of an environment that he creates to fit his fancy, a stage set for a play that may never be produced. If only he can project himself, being warm and supportive to the proper degree, his students will be so affected that in later years they will manifest the values implied in the instructor's efforts— or so he thinks.

All teachers, however, do not fulfill a mediating function simply by virtue of their ascribed status. But whether or not they *actually* serve as effective interlocutors, most teachers *think* they do. The things for which faculty members fight hardest are those that help them maintain what they perceive to be a position of direct involvement. The typical instructor will demand open arrangements, allowing the greatest amount of room for individual and spontaneous choice in conducting his classes. He wants to be free to support or to chastise the students through smiles or frowns, kind or harsh words, high or low grade marks. Whether his students learn more than they would if he were totally out of the picture never crosses his mind.

These are broad pictures. Perhaps the concept can be better understood if the extremes are pointed out, if the mediator is seen as a therapist or a mystic. Such views further describe the person who is focused on process rather than on product; on means rather than on ends; on the mystique of human change, not on the altered behavior that results; on his impact as a person, not his effect on student learning. Any instructor might well ask himself whether he is adopting a single pose or whether this posture is merely one among many facets of his teaching role.

The Mediator as Therapist

Several people have spoken of the parallels between instruction and therapy and of the common characteristics that run through such helping relationships as counseling, therapy, supervision, and instruction. Certain therapeutic agents were designated by Heine (1950) as factors commonly held by therapists representing three different approaches. Other investigators have concluded that the "good" teaching relationship, like the optimal therapeutic relationship, is in fact merely a good interpersonal interaction (Fiedler 1950). And Reitz, Very, and Guthrie (1965) questioned whether there were similarities between descriptions of "ideal" teacher–student relationships offered by university teachers and descriptions of ideal therapeutic relationships given by trained therapists. In their investigation, experienced and novice teachers from six colleges were asked to describe their conception of the ideal undergraduate teacher–student relationship. Although teachers generally agreed on the ideal relationship, experienced teachers agreed more closely among themselves than with therapists. Moreover, the instructors' years of experience influenced the types of relationships they set as goals.

What are the parallels between teaching and therapy? Among the many recent discussions of the helping or therapeutic role of teachers, Rogers's work stands out. More than any other contemporary writer, Rogers sees the teacher as therapist—with student learning depending

> . . . not upon the teaching skills of the leader, not upon his scholarly knowledge of the field, not upon his curricular planning, not upon his use of audiovisual aids, not upon the programmed learning he utilizes, not upon his lectures and presentations, not upon an abundance of books . . . [but] upon certain attitudinal qualities which exist in the presonal *relationship* between the facilitator and the learner. (1969, pp. 105–6)

Basic to this teacher (facilitator)–student relationship are certain attitudes—particularly realness, genuineness, and mutual trust. Rogers sees most teachers as wearing a mask and not allowing students to "get close," but "when the facilitator is a real person, being what he is, entering into a relationship with the learner without presenting a front or a façade, he is much more likely to be effective" (Ibid., p. 106). This, of course, is the ideal therapist–client relationship. And if "the client perceives his therapist as real and genuine, as one who likes, prizes, and empathically understands him, self-learning and therapeutic change are facilitated" (Ibid., p. 116).

Trust, then, freely and genuinely given by the instructor, is the key— the essential ingredient in the relationship between teacher and student. The instructor may set up many kinds of requirements for the students, but he must trust the group and its separate members. The hero or heroine of many novels about teachers has this quality:

McH [the supervisor]:	*You let him go out of the room unescorted?*
I [the teacher]:	He had to go . . .
McH:	He may have been looking at answers!
I:	I don't think so. He told me he wouldn't.
McH:	He *told* you.
I:	Yes.
McH:	And you believed him?
I:	I believe him. (Kaufman 1964, p. 269)

Trust is inextricably interwoven with the sense of identity, with the person's consciousness of his overt behavior as well as with his more private notions and desires. The teacher cannot fake trust; it is not a technique. It must come from within himself; it must be his own style. He is able to give it only to the extent that he is comfortable with it; to share himself only to the extent that he actually desires to.

People have the quality of openness in varying degrees. Pointing out that among school personnel, administrators find it most difficult to reveal their feelings (with college faculty a close second), Rogers concludes, ". . . the more prestige and status and intellectual expertise the person has to defend, the more difficult it is for him to come into a real basic encounter with other persons" (1969, pp. 338–39).

A common theme of much of Sanford's work (1962; 1966; 1967) also concerns therapeutic processes in education. If, as Sanford maintains, higher education can bring about changes in the development of the individual beyond the mere acquisition of a skill or the mastery of a particular field of knowledge, it follows that the institutions and the instructors should consciously attempt to bring about this change. But how—in terms of both cognitive learning and emotional maturity—does such development occur? How can it be encouraged? A student develops when he "is freed from the necessity of maintaining unconscious defensive devices" (Axelrod et al. 1969, p. 16). This freedom grows within a situation of mutual trust, when there is an awareness that unconscious defense processes exist that hinder learning.

The encounter group (T-group, sensitivity training course, human relations workshop) is an attempt to enhance mutual trust and to reduce the debilitating operation of unconscious defense mechanisms. Its techniques, frequently favored by mediators, build on "increasingly free, direct and spontaneous communication between members of the group" (Rogers 1969, p. 142). Their most powerful force "is the close presence of other human beings, without competition or one-upping" (Goodman 1970, p. 57). The mediator may see these kinds of groups as valuable aids and consequently attempt to introduce them in the schools.

At their best, encounter groups foster openness and communication and tend to enhance students' abilities to learn. At their worst, they allow voyeurs to pursue their own ends. If the encounter group leader has undefined goals for the group, is overly eager for progress, pushes or probes, acts according to a pat formula and unconsciously employs techniques that focus on himself rather than on the group, he has the least effect. In fact, he may actually be hindering learning.

But despite the parallels, education is not psychotherapy and the college is not a therapeutic community. The roles of therapist and teacher overlap, yet they are different. Both teaching and therapy are expected to lead to individual change. In therapy, however, the ends may be defined only generally in terms of eventual integration and self-actualization, whereas in education, teaching should lead to learning as defined in terms of specific outcomes. It is true that both therapy and instruction are applied arts, deliberately seeking to change the person. But the rationales behind the treatments differ.

A further difference between therapy and education is that in some cases the results of psychotherapy may be disappointing, but because the general approach is established, both successful and unsuccessful treatment may be evaluated and used as the basis for understanding the process. Education, on the other hand, often functions in the absence of a specific rationale for human development; thus, its failures rarely lead to greater understanding of individual functioning. The mediator as therapist must be aware of the differences between the two. He must recognize that student transference may be a source of motivation for intellectual work, not solely a means of giving the student insight into himself. Although they have a common denominator in terms of process, the goals of psychotherapy and education are different.

Problems arise when the mediator–therapist–teacher identifies exclusively with the therapist, adopting too many of his behavioral patterns. Students are sent to school to be taught—not treated. Jones argues that

> Any attempt to treat a student, when not clearly intended as subordinate to the aims of teaching, should be viewed with suspicion. . . . Mental health needs cannot be optimally served in classrooms *except* as a means to improve teaching. (1968, p. 160)

Pointing to "a typical first error made by many teachers who become persuaded that psychoanalytic principles can approve their teaching skills," he sees these instructors as not content merely to allow their students to confront emotionally charged issues. Instead, "they rush to *interpret* them . . . and therefore run contrary to the manifest purposes of teaching and to the attitudes of many therapists" (Ibid., p. 182).

In spite of certain dimensions held in common, then, education is not a therapeutic relationship. As Sanford and others have pointed out, teaching is not therapy and the teacher is not a therapist. But since the intent of the college is to enhance individual development, the role of the mediator in facilitating the development process looms large.

At his best, the mediator arranges a climate in which both cognitive and affective changes are allowed to occur. He recognizes both the strengths and the weaknesses of his students, and when their weaknesses extend beyond the province of education, he refers students to the proper therapeutic sources. But primarily he permits his students "to be"—and is able to do so because he knows who he himself is.

Certain psychological processes, on the part of both instructors and students, can minimize learning. Along with the therapist, the mediator in the academic situation takes account of—and frequently builds upon—such defenses as transference and identification. He believes that student-teacher relationships are affected by unconscious expectations and needs as well as by the observable interchanges within the classroom; that in order for real development to take place in the student, various dynamic forces must be considered. When these forces are brought into the open, when the student can acknowledge the impact of defense mechanisms and archetypal images on his own acceptance or rejection of cognitive content, he is then able to "learn." The teacher who has enhanced this process of awareness has actually facilitated learning.

THE MEDIATOR AS MYSTIC

The mediator as mystic is somewhat like the teacher as model. The mystic attempts to become a model through deliberate intervention. Just as the teacher as model possesses both positive and negative elements, the teacher as mystic mediator, drawing his students into his orbit, has both positive and negative effects. In fact, Adelson points out that "charisma, competence, and influence do not necessarily go hand in hand" (1962, p. 406).

As we suggested in the chapter on the teacher as model, it must be recognized—perhaps first by teacher, then by student—that the process of identification can both hinder and facilitate development. Adelson notes that the mechanism of identification, especially in adolescence,

> . . . sometimes seems to provide the means through which needed restruc-turings or crystallizations of personality take place. In some cases the student can become himself only by first becoming someone else. He may find it difficult to acquire new and complex skills unless he protects himself psychically by borrowing, through identification, the teacher's power. Or he may use the identification as a mask, as a form of camouflage . . . while he pretends . . . he is actually accomplishing the inner changes which will allow him to achieve an identity closer to his own talents and dispositions. . . . The identification serves as the means of achieving a new and necessary identity. (Ibid., p. 401)

Whether the student accepts or rejects the identity of his teacher, the power tied to the archetypal image of the model itself is related to the process of interaction and to the way that the teacher employs his power in influencing his students or clients. The difference between the teacher as model and the teacher as mediator is not in the perception of the image, but rather in the intent of the person. To the student in search of a figure to emulate, every teacher is a model, whether or not he wants to be. The mediator as mystic insists on being one.

Adelson uses the language of the anthropologist in defining the mystic as shaman, priest, and healer. The shaman consciously employs his personal powers of craft, charming, and cunning to bring about change. The priest acts as an agent of omnipotent authority, frequently so identi-fying with the authority that it becomes personalized within him. And the mystic as healer treats the source of illness itself, stressing the pathology of his subject.

The teacher as shaman is the most narcissistic of the three types of mystics. Unlike the true shaman (Boyer, Klopfer, Brawer, and Kawai 1964), who operates in non-academic situations, he may be humble and not exhibitionistic. But in common with all shamans, he keeps the audience's (students') attention focused on his own demonstrations of charm and skill. In some cases, this type of teacher has a strong impact on the student; more often, once the student moves away from his spell, the teacher's influence is seen to have been merely transient. The shaman–teacher's focus on narcissism is autonomous, and although his orientation may seem to invite identification, he tempts his students into regressions. Therefore, whatever power he held over his students at the time he was "teaching" is soon forgotten.

The teacher as priest claims his power through his office rather than through any personal endowment. He sees himself in terms of continued identity with the institution. Believing in the stratification of prestige and authority and in the resulting hierarchical system, the teacher–priest emphasizes discipline, trials, and self-transformation. He is powerful and effective for many reasons. Teacher and students are generally in close relationship and the student, presented with an ambiguous image of character and behavior, is encouraged to identify with this type of teacher. The "priest's" mode of teaching offers his students a stake in a collective, utopian purpose that is associated with power, position, money, and intellectual exclusiveness. Less obvious, but equally important, this ". . . collectivity makes its appeal to the student in helping him to resolve internal confusions. His participation allows distinct identity choice; it supports that choice by collective approval; it reduces intellectual and moral ambiguity" (Adelson 1962, p. 410).

The third kind of mystic mediator, the "healer," attempts to find a source of illness or pathology in the patient's (student's) personality. In the sense that he helps the student realize both his flaws and his hidden strengths, the mystic healer might be considered a positive influence. This image of the teacher is closest to that found in college brochures—the omniscient agent of guidance who helps the student realize all he is capable of becoming. The teacher who assumes this stance sets aside "his own desires and [his own] concerns, to devote himself, without hidden ambivalence, to the needs of another" (Ibid., p. 412). In common with all teachers who stress the mediating function, and parallel with Rogers's emphasis on genuineness, Adelson points out that this type of "altruism . . . is a fragile and unsteady trait. . . . If the teacher's selflessness is false, expedient, or mechanical, if it comes out of a failure in self-esteem, or if it gives way to an underlying envy—and . . . these are real and ever-present possibilities—then the teaching at best will not come off, and at the worst may end in damaging the student" (Ibid., p. 412).

Whatever the form taken by the mediator, he must be aware that his influence is not always effectual, not always positive, and not always lasting. His role as mediator deals with process; desirable ends may or may not result. Above all, the instructor must be conscious that viewing himself as a mediator is just one of many ways in which he may address his profession.

8

The Manager

Everyone studies the teacher in his classroom. A glance at the *Encyclopedia of Educational Research* (Harris 1960) or the *Handbook of Research on Teaching* (Gage 1963) reveals the magnitude of the efforts to understand him and his work. The acts of lecturing, conducting a discussion, or interacting with students in some other fashion are recorded, isolated, and examined for their own dynamics—as though we would find the magic formula for "good teaching." Teasing out the differences is certainly preferable to viewing all instructional forms and all kinds of instructors together as invariably forming a gestalt. But even so, such procedures exclude a potentially more promising mode of viewing instruction. There are many dimensions other than those generally considered in teacher observation studies.

It is the difference in intent that points up the futility of attempting to understand instructors by merely viewing their activities. The question is not "What does he do?" but "To what end?" Does he see himself as concentrating on process or product? This becomes apparent in many ways—for example, when an institution introduces reproducible media or when it plans a systematic study of student learning. In the one case, the mediator finds it difficult—if not impossible—to step back from stressing his involvement with the students. In the other, he may take as a personal affront any institutional attempt to gather evidence of his students' learning. ("The things *I* teach, *you* can't measure!") No "teacher observation scale" can measure these dimensions adequately or appropriately.

Perhaps it is the deeply felt fear that one can never really teach anything to anyone that prevents many mediators from assessing themselves on the basis of their effects. Accordingly, they may feel that they are avoiding the frustration of constant failure by refusing to study their products. "Stop worrying about learning," they say, "just go on and teach." Only those instructors who believe there can be teaching without learning can continue to reject assessment of their effects. They may well study process, but whether they maintain archaic classroom practices or "innovate" every third Tuesday, they are concerned primarily with effort expanded, not with results obtained.

The image of the teacher as model—with both positive and negative elements—was discussed in chapter 6. Chapter 7 described several approaches taken by the instructor who adopts the stance of mediator. In this chapter we discuss the *manager* of instruction, the person who, fully aware of his own identity, consciously focuses on the achievement of student learning.

TEACHING AND LEARNING

The teacher as instructional manager cannot be understood unless the term *instruction* (or *teaching*) is given a specific referent. From a philosophical point of view, the word *instruction* has two distinct meanings—one relating to the *task*, the other to the attainment of *success*. As Waks points out,

> Teaching, like law, is a recognized profession, and teachers engage in an activity called "teaching." . . . Teachers go to schools, try to get students to learn a variety of things . . . [and] are identified as teachers largely through these forms. . . . In one use of the verb *to teach*, anyone who is in this way identifiable as a teacher engages in the activity of teaching by virtue of that fact alone and without regard for the success of his endeavors. (1969, pp. 614–15)

The teaching task thus becomes a set of activities in which teachers typically engage—lecturing, committee service, chatting with students.

Teaching success, on the other hand, is the process of causing learning. In the success sense of the term, if an instructor said, "I just spent the hour teaching about verb forms" and was asked, "To whom?", it would be ludicrous for him to respond, "Oh, to no one; I lectured to an empty room." Similarly, when a person says, "I teach students," the implication is that he teaches them to *do* something, to *act* in particular ways. When the term is used in its success sense, if no evidence of learning can be gathered, the inference that "teaching" has taken place cannot be made. However, the inference that teaching has *not* taken place cannot be made either, we hasten to add. One simply does not know.

In common usage, the term *teaching* obviously has both task and success components. The person may engage in "teaching activities"—the task—without anyone's learning anything. He interprets and explains concepts, selects media, interacts with students—performs the tasks associated with the teaching act. In the task sense, he is "teaching," but unless at some point in time the students do, in fact, change—exhibit learning—he has not "succeeded." This differentiation points up the illogic of the argument between those who "teach students" and those who "teach subject matter." Both statements are foolish. One cannot teach subject matter to an empty room; one cannot teach students without teaching them something.

The Instructional Manager

In its task sense, then, "teaching" is an activity. In its success sense, "teaching" is a process that must, by definition, lead to discernible ends. There are further distinctions. Even though all instructors who deal with students are acting as media of instruction, some may be functioning as managers and others as mediators. The distinction depends on the way they perceive their purposes. Those who see themselves as managers recognize that their actions as information transmitters or as interactors with students represent only separate functions of the total instructional process.

The mediator attempts to inject himself into the life of the student, viewing interaction as the major focus of his work. Sometimes this intervention stops at the process of interaction itself; occasionally, it approximates a therapeutic situation. It may or may not lead to a definitive outcome. Conversely, the instructional manager is clearly outcome-oriented. Focused on student learning—tangible, measurable, identifiable cognitive and/or affective behavioral change—he is concerned with the product, with the outcome of his endeavors. He arranges the environment, selects the media, and gathers evidence of his effects and he structures situations so that learning occurs. He stands outside the student and attempts to intrude only when such involvement is clearly warranted for the achievement of designated ends.

How does the manager operate? In the usual teaching situation, each instructor, acting as an interlocutor (or medium), inserts himself into the space between the student and the potential knowledge to be gained. He may be far away, delivering a lecture-demonstration over television, or he may be very close, personally involving himself with the students. The functions are not wholly separate; rather, a continuum of space is suggested—the instructor touching the students in an encounter group, sitting within a few feet of them in a discussion section, lecturing to them from a raised platform at one end of a large room, and presenting himself to them over great distances, as in television.

However, the manager views these acts only as they relate to potential effects. If it seems important to organize an encounter group, he will. If television will achieve the effects he wants, he will use it.

Focusing on student achievement, rather than on self, he may or may not dispense the information, may or may not intervene. The film, programmed text, bibliography list, and auto-tutorial situation can be the tools for this type of instructor. None of those instructional devices requires his physical presence, yet all require his guiding hand in arranging the situations and in determining their effects.

SPECIALTIES
WITHIN INSTRUCTIONAL MANAGEMENT

As the teaching profession and the junior college develop and move toward identity, faculty functions will become more explicit. Classifications of these instructional specialties have been described by several educators. Wiegman (1969) sees clear-cut distinctions among faculty members who translate research findings into changed courses and programs, who are particularly adept at leading small group discussions, who specialize in lecturing to large groups, and who are particularly gifted in tutorial skills. And he claims that it is unreasonable to expect all teachers to be proficient in every function.

Another set of learning specialties has been developed by Cohen (1966). In this scheme, the aware faculty would subdivide itself into groups of specialists with distinct functions—setting objectives, preparing evaluation devices, selecting media, and diagnosing and aiding individual students with their learning problems. Each specialist is concerned with different groups of activities. The setter of objectives translates general curricular goals into specified outcomes for his division or department and works closely with the measurement specialist in preparing examinations to assess the attainment of these objectives. The media specialist sorts through available workbooks, films, texts, and other materials to select those he judges most appropriate for the students enrolled in the department's courses. The instructor who is especially skilled in aiding individuals with their own learning serves the department as diagnostician and tutor. Cohen sees the functions becoming ever more distinctly specified, with specialized educational techniques coordinated into ends-oriented systems.

In Trow's (1963) view, both administrators and instructors would act as specialists in the schools. Administrators would reallocate their present functions to such specialties as public relations, curriculum and learning resources, staff organization, and media construction. Staff specialists would accept more specific responsibilities in terms of student personnel services, appraisal and examination, and management and research, with appropriate provisions for feedback in terms of evaluation and the development of new techniques. Subject matter specialists would replace generalists, yesterday's instructors whose many roles require tremendous arrays of competences. Very specialized performances would be enacted by learning materials consultants, programmers, monitors, or standby instructors who would be stationed at the consoles in language laboratories or TV studios. Trow's scheme also allows for demonstrators who combine "scholarship and histrionics," for classroom directors, and for discussion leaders.

Where will such specialists come from? The attempt to introduce new techniques of instruction cannot produce them. Team teaching—a technique long discussed and as frequently attempted—is a case in point. As presently conducted, it has had some success; however, it has also revealed some basic problems. Working in a team requires a high degree of skill in interpersonal relations. Such skill may be hard to find, especially since it requires that individual participants possess such traits as flexibility, the ability to cooperate and work effectively with other adults, organizational skills, and the ability to accept constructive criticism. The people who are expected to operate within the mode remain the keys to its success. Even when members of the team are compatible, each typically concentrates on different subject matter areas rather than on specialties within the instructional process itself. Thus in the strictest sense of the term, team teaching rarely receives a fair trial.

Nor can new technology produce a breed of specialists in instruction. So far, at least, live teachers are the only reliable, standardized, prepackaged, flexible "hardware" currently available. No application of technology to education is going to change that in the near future. Oettinger says it well: "The technology-there-is fails in the schools-as-they-are. No one can tell for sure how to marry the technology-that-could-be with the schools-that-might-be" (1969, p. 219). Technology has far to go to fulfill its own promise. Machines do not operate themselves; auto-instructional programs are not self-generating. The specialist in instruction must create or select, accept or reject the materials. He must also keep the auto-tutorial lab running. The manager knows this. Administrators in colleges that are heavily "media-oriented" know it, too. If the instructor sees himself as mediator, not manager, the claims of the technologists and the exhortations of his supervisors will not alter his commitment.

The instructor who becomes a manager does so out of a sense of purpose. He insists on knowing his own impact. He tends to welcome different instructional forms as well as specialization within the profession. However, he appraises each new technique, each piece of hardware, and each specialty in terms of the way it enhances his students' learning. He is the manager of student learning and his satisfaction with his profession and with himself depends on their progress.

At no level of schooling is specialization of function well developed. Nevertheless, the instructional manager is appearing in junior colleges where some individuals have begun to operate with competence in the separate instructional specialties. These are the new heroic figures who handle large numbers of students. Administrators love them because they save money, they are "innovative," and they employ the new media and hardware that many institutions have purchased. Instructors who play these roles must invent techniques, use different forms of media, manage corps of aides, and build new instructional forms. Although some do all this because they are fascinated by the power implications of manipulating large groups—or perhaps simply because they want to be recognized by their peers for extreme heights of ability—others accept such broad challenges because they firmly believe they are performing a professional service. They are confident and competent and they exemplify the present-day professional instructor who is, in fact, a one-man team of specialists.

It is entirely possible that the junior college, standing as it does between the high school—predominately a custodial institution—and the university—in the main a research institute—will generate its own profession of learning managers. Who will they be? In his paradigm college, Cohen (1969) sees them managing a corps of aides that includes students as well as especially trained paraprofessionals. They select materials, create media, prepare examinations, and use tools and techniques that have been created by their fellows. They do not intrude between the students and the knowledge and skills to be gained; instead, they arrange alternative learning paths for students to follow. They are models of "manipulative man" rather than of "reflective man." They are not spiritual commuters to the campus, but rather involved practitioners using the tools of their trade. Their value to themselves and to the institution in which they labor is directly related to the learning manifested by their students.

The instructor need not await the millennium. Even now an individual may profitably begin to manage large numbers of students simply by making his own special arrangements. He can suggest to his administration that he be assigned double the number of students along with a number of assistants. The assistants are paid from the funds that would ordinarily go to another instructor. A total faculty may grasp the idea by fighting for a raise of a few hundred dollars per year and then saying, "Keep the money in a separate fund and use it to pay instructional aides." This may sound fantastic now, but the faculty that takes this step will be dollars ahead in the long run because it will become indispensable to the institution—a far cry from today's instructors, who are more likely to be viewed by members of their governing board as easily replaceable parts.

To the extent that instructors perceive themselves as managers of learning, the profession of teaching in the junior college gains stature.

Some trends in this direction are apparent. Teacher education at the present time is at least compatible with the notion of the teacher as a manager. And as teacher aides move into the colleges through New Careers programs and other measures, the instructional manager will be properly supported. Some two-year colleges have moved far in this direction. Even so, for the individual instructor the race is between gaining identity through managing the learning environment, and acquiring a pseudo-professionalism through ascription. Identity must be earned. There are no shortcuts.

As, on the one hand, new media are made more readily available, and as, on the other, students more stridently demand human beings with whom they can relate, the differences between the manager and the mediator become more obvious. Adults who nurture, sympathize with, and, in effect, roll around on the floor with young people may be getting close to what students want—but is this instruction? Adults who select media and remain aloof from the students may be able to advance principles of instruction—but are they satisfying students' needs? The situation is not easily resolved. However, examining instructional situations in the schools from the separate viewpoints of model, mediator, and manager can lead to new ways of viewing instruction as a discipline and to assessing the potential effects of educational institutions.

PARTS OF ALL

In this section we have described a way of viewing faculty roles. Our formulations are not mutually exclusive, but most faculty members will readily recognize themselves as belonging more to one group than to the other two. Model, mediator, and manager—to a degree every instructor plays all three roles. The differences between those who function as model, or mediator, or manager lie in their particular orientations toward work. Each instructor chooses to emphasize those activities that most accurately represent his interpretation of the teaching role and/or best fit his own life style. One person seldom achieves an equal balance among all three adaptations.

All activities may be represented in part, but the dominant function determines each instructor's actions. His focus probably relates more to intent or personal goal than to any characteristic of personality or cognitive style. When the choice is conscious and deliberate, conflicts among the situational demands that continually confront him may be more easily reconciled.

Today's junior college is not likely to include a faculty in which the three types of specialists are evenly represented. Because of selection practices and the attrition occasioned by instructors' unwillingness to stay where they feel unwanted—that is, because of the expressed or implied "That's not the way we do things around here, new boy!"—a faculty often tends to be skewed in a single direction. However, if there is a decided mix in orientation and style among the faculty, subsequent balance among roles may be developed. And this sort of balance appears desirable for education—today and tomorrow.

part four

Instructor and Student

Except for instances of extreme pathology, there is no form of human interaction that is not reciprocal, that does not in some way put its mark on all the persons involved. Parents and children, colleagues, students and faculty—all interact. The individual does not function in isolation. He both affects and is affected by other people and by the inanimate forces in his environment. We have described the instructor in terms of his traits, orientations, and typologies and also according to his role and the way he addresses his work. But such descriptions relate directly to the instructor as a person and to his professional orientation. What about his interactions with others?

Regardless of the instructor's personal traits and orientations and his choice to emphasize one or another facet of the teaching role, the people with whom he interacts have a distinct bearing on his success, on what he derives from his profession, and concomitantly on his satisfaction with himself. He interacts with members of various groups—colleagues, administrators, community representatives, parents, and students. Of all these, the students are foremost.

The instructor may follow institutional regulations routinely, and except for an occasional nod, ignore his colleagues. But regardless of his preference, students are always with him. He meets them daily, singly and in large numbers. They speak with him, attend to him—or ignore him. He facilitates or impedes their learning. Most important, because the college exists to serve the students, if they go away happy and well taught, he is by definition a success. If they leave disgruntled and no further ahead in their learning than they were when they entered, he has failed. His interactions with them thus relate directly to his effects, and indirectly to his own sense of achievement. In fact, his very sense of identity, his satisfaction with his work, and his relative success or failure are more dependent on his students than on any other facets of the institution in which he functions. Just as he affects his students, they affect him.

This section extends the discussion of the instructor's work more directly into his interactions with others. It is divided into two parts: chapter 9 describes junior college students, emphasizing the global rather than the singular dimensions by which they may be characterized. Chapter 10 discusses certain aspects of student–teacher interactions and the relationships that may tend to enhance or detract from both student learning and teacher satisfaction.

9

The Students:
Who Are They?

In previous chapters the instructor has been discussed primarily as an individual. Although we have not purposely implied that the instructor stands alone, the impact of his students—the most significant others in his purview—has not been considered. However, just as he affects them, they affect him. And, if we are to understand these mutual effects, we must know something about both groups involved in the interchange.

This chapter sketches junior college students. We are fully aware that there is no such thing as *the* junior college student—the variety of individual students with whom the instructor interacts is as broad as society itself. However, certain pictures may be drawn, both from hard data studies and from general perceptions about students in higher education. In this sense, we talk about "the student" in "the community college."

Few people would argue that there are many reasons why it is important to understand students. The argument, rather, concerns the depth and extent of understanding: along what dimensions must the student be known? How well? Is it necessary that the instructor recognize the range of abilities possessed by a classroom of students, or is a measure of mean ability sufficient? Does the teacher need to know how students perform on pre-tests before he can interpret the results of post-test data? Numerous other questions may well be asked about both cognitive and affective dimensions that relate to teacher–student interactions.

In a book concerned with the junior college instructor, it is unnecessary to review the many studies of students that have been conducted since the education field began to write about itself. It *is* important, however, to acknowledge the plethora of available literature about students at all levels of education, particularly regarding such topics as learning ability, attrition rates, peer group influences, student–faculty interactions, and relationships between individual needs and the environmental press of the academic institution. These and related research activities introduce numerous questions about whether the students' behavior fits the academic milieu, whether failure results from a lack of proper fit, and whether predictions of student potential actually fit student behavior. The concerned junior college instructor will want to be aware of some of the directions these investigations take and the implications to be drawn from them.

STUDENTS IN HIGHER EDUCATION

Research on students in higher education serves many purposes. Students are examined in order to measure previous school achievement, predict academic potential, select into and out of particular institutions, determine individual characteristics, evaluate environmental perceptions, assign positions in special occupational programs, and learn about the effects of education beyond the twelfth year of schooling. Whatever the intent, it is important that systematic knowledge about the entering student be available, particularly his potential for—and resistance to—learning and development. This type of information can point to appropriate changes in educational structures.

It is common practice for colleges and universities to require that their prospective students take certain aptitude and/or achievement tests. Different institutions may require different tests, but few people who decide to continue their schooling beyond the twelfth grade can escape one or more of these instruments. College admissions testing has become big business, and whether they be open-door junior colleges or selective four-year colleges or universities, most schools draw heavily on data derived from such inquiries.

Academic achievement tests are the most commonly administered instruments, and most institutions can readily provide normative data regarding their students' scores on these types of measures. However, looking at student bodies along the dimensions of academic talents alone is a limiting pursuit—especially if one subscribes to the notion that the college experience is presumed to affect individuals in a variety of ways. If the purpose of a college education is more than becoming able to perform certain requisite tasks, then it is narrow to look only at the cognitive domain. People develop along many dimensions.

We do not yet have either the sufficient data or the proper tools to show systematically the many ways in which college-going populations function. However, efforts are being made to develop different types of measures. In-depth studies have been conducted with Bennington, Vassar, and Sarah Lawrence women (Newcomb 1962; Webster 1957; Munroe 1945); with medical students at Johns Hopkins (Thomas 1965); with psychiatric residents at the Menninger Clinic (Holt *et al.* 1958); and with a host of students at other colleges. These examinations of student groups offer multi-dimensional bases for understanding young adults. They also provide needed information about college environments in general and the extent to which academic programs are directed toward meeting educational commitments. Much of this information is parochial—primarily relevant to single institutions—but certain studies also have something to say to all people concerned with higher education. In this sense, studies of college students are potential links to curriculum development, extra-curricular program planning, and other issues related to educational aims.

A major effort in much of the research relating to college students is directed toward questions of human change. A school's effect on its students or a course's relevance to its students' needs may be best observed by looking at the students themselves. When they are appraised both at matriculation and at the time they leave school, assessment of the college's general effectiveness may be gleaned from a measure of the changes that have transpired. Accordingly, such examinations become part of the total organizational scheme.

Just as the individuals comprising student groups differ, there are also differences in the kinds and extent of changes experienced while in college—if, indeed, they take place at all. In the sense of merely providing opportunities for the acquisition of information, education could proceed without any apparent changes in the personality patterns of the students (Sanford 1962); but in light of today's emphasis on the individual, and on the subsequent search for expansion in his "personal universe" (Pace 1969), such a limitation appears unfortunate. This is especially true if the kind of learning desired in college involves a change in the individual's personal development, differentiation, and integration.

Among the more compelling problems held in common by students, parents, schools, and communities at every level of education are high attrition rates, "superior" students performing in "mediocre" ways, transfers to different schools or to different fields of study in the same schools, motivational factors, and goal expectations. These issues continue to attract much attention, with gulfs still apparent between the knowledge acquired from research, its implementation in school systems, and its relevance to academic situations. Other concerns, springing from the posture that one important goal of the school is the adequate preparation of the "whole person," extend beyond the "merely academic." The problems, the issues, the confrontations, go on and on. But what about the junior college, its students and personnel, in all this research?

JUNIOR COLLEGE STUDENTS

Students in the open-door junior colleges represent a cross section of the communities in which the colleges are located. This is truer of the community college than of any other institution of higher education—a phenomenon noted by Clark (1960), who pointed out that the community college draws its people from all strata of society. Who are they? Why are they there?

Most—perhaps all—junior colleges collect data about their students. In the vast majority of cases, this is demographic material regarding each student's age, sex, high school grade point average, and often a statement about the program to which he is applying or the institution to which he hopes to transfer. Accordingly, a sizable body of information is available. Yet, although Pace (1962) points to the "long and distinguished history of research on the characteristics of college students," published research on the junior college student has lagged considerably behind research on the four-year college and university student. Synthesizing several previous studies, Cross concluded that

> Research on the junior college student is a new phenomenon. . . . Almost half the references cited [in this monograph] bear the date of 1966 or 1967, and no attempt was made to conduct any systematic search of the literature prior to 1960. (1968, p. 8)

In the relatively few—albeit increasing—studies that do include junior college populations, these students are usually grouped with others at different levels of education and/or different types of schools. For example, the longitudinal SCOPE study (Tillery 1964) analyzed data in terms of three subgroups: (1) individuals not enrolling in colleges immediately after high school graduation, (2) individuals entering junior colleges, and (3) individuals entering four-year colleges and universities. The focus was on high school students moving into work, marriage, and all types of post-secondary schools, not specifically on junior college students. The project TALENT study of high school graduates across the nation (Goldberg and Dailey 1963) reported innumerable changes occurring in the top quarter of students then attending college. From such data, Cross anticipated that "The student new to higher education—the student now entering the junior college—is of necessity going to come increasingly from the second, third, and lowest quartiles [on measures of academic ability] (1968, p. 14).

Another study of high school graduates surveyed 10,000 subjects (Medsker and Trent *et al.* 1965; Trent and Medsker 1968). Various differences were noted when students who persisted in college for four years were compared with those who attended different types of institutions and those who either did not enter college or withdrew before obtaining degrees. And Warren (1966), looking at particular personality dimensions, found that his sample of junior college men and women differed from samples of students in a state and a private college. The private college students were found to be most adventuresome, impulsive, and involved, while the junior college students were described as being cautious, prudent, and controlled; they were also the most apprehensive and rigid in their concern over academic standings.

In all these studies, there is an implied—if not an explicit—lack of homogeneity among students in different institutions. However, while tendencies toward heterogeneity may accurately apply to such dimensions as age, previous academic achievement, and educational aspirations, examinations of junior college students do not warrant a description of mix on the basis of personality or cognitive style. Just as the "highly diversified" nature of students in four-year institutions does not yield a "typical" portrait (Sanford 1967), an accurate picture cannot yet be drawn of the typical community college student. We simply do not have sufficient data. Yet, Cross's synthesis of junior college student studies reveals certain patterns, which may be summarized as follows:

1. Carefully designed research studies find that junior college students in national, regional, or statewide samples achieve lower mean scores on academic ability tests than comparably selected students at four-year colleges and universities. Some junior college students, however, score high on measures of academic aptitude. Little is actually known about patterns of special abilities among junior college students.

2. The junior college is presumed to play a significant role in the democratization of American higher education. The parents of these students tend to have lower socio-economic status than parents of students in four-year colleges and universities.* But much more information is needed about junior college students' home environments, parental encouragement, financial standing, and related matters.

3. Clear-cut differences in occupational aspirations exist among non-college, junior college, and four-year college groups, with junior college students generally appearing less settled about future plans than either of the other two groups. However, little is known about those junior college students who do not subsequently transfer to four-year colleges—for example, the vocationally oriented students, the dropouts, or the older students returning to pick up new skills simply to revitalize their education.

4. Junior college students hold more practical orientations to life and to college than their four-year college peers. They are less intellectually disposed, score lower on measures of autonomy and non-authoritarianism, appear more cautious and controlled, are less likely to be adventurous and flexible, and are less sure of themselves. Yet research on the personality characteristics of junior college students is meager, and more information is needed regarding their values, feelings about self, and inter-personal relationships.

*Jencks and Riesman disagree with this point, suggesting that "The parents of students who enroll at community colleges are slightly *richer* than the parents of students at four-year institutions" (1968, p. 485).

Cross raises some important points; there are others as well. In terms of their preparation for college, general academic abilities, and confidence in previous academic achievements, junior college students in general consistently fall below four-year college students. However, they may well excel in other areas, which need examination. If previous lack of satisfaction in academic activities can be understood, such dissatisfaction may be overcome eventually and/or compensated by competence in other roles. If the community college student is given a chance to demonstrate success in non-academic avenues, can he then cope better with academic tasks? Would a year of delay, a kind of "moratorium" (in Erikson's sense), better allow him to assess his motives and interests, and eventually to function successfully with other kinds of students who had not needed this time for personal evaluation? Perhaps one of the underlying, even unconscious, cries of the youth who asks for "relevance" is actually a plea to be allowed to assess himself in terms of what the schools are all about, without untoward pressures from the educational system.

Another issue regarding junior college students deals with their similarities and differences. It has been rather common practice to describe community colleges as extremely "heterogeneous" institutions. This stress on diversity usually refers to the variety of courses and curricula and to the people involved in the total system of which the schools are a part. Frequently, junior college students are characterized as heterogeneous on the basis of measures of their academic abilities, aspirations, and socioeconomic status. The college that enrolls large numbers of "transfer," "vocational," and "remedial" students with apparently equal investment must, by implication, serve a mixed population.

Descriptions of heterogeneity or homogeneity, however, are meaningful only if the exact components are spelled out. Which dimensions comprise diversity? Which uniformity? Most studies of community college students examine their grade point averages, measures of general ability, ages, and the miles they travel to school. Certainly the students vary greatly along these dimensions, but such data do not indicate that the ascribed diversity is actually a general quality. In spite of apparent heterogeneity on demographic dimensions, little is known about relative heterogeneity among students on other measures.

Indeed, when each component is carefully considered, doubt is cast on the generality of diversity among junior college students. True, community college students as a group achieve lower mean scores on tests of academic ability than do comparably selected samples of four-year college and university students. They indicate lower educational and occupational aspirations and show less confidence in their academic abilities. However, these data do not point to greater *intra*-population diversity along the dimensions cited.

In their study of freshmen at one junior college, Cohen and Brawer (1970) found *less* heterogeneity among the students on 13 of the 14 Omnibus Personality Inventory Scales (Heist et al. 1967) than there was in the comparison group composed of freshmen at the University of California, Berkeley. In addition, the junior college freshmen tended to cluster on another measure, that of adaptive flexibility (Brawer 1967). It was concluded that the phrase "a heterogeneous student body" needs qualification—how heterogeneous? Along which dimensions?

Why Are They There?

We know, then, certain things about students relative to demographic data, personality characteristics, and cognitive styles of behavior—in general, who they are. But knowledge *about* them is hardly sufficient for understanding the person or the group. It is important to know them, but we must also know why they are there. The concerned faculty member can use such information not only to understand his students as individuals, but also to understand his own interaction with them.

Many commentators have described the community college as an instrument of social mobility. In their view, the college allows the most able young people to go on to further higher education and/or to higher social status. However, the argument that the college is an instrument of social mobility loses much of its force when a majority of the high school graduates go on to college because they have nowhere else to go. Dropping out of the mainstream of schooling is not easy. Von Hoffman (1970) speaks of "a vast social conspiracy to force a kid onto welfare, into the Army or back to school!" And Jerome (1969) points out that "college education has become, *de facto*, compulsory." Why are they there? Where else can a young person go?

The question of why these students attend school also relates to their search for identity. Not unlike many instructors, large numbers of freshmen are looking for a sense of being. As Erikson points out, the growing and developing youth, faced both with a physiological revolution and with tangible adult tasks, is concerned about how others see him. He is confronted by the problem of integrating previously developed roles and skills with occupational prototypes. This integration

> . . . now taking place in the form of ego identity is . . . more than the sum of the childhood identifications. It is the accrued experience of the ego's ability to integrate all identifications with the vicissitudes of the libido, with the aptitudes developed out of endowment, and with the opportunities offered in social roles. The sense of ego identity, then, is the accrued confidence that the inner sameness and continuity prepared in the past are matched by the sameness and continuity of one's meaning for

others, as evidenced in the tangible promise of a "career." (1963, **pp.**
261–62)

Sanford emphasizes the importance of goal setting in a student's
attempts to establish his sense of self. "To survive, grow, and have an
identity in the complex and changing environment that is every person's
lot involves the setting and achieving of diverse goals" (1970, p. 21).

While these comments relate to many recent high school graduates,
they have little pertinence to the vast numbers of adult and mature young
people who seek precise occupational upgrading and, frequently, upward
mobility. An ever increasing effort in the community college is directed
to vocational preparation. Generally speaking, these students have fairly
distinct goals and look for specific curricula to help them achieve those
goals. Most of the research on junior college students fails to discriminate
between this group and the more immature adolescent. Nevertheless, the
instructor must deal with both.

Students All,
Individuals Each

Only a rare person finds mass student surveys of more than passing
interest. Accordingly, the broad pictures of students presented in this
chapter have limited appeal. The instructor is more likely concerned with
individuals: Sam, slumped in his chair in the corner; Mary, who has just
confided her fear of pregnancy; John, making his usual complaint about
a grade mark; Frank, who needs a drop slip signed because his appeal for
financial aid has been turned down; and the dozen others who have simply
stopped coming to class. Or he sees his students as a faceless mass and
builds his own categories in an effort to sort them out, labeling those he
sees currying favor by being fawning or deferent; those who have an
attitude of "I'm here but that's all. Tell me what I have to do to pass";
and those blessed few for whom high school has not knocked out the
desire to learn.

Confronted by multitudes of students, the instructor frequently
longs for fewer, more dedicated individuals. The question is whether he
can retain a sense of responsibility to all the students in his charge and
not fall back on the fond dream of a room full of eager learners—who may
exist in his fancy only. For, as Jerome notes, few students would remain
if the college were to cull out those who were there "not to learn but to
qualify, . . . the anti-intellectuals, the militants, the experience seekers, the
group-groupers and T-groupers, the great washed masses who are none of
these but who are content to be herded along, not wanting to rock the
boat, not wanting to risk their degrees and jobs and deferments" (1969,

p. 41). If, in addition, the college were to cull "the sycophants, the hustlers, the socialites, the influence peddlers and seekers, the red-necks . . . ," fewer still would remain. And, in addition, if it were to cull "the lost flower children, searching for their identity, confused about their goals, drifting in fuzzy clouds of introspection . . ." along with the "draft dodgers, . . . the inadequately prepared, the products of poor schools, the stupid, the lazy, the disadvantaged, the spoiled, . . . and the blacks who are not willing to accept the standards and goals of our educational institutions," there would remain only Mark Hopkins on one end of a log and a mirror on the other end (Ibid., p. 41). But perhaps this is what some instructors want, anyway.

The students, drawn by the open admissions policies, drop in and out, visiting the institutions intermittently. Fitfully they drift toward graduation, desiring only to be something other than they were when they matriculated. As Jennings puts it, "Here they come . . . recent high school graduates and dropouts, young adults now at last ready to settle down to the business of getting and holding an education, middle-aged men and women seeking the insurance of a second career, and assorted other students of all ages who like to take a course once in a while" (1970, p. 16).

The instructor meets them all.

He can easily scan the scores his students have made or the scholastic achievement tests they have taken. If he has time, he can talk with them individually about their own plans and aspirations. He can read the papers they submit, note the ways they respond in class. And with a few, he can perhaps strike up personal associations. Drawing on these meager data, and perhaps integrating them with the information available about large groups of students, he forms his own impressions. The students affect him just as he affects them. It's a two-way street.

10

Interactions

The extent to which we understand students and the role played by the college in shaping their development are open questions. We do know that peer and parental influences along with individual dispositions play a large part and that the college accounts for only a portion of each student's progress. Determining the impact of the college itself is not easy; accounting for the impact of an individual instructor is even more difficult.

The instructional staff as a whole and each teacher individually is responsible for designing procedures that will bring about changes in students' aspirations, personality development, and capabilities. However, these changes—called "learning"—are the result of more than direct instructional effort. The instructor also affects his students inadvertently. What are the subtleties that create this effect?

The effects are reciprocal—both students and instructors are involved. What are the students' effects on the instructor? To what extent do they shape his behavior within the classroom and as he plans his activities? Can he be callous and maintain his own pace? Can he shift gears a hundred times daily and still be himself? How deep can his relationships be with any of the students? Perhaps his involvement must remain superficial because, as Rossi and Cole suggest, "Teachers . . . have to fall in love in a hurry with anybody who comes their way. Afterward there is no time to cry. . . . There are so many others to serve" (1970, p. 35). Influences are like two-way streets; but what are the processes of interchange?

The question of what passes between college students and their instructors is one of the thorniest in education. Although students and instructors separately are studied up, down, and sideways, the element of mutuality is too often overlooked. Yet each person affects the other and, while young people have needs, adults have needs, too. The many dimensions of the relationship mesh. Commentaries on the people who function within the schools and discussions of ways to improve education frequently neglect this point even though, as Jones (1968) notes, the needs of the instructor and the way they interface with the needs of the students are germane to *all* questions in education.

This chapter deals with faculty–student interactions—relationships in which members of both groups are involved. Only a few of the possible interactions are included here: relationships in class; out-of-class contact; and potential effects of interactions on student attrition, cognitive learning, student development, and faculty satisfaction.

The Concept

Interaction occurs when two or more persons behave overtly toward one another so that one receives perceptions and impressions of the other that are distinct enough to incur reaction (Bales 1950). This definition allows the phenomenon to be examined in terms of its effects on the people involved. Yet, even without attempting to assess effects, it is not easy to stabilize systems for merely describing what goes on between the members of two groups.

The study of teacher–student interaction occurs in many different ways. Students "evaluate" the instructor according to their perceptions of him. Thus, the study of student ratings of instructors is, in fact, one type of investigation of interaction. When outsiders visit the classroom and describe the numbers and types of comments made by instructors and students, they too are assessing interaction. A third area of study has to do with teacher–student interaction in other than formal classroom situations.

Certain problems are common to all attempts to study human interaction. A recurrent problem is rater bias—that is, through whose eyes are the assessments being made? Another is establishing the categories, determining the kind and amount of inference that can be drawn from the ratings themselves (Rosenshine 1970). The most difficult problem, of course, is in extrapolating from any type of interaction study to the broader questions of human change.

A major reason for the failure to develop systematic knowledge of teacher–student relationships is that such information still awaits the emergence of a serviceable psychology of personality development. Whatever the reasons, we must study interaction as best we can. Sanford very aptly set the scene for this type of inquiry:

> Very little is known about the influence of college teachers' characteristics upon students' learning and development. Although studies of this aspect of the educational process have often been carried on in elementary and high schools almost nothing has been done in the colleges. Here is a vast and significant area that awaits investigation. (1962, pp. 54–55)

The importance of studying faculty–student interaction is also suggested indirectly in the large body of "inspirational" literature in the field of education. Prospective teachers are exhorted to be warm, friendly, kind, sympathetic, and so on. Why? Ostensibly so that they will have some positive effect on their charges. But how or when the warmth and friendliness translate into impact on an individual remains in the realm of mystery. The mechanism of transference is ambiguous; consequently, devices to assess the quality and extent of faculty–student interaction are often gross and crude.

The immediate reaction to the question of whether individual instructors affect students is to say, "Of course." The evidence, however, is sketchy, more anecdotal than empirical. In his study of colleges and their impact on student values, Jacob (1957) used testimony provided by educators and counselors to show that profound influences were exerted by some teachers, even to the point of causing certain students to re-orient their philosophies of life. However, because the influence that ignites "the certain spark" is personal and often indiscernible, it could hardly be identified.

Many other types of investigations attempt to grasp the same issues. Perceptions of students, teachers, and trained outside observers have frequently been examined in regard to dimensions of classroom activities—Morse, Bloom, and Dunn (1961), for example, studied development, mental health, and group process and Gordon, Adler, and McNeil (1963) have emphasized inter-personal perceptions and teacher leadership styles. Other investigators have used various observational techniques to assess the spontaneous behavior of instructors.

Some investigators suggest that faculty who have powerful effects on students are likely to be individuals whose own value commitments are firm and openly expressed, who are outgoing and warm in their relationships. Their influence is more pronounced in institutions where associations between faculty and students are frequent and where students find their teachers receptive and unhurried in their classroom conversations. But these assumptions are usually based on superficial observations; they are not well substantiated.

Limited knowledge about the interaction process has not deterred today's instructors. Building on minimal knowledge that implies that more students are positively affected by warm and friendly people than by cold and aloof individuals, a school of "maximum interaction" has recently developed. By the end of the 1960s, practically every institution had at least one instructor who insisted on "revealing himself" to his students. In the classroom this revelation took the form of everything from frequent personal references to confessionals to arranging situations in which there was much physical contact. This type of intense personal interaction was usually justified by the practitioner as a way of putting the student more in touch with his "real self" and "freeing" him for greater heights of awareness. Although this "touch and tickle" school of classroom instructors claimed that it intended to enhance intellectual work, many of its devotees allowed the process to override the potential learnings and were often likely to perceive the personal contact as an end in itself.

INTERACTION ANALYSIS

Interest in measuring classroom interaction more precisely has led to various systematic rating schemes that can be classified under the general term *interaction analysis*. By definition, interaction analysis refers to "a system for categorizing, observing, recording and analyzing the classroom behaviors of teachers and students" (Crispin 1970). Trained raters note the form and extent of interaction in the classroom by observing the numbers of times that one or another person speaks, makes positive statements, asks questions, and so on. They tally these behaviors along such dimensions as "direct" and "indirect" statements—that is, statements that tend to minimize or maximize student freedom to respond. The implication is that a student's learning is enhanced when he feels free to express himself in an open environment.

When interaction is examined by viewing the classroom "game" (Bellack et al. 1963), more than half the classroom talk is frequently attributed to the teacher. Amidon and Flanders (1963) discussed this finding at length when they reported that in the average classroom someone is talking two-thirds of the time and that two-thirds of this is teacher talk, of which another two-thirds consists of attempts to influence students directly. Thus, despite recent cries for student involvement in every educational process, the teacher still sees himself as properly the single most active person in the classroom. The higher the level of schooling, the more this is true. Whereas the elementary school teacher frequently has the students recite, read, and report, the image of the college classroom is more often that of a professor giving a 50-minute lecture to a silent room. Arguments are frequently raised against this teacher-dominated situation. In fact, Postman and Weingartner (1969) go so far as to insist that each teacher be limited to three declarative sentences and fifteen interrogatives per class. They even suggest fining a teacher for each sentence above the limit, with the students doing the counting and the collecting!

Tallying overt classroom behaviors is a seemingly crude way of assessing anything, but the practice does show promise of assisting instructors to become aware of their own actions. An instructor may genuinely feel that his classroom is free and open. Yet, after trained and objective observers appraise the environment, they may present him with data that suggest quite the opposite. The resultant surprise can be most enlightening.

OUT-OF-CLASS INTERACTION

To educators who view the closeness of a college environment as positively affecting students' lives, extensive contact between faculty and students outside regularly scheduled classes is a fond dream. They see this type of interaction as part of the total immersion of the student in his environment—a feeling that stems from the residential college concept. Unfortunately for their hopes, relatively few junior college students live on campus. Hence, possibilities for contact out of class are frequently limited to scheduled visits in instructors' offices, chance contacts on the way to parking lots, or association with instructors in sanctioned student activities.

Only a few studies systematically examine the degree of student contact with faculty members outside the classroom. Feldman and Newcomb (1969) summarize the results of eight such studies, but none of these deals with community college populations. Except in the smaller schools, such contact is probably minimal—a phenomenon that leads to charges of depersonalization. Depersonalization, however, does not necessarily imply that all students would have it otherwise. Some prefer it that way.

An extensive study of out-of-class interaction in the junior college was conducted by Machetanz (1969), who surveyed 5,400 students and 546 faculty members in 21 Southern California institutions. Most out-of-class contacts were found to occur either in the instructor's office or in the classroom just before or after class. Very few students sought out their instructors to talk about personal or social problems or academic questions in general; instead, they questioned course assignments or grades. And, although most students reported that they found it rather easy to meet instructors outside class, they did so very infrequently—rarely more than once a month.

Approximately half the instructors surveyed in the Machetanz study held off-campus jobs and a fourth more were involved in graduate studies of their own—even though the sample was composed of "full-time day faculty" only. The instructors who were most committed to non-teaching activities interacted least with their students outside class. "Full-time" is apparently more an artifact of payroll categorization than a description of individual commitment.

Machetanz's report suggests a phenomenon not easily overcome in the current structure of the community college. One gains the picture of both students and faculty members driving to a campus, walking to a classroom where they meet together, and then leaving to engage in work, study, or play unrelated to the college. And who meets whom in the process remains a "potentially researchable question."

Many two-year colleges attempt to stimulate interaction by organizing activities designed to bring students and instructors together outside class. Their success, however, is not great. When both students and instructors are commuters, the ideal of a campus where chance contacts are a possibility throughout waking hours cannot be realized. This ideal, so desired by those who base their vision of a college on the English boarding school, is far from reality in the community college. Commuting is a state of mind as well as a physical fact.

INTERACTIONAL EFFECTS

How important is it for college students to maintain close relationships with faculty members? White argues that the instructor as a person is less important to the college student than he is to the high school student—and considerably less important than he is to the elementary student. Whereas the child does not compartmentalize, but rather interacts holistically with the adult, the college student is "capable of interacting with the instructor at almost a purely intellectual level, in a manner that makes many of his personal characteristics irrelevant" (1969, p. 68). Wise corroborates this observation, suggesting that students "are not nearly so eager to learn to know faculty members as people as they are to know them as teachers . . . as 'experts', [and] to have further opportunity to explore with them the new ideas met in their courses (1958, p. 28).

However, many college students do attend to their instructors as people. This was demonstrated in a study of approximately 2,000 entering freshmen at three junior colleges. Students ranked "instructors' personality" second in a list of eight "things they look for" when they enter a class for the first time. ("Specific learning objectives" was ranked first; "course reading list" was last! [Cohen 1970c]). These new students apparently saw value in learning about both the objectives they would be led to attain and the personality of the individual who would teach them.

If, as Sanford (1967) argues, optimal student development comes from a highly personal student–faculty involvement, and if people differ in their goals, personal objectives, and feelings—then different students also vary in their needs for close contact both in and outside the classroom. Feldman and Newcomb substantiate Sanford's position by suggesting that "Different kinds of students . . . do not always agree about the desirable degree and nature of student–faculty contact" (1969, p. 251). They point to one study that found a sizable majority of high-achieving students wanting closer contact with their professors but only a minority of low-achieving students seeking such closeness.

If mutual interactions are to be understood, then the consonance and dissonance among various dimensions of faculty and student groups must also be considered. In a project comparing hierarchies of values of junior college instructors and students, both groups ranked, in order of importance to them, lists of *instrumental* and *terminal* values developed by Rokeach (1968). The importance attached to different values by both participating groups was widely disparate (Brawer 1971). And if there is marked disagreement, what, indeed, can be the mutual effect of academic inter-action? If people are so different in characteristics as basic as values, one wonders if there can be any direct reciprocal effect at all except on the most superficial level. However, it might well be asked whether one has any right to expect congruence in value structures—and thus, ulti-mately, in behavior—among people representing different generations and different role orientations.

Processes of interaction relate to other issues in the academic setting. Student attrition is one prominent concern; another is individual and institutional purpose. The two may be related in ways not yet fully under-stood. We have, for example, certain information about student with-drawal from college, but as Summerskill (1954) points out, after 40 years of study the dropout figures—and presumed causes—remain the same. One class dropped does not make a college dropout; yet each class that a student attends and each instructor with whom he interacts contributes to his chances of staying or withdrawing from school. What indeed are the relationships of students and teachers that lead to persistence or withdrawal?

Terminal interviews with students who are withdrawing from college often reveal a major cause of early departure to be general dissatisfaction with instructors. While the teachers' abilities to sustain the interest and attention of their students would seem to be major determinants of success in teaching, such variables are rarely included in investigations of academic mortality rates. Although it is the instructor who formulates his own courses, develops and uses certain instructional methods, and establishes practices that may activate students' decisions to stay in or drop from school, few studies have been concerned with the differential retentive capacities of instructors.

Certain instructors probably account for more dropouts than other faculty members, but no one really knows why this is so. Is the phe-nomenon related to the personalities involved? Marking (1967) examined the extent of similarity in attitudes and personality characteristics between students and their instructors, noting their social class identification, values, masculine–feminine traits, and liberalism versus conservatism. Whether or not the students were "like" their instructors did not relate to their staying in school. Nothing that could be identified made a significant difference in the variables "persist" and "withdraw from" junior college.

Does the dropout issue relate to the instructor's methodology? If certain instructors have fewer students who withdraw from college before completing their programs than other instructors, these staff members might be communicating a sense of purpose and/or direction to their students. One way this sense of purpose may be transmitted is through the outlining of specific learning objectives. Theoretically and logically, objectives are important to achievement. If the attitudes of both faculty and students are essential to the learning experience, it is assumed that students would learn more from an instructor who has a clear notion of his own direction than they would from one who conducts his class in a vague, ambiguous manner. It follows, then, that the instructor who specifies the ends of his teaching—who focuses his students' attention on the goals rather than on the media of his instruction—is more likely to hold students than other kinds of instructors. Students do seem to prefer this type of direction. As Arrowsmith says, "If a student is serious, he rightly asks of his education that it give him some sense of the end on behalf of which the whole process takes place. Finding no such end, he calls his education 'irrelevant'.... The student rightly expects his teachers to have some sense of the same end, or to be busy about remedying the lack" (1970, p. 60).

WHICH TEACHER? WHICH STUDENT?

All schemes for observing classroom interaction and all questions of the effects of individual instructors run afoul of the phenomenon that different teachers affect different students in ways that are still unknown. Several investigators have reached this same conclusion.

In studies of the elementary school, teachers and students have been classified into several types on the basis of classroom observation. Noting responses to an interest–personality inventory, to role playing, and to scores on an educational examination, Heil (1960) found that only the interest schedule yielded clear results. This verified the major hypothesis that different kinds of teachers impel different kinds of achievement from different kinds of children. The self-controlled individual was found to stimulate the most achievement from certain pupils, while the fearful teacher was associated with the least achievement. With children classified as "conformers" and "strivers," the turbulent teacher was almost as successful as the self-controlling one, but he was less than half as successful with children who had been classified as "opposers." The salient point is that no one kind of teacher did well with all kinds of students, nor did one kind of student do well with all kinds of teachers.

For some time, McKeachie and his associates have been concerned with the interaction between student motives and instructors' cues (McKeachie, Lin, Milholland, and Isaacson 1966; Isaacson, McKeachie, and Milholland 1963). They find that college men who are high in affiliation motivation (the need for affiliation and relatedness) make relatively better grades in classes that are characterized by a high level of affiliation cues coming from the instructor. Conversely, men low in affiliation motivation do relatively better in classes low in affiliation cues.

Thus, if one type of teacher or teaching style affects some students positively and others negatively, the effects of any variable cancel out. This point was corroborated by Dubin and Taveggia (1968), who reanalyzed the data from nearly 100 studies of comparative teaching methods. Finding no significant differences between any pair of methods, they suggested that some students react favorably to one technique, others to different approaches. The results of studies comparing different teaching procedures must, therefore, be inconclusive, if only because each different type of student–subject reacts differently to the same treatment.

Nevertheless, certain gains in both comprehension and factual information seem to be influenced by different types of teacher behavior. Apparently, teachers need to be very clear about their objectives and need to develop those aspects of their natural styles that best lead students to attain those objectives. Certain teaching modes are probably better suited to some groups of students than to others, and eventually it may be possible to select instructors especially adept at teaching certain student types and to help teachers develop styles most appropriate for particular audiences.

Heath (1970) reports that the ability of teachers to relate to students may vary according to the ethnic background of the students, and that certain elements of teaching style contribute to this ability differentially, again depending on the students' ethnic backgrounds. Most research reports, however, are inconclusive regarding the key question of how affinity relates to learning. Although a student may generally *prefer* certain types of instructors, just how they *affect* his learning or development is not presently known. It would seem logical that faculty members who are attentive to individual students are more effective than those who are less responsive. Yet we cannot predict which instructors will tend to be attentive. Further, except in very limited cases where single classrooms are examined, we do not know how individual students react to special teaching situations.

STUDYING CONGRUENCE

What can the study of interaction offer the community college instructor? The attempt to discover the impact of the individual whose personality structure is essentially congruent or dissonant with his students seems potentially fruitful. We do not know whether common characteristics or mirror images are more influential in determining effects of teacher on student or of student on teacher.

The general issue of congruence/dissonance gives rise to certain questions: Do teachers who tend to be extraverted relate better to students who are similarly oriented? In terms of a taxonomic scheme of cognition, is the individual who functions at the level of "synthesis" better able to learn from the teacher who functions at the same level? Or does the student's learning to synthesize really stem from his exposure to a potpourri of cognitive styles? Dealing with the more global aspects of individual personality, it would seem important to ascertain whether students who are relatively high in ego-strength are better able to learn from teachers who are spontaneous and flexible. Similar lines of inquiry could employ almost any variables.

Some investigators have indicated that differential cognitive preferences affect interaction in the classroom. In this vein, Smith and Meux point out that

> ... some teachers prefer to deal with details and thus neglect the general ideas of the material they are dealing with. On the other hand, other teachers prefer to discuss generalizations, and, in consequence, overlook the details which support the more general conceptions and principles. The same sort of preferences may also be found among students. These sorts of preferences will probably influence the quality of classroom discourse, shaping its various twists and turns and determining, in part, who will participate. (1964, p. 117)

Many alternative arrangements have been posed as ways of capitalizing on different styles or modes of approach. Instead of grouping students solely by ability, we should try grouping them by style or approach. It is feasible in larger classes to let some students gain information from library learning rather than from class attendance. Other students could be encouraged to do laboratory work, and still others to gain experiences in field settings. The point is that a variety of approaches to the same ends should be offered, since we do not presently know which students best achieve which goals under which instructional conditions.

Many students have opinions about what and how they can best learn. Although these opinions are not generalizable, giving students the opportunity to determine their own conditions of learning, to suffer the consequences of bad choices, and to learn from these experiences may be the most important way in which education can be personalized. Information on the interaction of student and teacher characteristics as it relates to and affects learning may even suggest that it is best to feed all pertinent data into a computer and assign students to classes with those teachers who would best fit their needs. However, this seems to be an unlikely and possibly even an undesirable consequence. We might do better to teach a student to learn from a variety of teachers rather than to restrict him to teachers to whom he can adjust more easily.

Still, research on the phenomenon of cognitive style or preference may be one of the most promising elements in understanding classroom interaction. For if the classroom is to be viewed as a prime medium for student–faculty interaction, personality and cognitive preferences must be considered. It seems rather presumptuous to maintain the existing patterns of classroom dominance by the instructor or to plunge into the uncharted waters of intense personal relationships bordering on the therapeutic without bringing other variables to the surface. Personality development, a desired but unknown outcome of college, is more difficult to measure than cognitive preference, but both might be enhanced if we better understood either.

The process of interaction also relates to the study of instruction. Because most classroom teaching shifts at the whim of the individual instructor, it is extremely difficult to separate the effects of instructional techniques from the total configuration of the person. Instructional methods cannot be assessed apart from the individuals who employ them, and in spite of the emphasis being placed on hardware and reproducible media, teachers continue to play the major role in college level instruction. Where instruction is "live," the teacher as a person is a more important variable than the presumed instructional treatment. Mutuality affects the process of instruction itself, but here again we know little about how to measure the variable.

In the final analysis, the raison d'être for any study of faculty–student interaction must be to perceive its relationship to learning. To understand how the instructor affects student learning, it is necessary to examine those phenomena that act on the individual by enhancing changed attitudes or behavior patterns. One reason the research is so inconclusive may well be that the classroom is the wrong place to seek patterns of interaction that lead to change in human functioning. To search within the classroom is to ascribe to it a value as an instructional form that is probably far beyond its real worth. And to remove "instruction" from the view of people interacting within the classroom is to change the pattern of observation so that the ostensible purpose of the meeting is removed from the model. We are far from being able to make definitive statements about the process of classroom interaction or about the way it affects the individual. We are even farther from specifying the types of teachers who are most likely to influence particular types of students.

DIFFERENTIAL
EFFECTS ON THE INSTRUCTOR

The student is not the only one affected by student–faculty interaction. Students affect the instructor as a person, subtly warping his personality, perhaps causing him to become something other than he might have become if he were in a different field. The effects reverberate. The students' social behavior, their diligence, and their levels of intelligence all bear on the types of instructors who apply for positions at the schools; accordingly, they serve as a potent selection factor. They also influence the instructors' behaviors in the classroom. Students thus play an important indirect role in their own teaching. Lombardi (1969) has documented the extent of student activism in junior colleges. In time, this form of student behavior will have its own kind of impact.

Special types of students have lasting effect on the instructors; students of marginal ability offer a good example. Despite the pronouncements of administrators and other leaders who insist that the junior college is uniquely qualified to meet the needs of the community, many instructors chafe at teaching students so classified. Whether community college psychology teachers (Daniel 1970), teachers-in-training (Cohen and Brawer 1968), or teachers in general (Garrison 1967) are being surveyed, the same feeling is frequently evident.

Similarly, institutional reputations for attracting students of high or low ability affect instructors' predispositions. Teachers may be drawn or repelled by the institution's reputation for student abilities and attitudes. Or they may accept employment only by default—because their first and second choices were unavailable. These attitudes can result in a self-fulfilling prophecy: "The students are poor, unappreciative, lacking in basic skills, and unmotivated. Why should I bother to try?" And the dropout and failure rate grows apace.

What kinds of effects might "low-ability" students have? Instructors who teach remedial classes frequently feel they have a role different from other instructors, that they have been isolated from their preferred reference groups. These instructors may even feel that they are not college professors, and may show their resentment to the detriment of the students, the college, and themselves—a phenomenon explored by Moore (1970).

Unmotivated students can also cause an instructor to shrink away from them as human beings. As Riesman says, "One might even contend that a certain amount of poor communication and distorted feedback may be necessary if faculty are to maintain their morale in the face of an enervating environment of mediocrity" (in Dunham 1969, p. 172). In self-defense, the instructor of remedial courses may resist close interaction with his students. This can lead to charges that some instructors do not care about students, that they actually see students as a mass of unidentified people, not as individuals. Yet the instructor may actually be attempting to save himself from despair and fears of self-doubt.

The phenomenon of personal withdrawal was reported by two of the new secondary school instructors who contributed to Ryan's book:

> As I began to recognize the shells into which many of the more established teachers withdrew, in their professional roles, I also began to understand why this happened. They were afraid of the new student body, which few of them were prepared to educate. (1970, p. 109)
>
> . . . I never became deeply involved in school affairs or with any of my students. I held myself aloof, jealous of demands on my time and on my emotions, as though protecting myself, from what, I didn't know. (Ibid., p. 141)

Activist or vociferous students take their toll in another way. Faced with accusations that his subject area is "irrelevant," the instructor may abandon his field and begin to make unsubstantiated pronouncements on contemporary issues. But this form of intellectual suicide can adversely affect both students and instructors. By pandering to the needs of the students who challenge his authority, the instructor may think he is helping them. However, "The teacher who makes the students' point of view his own not only yields to dishonesty but runs the risk of destroying the students' vision" (Kriegel 1970). Students may sincerely wish to confront the establishment as a way of testing their own boundaries. Unfortunately, they are often greeted by "professional masochism," exhibited under the guise of making the course relevant. The student challenges; opposition evaporates. Neither instructors nor students are well served.

A similar effect occurs when students who are in college principally because of the draft or because they simply have no desire to go to work demand relevance. The instructor may feel forced to relieve the students' boredom with school by catering to their need for excitement. In fact, the students may have brought to the fore the instructor's own lack of commitment to his discipline, his failure to maintain currency in his field, or his plain and simple laziness.

Changes do occur, in both instructors and students. But as McKeachie so perceptively notes,

As faculty members it is easier for us to accept the possibility that students may have personal barriers to learning than to recognize that we as teachers often defend against real change in ourselves. If we accept Roger Heyns' definition of college as a community of learners, every teacher–student interaction carries potential for learning of both teacher and student. . . . Teaching should be a two-way process in which both students and teachers learn from one another; as long as teaching conditions facilitate two-way interaction, we can place substantial reliance on the good sense of teachers and students. (1967, pp. 31–32)

The instructor who understands his own dynamics as well as the reciprocal interplay that goes on between himself and his students is in a better position to gain a sense of personal and professional maturity.

In Summary

This chapter has stressed the problems of determining mutual effects— especially in an institution where few contacts between teachers and students occur other than in the classroom. Interaction analysis, a recently popular line of research, can potentially reveal what goes on in the classroom, but the interaction processes themselves are still unknown. Experimental situations in which students and instructors meet together in groups without the artificial constraints of the classroom are warranted, but these conditions seem unlikely to develop in the community college as we know it. Our knowledge about the process of interaction seems destined to grow slowly.

The chapter has also referred to the problems of the instructor who must cope with large numbers of young people, many of whom have been classified as remedial, unmotivated, or low-achieving. These students are a fact of community college life in the 1970s, and no yearning for independent, knowledge-seeking learners will make them vanish. Nevertheless, if the instructor acknowledges them overtly, accepts them for the human beings they are, and genuinely commits himself to furthering their development, he may find his interactions with them very rewarding. By putting his own person on the line, he may not only help his students, but his own growth as a professional being will certainly also be enhanced. The challenge can be its own reward.

part five

On Becoming
a Teacher

Beginning instructors are frequently advised to have humor, will-power, a good memory, kindness, and breadth of interest. They must know their academic subjects and their students. They must be well prepared and able to communicate. And on and on. Unquestionably, there are merits in the frequent exhortations in books that provide teaching tips or that speak of teaching in terms of art and beauty. Although the catalog of human virtues typically ascribed to the "good teacher" often sounds like the Boy Scout laws, who can argue with virtuousness? The instructor is told that a good teacher is a good person and that decades of research on teacher characteristics have supported these contentions.

Such notions make comfortable reading and may even help the instructor feel that he is joining a noble calling. However, there are some debilitating considerations in this type of advice that must be faced if teaching is to become a profession. Telling an instructor that he must possess a full array of human virtues if he is to be "successful" is like telling a doctor that he must have no vices if his patients are to get well. Without doubt, the profession is better for the better people in it. But by excessive concern with the teacher's traits as such, the prospective in-structor—and indeed, the field at large—loses sight of the qualities that help make a profession. The doctor must still be considered a success to the extent his patients are cured, no matter what his faults. And the measure of an instructor's success can only be the learning manifested by his students. The qualities of goodness that either possesses may enhance his capabilities, but they are not sufficient conditions for effective professional practice. Neither are the methods he employs.

If one assumes—and judging from their actions, most junior college instructors do—that there is no reliable pedagogical knowledge that can be applied absolutely, it follows that there is no universally applicable prescription for teaching. Why, then, these chapters on teacher selection and preparation? This book is dedicated to enhancing individual self-awareness as it relates to personal and professional maturity. We submit that an instructor cannot use a technique effectively without being intellectually and personally involved in the method. No one can give what he does not have. Basically, before he can use any approach to good effect, the instructor must internalize the meaning and consequences of his action. Unless he knows what result he is striving for, he has no basis on which to evaluate his own effect. And further, unless the instructor is aware of his own motivations, he is in a poor position to select the most effectual methods.

The instructor himself, the techniques he employs, and the results he obtains operate reciprocally. Both intrinsic and extrinsic forces demand recognition. Extreme conflict among them weakens all. The instructor who attempts to have his students learn what others have decided are appropriate skills or attitudes cannot, unless he has accepted them as his own, teach them well. The instructor who adopts a method or technique just because he has heard it is valuable cannot employ it appropriately. And the instructor who has not searched out his own motives, objectives, and best modes of procedure is doomed to constant frustration as he tries to achieve ends and uses methods that run counter to his own predilections.

Taking the position that the individual entering the profession or seeking employment at a particular institution should be well aware of what the profession—or the college—will mean to him personally, the first chapter in this section deals with processes of selection. As Riesman notes, "... it is important to recognize without cynicism the fact that all occupations and professions must serve the people in them as well as the clients of those people" (in Dunham 1969, p. 177). The employing administrator can help the individual gain satisfaction in his work if he tends to select people for the particular jobs that must be done, not only on the basis of the personal qualities of the applicants.

The review of certification requirements and professional associations in chapter 12 is included with dual intent: first, because they are extrinsic forces that influence the individual instructor through their effect on the profession at large, and second, because of what they reveal about the belief systems on which the junior college and the teaching profession are based.

Junior college teacher preparation programs are discussed in chapter 13. We recognize that no one program can do everything. No matter how they are organized, most programs provide little more than a few tips on techniques of teaching, some data on institutional organization, a certificate that enables one to apply for a position, a chance to try out one's stage presence with a group of students, and some suggestions for a philosophical framework on which he can build his own activities. Nonetheless, any of these can be useful to the individual in his move toward self-awareness, identity, and maturity within a profession. Although the person enrolled in a teacher preparation program is usually not concerned about its organization, the structure of these programs and more important, the premise upon which they are based, might suggest what they can mean for the individual—in terms of both personal and professional growth.

Chapter 14 sketches a program based on a defined learning approach. This program forces its matriculants to discover and identify their own objectives, to reconcile their commitment to a field of knowledge with the realities of junior college instruction. The effect that specific, measurable objectives have on the instructor has rarely been articulated elsewhere. Too frequently, objectives are accepted or rejected on the basis of what proponents feel they will mean to the students who are confronted with them. In the program described in chapter 14, objectives are seen in terms of what they do for the instructors who specify them. We feel that this program is significant because requiring the instructor to specify the objectives of his own teaching turns him back on himself in a special way. In effect, it backs him into a corner where he must answer a question he poses to himself: "What am I *really* trying to do?" In our opinion, the instructor who can articulate his real intentions is well on the way to understanding himself and his profession. His specifying learning objectives for his students thus enhances his own personal and professional maturity.

11

Selection:
A Two-Way Process

Vocational choices are made at various stages of life. Indeed, as society becomes more complex and as alternatives increase, the individual may explore many avenues before he settles on a particular vocation. Even the notion of "settling" may be erroneous, since it is common for occupational changes to be made at frequent intervals—even by those who have had a fair amount of educational preparation and are well integrated in terms of personal development. Certainly those occupational patterns that were important in the past are seldom found intact in the present. It is no longer usual to assume the same occupational role that was accepted by one's father or grandfather. The person who engages in any occupation may find his role changing with the times.

By the time a person decides he wants to teach, he has already made certain resolutions. If his selection of profession is carefully made, if he is aware of its concomitant responsibilities and of what the teaching role entails, we maintain that he is in a far better position to derive satisfaction from his work and to direct himself to student achievement than is the person who is ambivalent about—and uncertain of the reasons for—his occupational choice.

Selecting an occupation represents much more than merely choosing to exercise a set of skills and functions. An occupation is a way of life. Indirectly—but very importantly—it provides the individual with much of his social environment as well as with his actual working environment. It strengthens the special characteristics he must use in his work role, diminishes other traits. It carries a certain status in the community, providing patterns for living as well as for the adaptation of social roles. And, in large measure, it determines the sorts of people with whom he spends his life ("... why would grownups spend whole days hanging around adolescents and callow collegians?" [Goodman 1970, p. 77]).

There is a chicken-and-egg relationship between vocational choice and the total personality constellation of the person. Selection of an

120

occupation has a marked influence on the person's value judgments and ethical standards, but the act is also an outgrowth of those same dimensions. It cannot be divorced from any part of the person. "Occupation and personality traits are intimately related," says Lidz (1968, p. 369). The two interact continually.

Selection is a two-way process that feeds into a common denominator. The individual who is making decisions about entering a profession or applying for a particular position is at once a selector and a selectee. Similarly, the agency that is in a position to accept or reject him is simultaneously selector and selectee. Each chooses the other. Both are affected by the resultant decisions.

This chapter outlines certain premises of selection—both into teaching in general and into particular institutions. It also discusses the process of selecting out of teaching and views teacher self-selection in terms of the interactions that exist among the instructor's needs, the employer's criteria, and the many dimensions of the college environment.

DIMENSIONS OF THE PROCESS

The practice of viewing people against particular paradigms has a long history. Predicated on the premise that certain individuals with particular characteristics are or are not likely to succeed in particular situations, the selection of candidates for occupational positions, academic fields, and special organizations is part of this history.

When viewing patterns of selection for employment in any occupation, we must consider four distinct elements: the individual applicant, the prospective employer, the interactions between employee and employer, and the occupational environment. And even though job markets fluctuate and the supply–demand balance waivers, both prospective employer and prospective employee must be aware of alternatives. Neither the applicant nor the person offering the position is always free to choose among several alternatives, but just as the potential employer may inquire about the candidate's experiences and expectations, the candidate too may inquire about the job opening. Knowledge of a situation combined with an awareness of one's own mode of functioning facilitates the process of inquiry. The chance for future occupational satisfaction is increased when one is sure of self and aware of situation.

The actual situation in which the individual will work is another dimension that must be considered in the selection process. The person applying for an academic position should ask questions about special features of the school, regulations and institutional goals that have been established and to which he must adhere, and other pertinent factors.

Much general information may be gleaned from college catalogs and faculty handbooks, but how many people apply for jobs without examining even these documents?

Teaching has been accused of being an ahistoric profession—that is, one that does not learn from its earlier practices. This contention is verified by the profession's failure to stabilize criteria for selection of instructors. The absence of systematic information about the specific conditions that applicants will meet can make selection a haphazard exercise. Without adequate descriptions of the major activities intrinsic to the profession, the selector must rely on vague notions of the types of people who seem to be likely to teach well. The lack of definite criteria of effectiveness also presents a problem to the employing administrator. Without specific criteria against which his predictions may be validated, even the best selection procedures become exercises in the assessment of people along ambiguous, often irrelevant, dimensions that blatantly ignore any consideration of future evaluation.

Understanding the applicant and the dimensions of the profession are two requisites for successful selection. Another is the interaction between the person and the environment. More often than not, the influence of extrinsic forces has been ignored by those who study processes of selection. Stemming from Murray's (1938) theory of motivation, however, there is now a body of inquiry that considers both person and situation. Murray's system advances the concepts of individual needs and environmental press, seeing the interaction between them as a significant determinant of behavior. Stern, Stein, and Bloom (1963) base their personality assessment schemes on this dual consideration. From these beginnings, others have described pertinent variables centering about individual traits and college characteristics (Astin and Holland [1961]; Astin [1964]; Pace and Stern [1958]; Pace [1960, 1962]). These studies emphasize the importance of interaction as a dimension in its own right and provide a basis for better understanding the reciprocal nature of the selection process.

INTO THE PROFESSION

Self-selection suggests that the individual has undergone certain processes of thought—and in some cases, of preparation—before deciding on a particular career. It also implies that a number of significant others have contributed to his decisions. Although much work has been done in the area of vocational and academic counseling, little is known about why people choose certain fields or about the relationship of subsequent success to their decisions. There is general agreement on which occupations hold highest prestige, but it is uncertain why some people enter specialized high status fields while others with apparently equal ability enter occupations with less attractive images. Heist points out that ". . . fundamental in the personal development that leads to an occupational decision is the self-perception or self-concept of the individual. The image of the expected occupational role must coordinate to that of a person's self-concept" (1968, p. 163). Since concept of self is an important dimension in the total personality picture, it might consequently be surmised that self-image as well as past experiences are both major determinants in the decision to enter a particular occupation.

Questions of selection are usually left to those engaged in vocational guidance and counseling psychology, but the issues are also directly related to the teacher's view of himself. Knowledge of the reasons why someone is attracted to a particular field may well provide information which the individual can use to better understand himself and his chances for attaining satisfaction in his profession.

Many reasons for entering the teaching profession have been postulated. Responses from former teachers, teachers currently employed, and graduate students suggest that men and women become college teachers because of the kinds of people they are—intelligent, middle class, responsible, and academically ambitious. As a group, they believe that self-improvement requires hard work. They prefer essentially solitary and intellectually stimulating activities and are willing to defer immediate desires in favor of long-range goals (Gustad 1960). Women generally become teachers because they like to work with young people, while men do so because they are primarily interested in particular subject areas. Other superficial reasons that have been advanced include the desire to hold a managerial position; interest in things of the mind (with teaching serving as a compromise for those not sufficiently talented to make a living in the creative arts field); training not sufficient for another profession; and desire (or need) for ready money.

Any discussion of why people embark on teaching careers must include the contention that, at least in the initial stages of their work, instructors crave affection. The sensitive statements tendered by six secondary school instructors at the end of their first year in the classroom (Ryan 1970) include such remarks as:

> "I didn't want them to be mad at me. I wanted to be liked." (p. 7)
>
> "I care very much if a student despises me personally." (p. 18)
>
> ". . . I wanted to be accepted, to be liked, to succeed, to feel strength or, perhaps, power." (p. 117)
>
> "I wanted very much to be liked by the students; I probably wanted their affection and acceptance more than I wanted their intellectual growth during most of this first year." (p. 118)

These types of motives cannot be ignored.

Occupational interests develop at various periods of time. Just how or when the precise decision to enter the profession is made remains unclear. For the college instructor, the decision to teach is often the result of his own drift toward more education. Interest in certain major fields comes earlier than the decision about how to apply the acquired knowledge. An investigation of career choices of 250 University of Minnesota faculty members found that, although 25 percent had first considered college teaching as a career while they were undergraduates, 53 percent had not seriously thought about the possibility until after their highest degree had been earned (Eckert and Stechlein 1958). Only 2 percent of the university faculty had held college teaching as a definite goal before they entered college.

The impact of reference groups varies. In some instances, high school teachers stimulate a particular occupational focus (Roe 1956). Top men in specialized fields who direct students to one discipline or another—and conversely, poor teachers who direct them away—also influence choice. Feldman and Newcomb do not find it surprising that ". . . faculty are a particularly crucial influence in the decisions of students to become teachers, especially college teachers" (1969, p. 253).

Beyond the precise source of influence, people in different academic disciplines report a variety of types of influences. Chemists, for example, most often stress the force of their own teachers on their choices, while psychologists are less inclined to attribute much influence to any one source. Eiduson (1962) found certain developmental patterns that differentiated creative scientists from other groups. But there is no consensus. The ambiguity is perhaps best explained by Waller: "Rarely does an occupational choice result from a process of rigorous reasoning. More often it is the social experience of the individual which gives him a push into teaching that he cannot resist and the advantages and disadvantages of teaching remain unconsidered" (1960, p. 331).

INTO THE COLLEGE

There is no single institutional environment. The applicant for a teaching position must be aware of the differences among colleges if he is to recognize the available alternatives. He is not taking advantage of his options if he does not realize that he has the opportunity to select as well as to be selected. It is true that employers can deliberately choose the kinds of people employed in their institutions, but the incumbent teacher who desires a change of employment or the candidate who is anticipating his initial job should recognize the dualism of the employment interview. He must answer the interviewer's questions about educational experiences and theory, but he can also ask his own questions about the roles he will be expected to assume, the types of students he will encounter, and the extent to which the institution has formulated its own objectives.

The applicant's first real contact with the college environment takes place when he presents himself for employment. The phone calls and letters, the personal introductions and interviews, the campus tours—all make impressions that may never be dispelled. Consciously and/or unconsciously, the candidate rapidly gains impressions and forms opinions. Similarly, each interviewer—dean, division chairman, prospective office mate—gains impressions of the candidate. Each has his own vision of the institution and what it represents for him. As he speaks with and views the prospective instructor, opinions are formed. Assessment is a continuous dual process, with the interviewers measuring the newcomer through their own eyes and making their own judgments of how well he will fit into the environment—and the candidate similarly viewing the interviewers.

The processes of employment and acclimatization affect job satisfaction in at least the initial stages of the teacher's career. In the junior college, new instructors are phased into their positions in a variety of ways, ranging from "Here is your office. Let me know if you have any problems" to elaborate first-year orientation programs such as those described by Kelly and Connolly (1970). In many cases the importance of the early exposures is ignored by everyone but the new teacher.

The issue has been viewed at other levels. Studying new faculty in two institutions—a sectarian college and a private university of a different denomination—Allen and Sutherland conducted interviews with 20 teachers soon after they had reached the campus for their initial employment. The same instructors were interviewed again eight months later. In spite of the small number of subjects, the findings of this study are of interest. New faculty members seemed to be compatible with the college if (1) employment interviews had been held in person with the college administrator or the departmental chairman on the campus itself; (2) the employment terms were made clear, in advance, in both oral and written contracts; (3) the faculty member's responsibilities were explained in terms of the college's expectations; (4) the policy and procedures of promotion, including the criteria used, were made explicit; (5) private offices were provided; (6) assurances of freedom of inquiry in teaching and of opportunity to pursue personal interests were given; and (7) the "cultural atmosphere of the college assured the new member that his own professional development was valued" (1963, p. 10).

The employment process affects not only the new teacher's perceptions and degrees of satisfaction but also the college's staffing patterns.

In the study of community college personnel described in chapter 3, Pratt (1966) found that presidents were inclined to hire applicants with whom they shared certain tendencies toward authoritarianism. However, the faculty members who retained their positions longest were unlike the presidents. The more flexible instructors were apparently more comfortable in the institutions in which the president was less flexible, while conversely, more rigid faculty members felt less in conflict with more pliant presidents.

Training experiences are important in developing role orientations (Medsker 1960). Both selector and selectee may gain insight into the congruence between institutional and faculty approaches to education by noting the kinds of training institutions attended by the instructors. Considering the similarities and differences between the training and employing institutions has direct implications for selection. When teachers who are prepared in schools with fairly closed belief systems eventually enter liberal, open-minded schools, they often experience confusion and conflict. Similar turmoil ensues when teachers move from non-authoritarian, open-minded training institutions into narrowly oriented schools.

The attitudes of the instructor's colleagues and administrators also bear on his attitudes toward the college. If the focus of the institution is toward the community, the instructors are more likely to be community-oriented. If the staff in general takes the university as its primary reference group, each instructor tends to act accordingly. This type of adjustment is effective and relatively permanent, however, only if it is truly consistent with the individual's basic orientation. The person who professes to be community-oriented only because his colleagues are so directed may soon return to form; the reverse is also true. If a college has a particular emphasis, its administrators should attempt to find teachers who already accept that philosophy rather than expect to mold them after they have been employed.

The precise definition of goals can act as a critical selection device. When goals are defined and directions spelled out, students can better judge whether or not a particular course, a discipline, or even a school fits their own needs and goals. Similarly, the specification of institutional objectives provides prospective instructors with a basis for deciding whether a particular college is one with which they would want to be identified and to which they may become committed. A small religious school, for example, would not answer—either superficially or temporarily— the needs of an agnostic instructor. Nor would a heterogeneous public college provide a tradition-oriented Ivy League representative with an environment that would be familiar and agreeable to him. These are the obvious disparities; however, the translation of governing board and administrative philosophy into precise goal statements would reveal others.

If a particular junior college prides itself on its innovative practices, it would seem that teachers who are able to shift focus readily would better adapt to the college's frequent changes of course. Both institution and individual would be better served if these matters were given more consideration than they are at present. When schools define their purposes and criteria of effectiveness, they can then select teachers who are consistent with institutional purpose. This does not imply that students do not need a variety of instructors to serve as models. It does imply, however, that schools, like people, must honestly recognize and know themselves for what they are. Undoubtedly both the institution and the individual would prosper if guidelines for faculty selection were spelled out in the context of the college's purposes.

The community college is frequently characterized as an institution where the student body meets a heterogeneous faculty—a description that concurs with the idea that students need varieties of adult models to enhance their learning. However, as Jencks and Riesman note, there is some doubt about the heterogeneity of faculties: "It would be pleasant to report that the community colleges' relative freedom from the Ph.D. fixation had enabled them to bring together men of diverse interests and talents. It would be doubly encouraging if these men had provided their students with a wide variety of relevant adult models ..." (1968, p. 484).

But "it would be nice if—" anticipations are not always realized. Jencks and Riesman go to explain this lack of diversity, citing as reasons the colleges' insistence on "just enough academic certification to bar the employment of gifted amateurs"; their inability to offer sufficiently attractive "salaries, working conditions, or social status"; and their "quite conventional academic vision." The net result is a group of people who look and act much like teachers at other levels of "the larger academic system" (Ibid., p. 484).

What kinds of individuals best serve an institution with a wide variety of ambiguously defined goals? Perhaps the most essential characteristic is the instructor's ability to adapt to a varied student body with a certain degree of flexibility. Merely saying, "We need flexible instructors," however, is not enough. Procedures to attract and retain these types of people must be established.

Notwithstanding the apparent desirability of stating clear institutional goals and developing faculty employment and orientation procedures accordingly, only a few junior colleges have taken such steps—for example, William Rainey Harper College (Illinois) and John Tyler Community College (Virginia). The guidelines regarding general recruitment and selection procedures rarely include precise statements of institutional objectives. Job descriptions are also nebulous. From several studies of these issues, it was concluded that more information regarding faculty employment procedures would be helpful to applicant and institution alike (Gaddy 1969). Gustad summarized the situation well:

> It is axiomatic in the field of personnel management that policies and practices must, if they are to have the desired effects, take into account the characteristics of the individuals and groups for whom they are designed. For many years, higher education has provided industry and governmental agencies with consultants on personnel management. It is astounding that so little has been done to apply the knowledge gained from research to the personnel practices of higher education itself. (1960, p. 5)

The Decision to Leave

Related to the broad issue of self-selection are the decisions to remain with—or abandon—the teaching profession. Satisfaction with the teaching role in general and with the institution in particular affects such decisions. However, college teachers actually abandon academia for a variety of reasons. Sometimes their resolutions to leave result from inadequate salaries, sometimes from personal and interpersonal conflicts. Whatever the ostensible reason, they leave only when their situations become intolerable or when other work becomes decidedly more attractive. And when they do leave, as Gustad (1960) notes, the decisions to do so—difficult at best—are made only under extreme duress. It is interesting that many instructor dropouts later go to great lengths to find part-time teaching opportunities.

The reasons given by instructors who choose to abandon their institutions are superficially very reasonable. Most instructors who left Florida junior colleges between 1962 and 1964, for example, reported that they wished to embark on graduate study in order to "advance" in the field of education (Cottingham 1964). However, this seems to be merely an excuse to satisfy their colleagues and themselves. If the jobs had really been attractive, the instructors who wanted further graduate study could have taken temporary leaves or made other arrangements to retain their positions. Perhaps these instructors never intended to make a professional career of junior college teaching. Any institution—especially in a period of expansion—attracts large numbers of transients who, when they get ready to leave, feel obligated to give socially acceptable reasons. Those who had initially planned to stay on may feel an even greater need to excuse their leaving.

A look at the problems listed by new faculty members in community colleges may provide a clue to why some instructors eventually drop out. In a study of 3,220 new instructors in 429 junior colleges, the single problem most frequently mentioned was "lack of time for scholarly study" (Siehr 1963). Other highly ranked issues were the necessary adaptation of "instruction to individual differences," "dealing with students who require special attention to overcome deficiencies," "understanding of college policies to be followed in curriculum development and revision," and "acquisition of adequate secretarial help." It is likely that new instructors had not anticipated the amount of time they would spend simply in "handling" large numbers of students. Their preconceptions of college teaching probably had them walking through the Groves of Academe, deep in scholarly thought. Need we point out that such idyllic situations exist hardly anywhere?

Garrison's interviews with nearly 1,000 faculty members in 20 different junior colleges throughout the nation corroborate the "lack of time for scholarly study" problem isolated earlier by Siehr. "With the unvarying insistence of a metronome's tick, faculty pinpointed their most pressing professional problem with one word: *Time*" (Garrison 1967, p. 30). Similar findings were reported from a national survey of 118 instructors (Kelley and Wilbur 1970). In response to the query, "What do you like *least* about your job?" the most frequent comments revolved about high work loads and the unavailability of aid.

Even though many junior college instructors moonlight at other jobs, the prospective teacher who hopes for time for intellectual pursuits should heed such warnings. He might similarly anticipate other problems cited by faculty members: the ambiguous image of the junior college as simultaneously a public school and a segment of higher education; the inflexibility of colleagues who reflect "the Standard Academic Mind" in their concern with courses and degrees; rigid teacher certification requirements; the lack of scholarly interchange with fellow faculty members; and the continuing frustrations associated with the attempt to "teach the unteachable" (*Ibid.* 1970, p. 194).

The changes that teaching itself effects in the person underlie many of the decisions to leave the profession. Waller insightfully notes that

> Teaching does something to those who teach. Introspective teachers know of changes that have taken place in themselves. Objectively minded persons have observed the relentless march of growing teacherishness of others. . . . The drudgery of teaching, combined with the many restrictions which the community places upon the personal conduct of teachers, may eliminate from teaching many of those virile and inspiring persons of whom the profession has such need, for it is a known fact that such pronouncedly individual persons often have little respect for purely negative morality, and react vehemently against living within the community stereotype of the teacher. (1960, pp. 329–30)

In short, who needs it?

As junior college teaching becomes a mature profession in its own right, many of the frequently cited problems will be overcome, or at least overbalanced, by the positive aspects of the job. In the meantime, if the prospective teacher is conscious of the many parts of his own being as well as of the various roles he will play, if he can anticipate the kinds of colleagues he will meet and the many demands made by the teaching environment, he will be better able to assess himself and the situation realistically. And perhaps he will avoid some of the negative aspects of the instructor's position.

THE ROLE OF THE SELECTOR

Selection is a process of interaction between selector and selectee. The prospective faculty member chooses to enter the teaching profession and subsequently—or in some cases, simultaneously—decides on a particular college. In turn, the college and the people who man the gates of the credential- or degree-granting institutions exercise their own judgments about the people who become instructors. Many behavioral scientists—Rogers, for example—have proposed "a rigorous selection system, which would weed out, so far as possible, those who seem unlikely to become creative scholars or practitioners" (1969, p. 191). However, this is easier said than done. We simply do not know how to measure the kind of intelligence, emphatic understanding, or spontaneous curiosity that Rogers finds essential.

The degree-granting institutions do not—cannot—make accurate measurements of requisite personal qualities; the junior college deans and division chairmen who do the interviewing are similarly unequipped. Junior college administrators employ a variety of vague criteria to select instructors, often making individual decisions—or seeking collegial consensus—on the basis of "that certain spark." Even so, greater care could be exercised if only they knew what they were looking for.

What about role specialization? Most occupational groups are built on specialties—why not teaching? MacLean notes,

> All community college teachers are not suited, either by personality or by training, to all of the many roles most of them are now required to play—stimulating teachers in the classroom, expert testmakers, accountants, secretaries, typists, file clerks, advisors, counselors, effective community and public relations operators—since each of these roles demands special aptitudes, abilities, interests, and skills. To be aware of these myths and their destructive effects is the responsibility of both the administrators and of the teacher himself. (in Brawer 1969, p. iii)

In the process of selection, emphasis can be placed on the teacher as an individual specializing in the teaching tasks that fit his interests and orientations. This presents a new kind of challenge because, as Hall and Vincent point out, if

> . . . the teachers who receive satisfaction from teaching are the most effective, then the assignment process itself must guarantee the teacher certain personal satisfaction on the job. This demands a tremendous amount of information about the teacher and about the kinds of jobs and situations in which [he] finds satisfaction. (1960, p. 377)

The available research suggests that different kinds of personalities are suited to play different roles within the overall framework of teaching. It seems desirable, then, for deans of instruction to select teachers who fit special teaching functions rather than to employ people with ability in a particular subject area. Instead of choosing teachers in English, for example, the dean might do better to select people on the basis of their ability to lecture, to build tests, or to do public relations work. If institutions are very large, it might be possible for each specialist to assume a single role. In smaller schools, individuals would have to engage in more than one function. But in all cases, if specialization were recognized as legitimate, instructors would be responsible for fewer different activities. They might then tend to gain greater expertise in their accepted tasks.

Specialization appears to be a particularly worthwhile approach to selection since teachers have, in fact, been found to differ in their interests, their abilities, their motivations, and their personal approaches. Some are effective in demonstration teaching or in evaluating products but less effective in drill and in follow-ups; others work better with individuals than with large groups; while still others are best at presenting lectures or a variety of reproducible instructional media to their students. Each faculty member should be encouraged to say, openly and honestly, "I would rather lecture to large groups than work with single students on a one-to-one basis," or "I want to develop curricula, but I don't want to deal directly with students." Ideally, these decisions would be made not because they are expedient but because they are congruent with the personality pattern of the teacher.

Another way to enhance the selection process is simply to explain the school environment to the teaching candidate as carefully as possible. The dean and the department chairmen can define the institutional objectives to prospective teachers and, on the basis of information available to them, determine whether these objectives appear congruent with the teacher's own orientation. Similarly, they should explain to the prospective instructor exactly what is expected of him—both as teacher and as community member—and help him decide whether the institution is truly consistent with his personality. This, of course, assumes that the teacher knows himself. However, merely describing the institution accurately, pushing aside the clouds of grandiloquence in which statements of college purpose are typically couched, can be helpful.

Administrators should be given information about prospective teachers that goes beyond the academic and normative data supplied in conventional applications. This does not mean that they should test candidates themselves, or that they should have direct access to personality and interest inventories. In fact, they should not. It does mean, however, that they should be given reports from independent agencies (personnel bureaus, placement offices) that provide valid but non-clinical appraisals of prospective faculty members. In the absence of personality data, interest patterns derived from inventories and previous vocational/non-vocational participation may provide important information.

Certain types of people should be selected out of teaching. The authoritarian person appears to be especially amiss in situations where students are openly fighting the establishment—not merely for the sake of argument, but in their various sincere attempts to establish their own identities. If junior college faculties include dogmatic, inflexible individuals (as many schools at all levels do), other arrangements might be made for them. They could be kept out of the classrooms and assigned other tasks with equal status and usefulness. Their identity as "teachers" might be maintained, but their powers would be exercised in situations where they might not "turn off" or, in the extreme, damage the students.

Awareness is a key element in satisfaction and effectiveness. If the authoritarian person finds himself in an open environment, he may learn to develop a less structured approach—depending, of course, on the degree to which his beliefs are firmly embedded and on his ability to adapt to the situation. A flexible person is better able to adjust to the philosophy of a school, even one incongruent with his own orientation. In time, however, this kind of superficial adaptation will fail for the well integrated person; if he is really true to himself, it will never be palatable. If, however, both institution and individual are able to spell out honestly what they are looking for, choices will be more satisfying and, presumably, schools more effective.

Many questions remain unanswered regarding the issues of selection. The important point here is that the selection of a career must be undertaken with care, since it is a decision critical to the individual's entire life. If the individual instructor's choice is sincere, if he is open to understanding the teaching situation, if he is aware of his own strengths and shortcomings, he is in a better position to make appropriate career choices. If he is aware of the reasons for his own decisions, he is more likely to contribute to the institution as an integrated, mature faculty member.

12

Who's
In Charge
Here?

Teachers have less to say about their work than any other group licensed by the state. . . . It is doubtful that they are so ignorant, indifferent, and incompetent that they should be deprived of a voice in the formation of educational policy. A record of the lay groups who have been in charge of education is not such as to suggest that improvement is impossible. (Hutchins 1970, p. 85)

It is doubtful whether anything has retarded professionalism more than teacher subservience to lay opinion on matters which should be settled by teachers. (Lieberman 1956, pp. 472–73)

If teachers are to maintain authority over their own enterprise under the stress of chronic change, they must seek and be granted a prominent part in evaluating the flood of new ideas. . . . They would make a grave mistake to leave it entirely to others inside and outside the scholastic community to determine what innovations in curriculum and teaching practices should be accepted and what rejected. (Friedlander 1966, p. 11)

These are the frequently reiterated positions. The instructor should control his own profession, police it, set standards of entry, select goals and methods, and so on. His professional associations seize on statements like these and demand authority. But certification controls remain in the hands of state officials; institutional policies continue to be mandated by governing boards and administrators. Adversary relationships become the norm. Each side gives ground grudgingly.

Where did it all start? Higher education has a long history of participation by faculty members in institutional planning and control. In fact, early American institutions followed the European model of the professors as the primary agents of institutional governance. But the two-year college stems from a different line. Public school–type principal–teacher relationships and a combination of state and local governance are its heritage. With few exceptions the roles have always been separated into "administrators" and "faculty members"—or, in the words of some instructors, "them versus us." Hence, control of the institution and of the profession never has been in the hands of the faculty. Standards for faculty certification, student entrance, curricular decisions, even instructional forms, have been and still are administrator–, governing board–, and/or state level–dominated.

How does this situation affect the individual instructor? It is impossible to separate him from his environment; intrinsic and extrinsic forces relate. Self-perceptions, his reactions to significant others, and a variety of other intrinsic variables all push the instructor toward or away from professionalism. Similarly, the extrinsics have an effect. Teacher certification requirements and professional associations, for example, are extrinsic to the faculty member; in fact, he may hardly be aware of their existence. However, they impinge directly on the instructor. Because they affect his status, his self-image, the way he addresses his work, and the satisfactions he derives from it, they must be seen in the light of the instructor's move toward personal integration and professionalism.

CERTIFICATION

Teaching is a licensed activity. All publicly supported educational systems require some form of instructor certification—defined here as any obligatory requirements for obtaining a position. This may be as elaborate as the state-mandated preparation sequences for elementary and secondary school teachers, or as simple as a set of locally developed and locally maintained rules for employment in the community college. Nevertheless, requirements do exist.

There is much nationwide consistency in certification requirements, although the details vary from state to state. The norm is a master's degree to teach in academic subject areas, and equivalent trades experience to teach in vocational programs in the junior college. The number of required courses in education has declined in recent years.

Data regarding state requirements for junior college teachers are easy to find—the American Association of Junior Colleges collects them from time to time. However, although examination of trends in certification is instructive, it fails to tell the complete story of instructor selection. The junior college is as susceptible as any other institution to reacting to emergency personnel situations with relaxed requirements. When, for example, pressing needs demand the establishment of certain vocational programs, instructors are employed whether or not they meet standards. Most districts also allow college administrators to employ non-certified instructors in any teaching area, with the proviso that the position be temporary pending successful fulfillment of prerequisites. On occasion, if suitable replacements cannot be found, these "temporary" positions become permanent.

For the profession at large, certification is the passport to respectability. The teacher is dependent on certification for his professional standing for at least two reasons: first, because his salary does not depend on his individual competence, and second, because he is not paid on a fee basis but in terms of salaries that are contingent on the community's evaluation of the faculty—and the profession—as a whole. At the present time, the public at large cannot distinguish competent from incompetent teachers on the basis of service criteria (the profession does not do well at this, either). Hence, all "certificated" instructors are "good" instructors, deserving the same pay and job responsibilities.

"Professionalism through ascription" differentiates teaching from most other professions. Teaching also differs in that, as Lierheimer points out, "... the student is compelled by law to accept the professional ministrations of the teacher assigned to his class. In most other professions, the client has some choice in the matter ..." (1970, p. 21). Individual members of other professional groups—doctors, lawyers, engineers—tend to be selected by the people they serve, to be differentially rewarded, and to be discharged if their services prove unsatisfactory. Hence, some of the deficiencies in their licensing procedures may be excused.

State-mandated certification has supporters and opponents. Those who speak for it claim that the need for a certain expertise in teaching demands that state and local agencies exercise a measure of control over practices in tax-supported institutions. Some of the arguments in opposition to teacher certification are that it guarantees nothing of value in an instructor's preparation and that it only assures a prolongation of junior colleges' identification with the local school districts from which, in most states, they arose; thus, certification detracts from the junior college as part of higher education. In those terms, certification is viewed as it contributes to perceived status or as it adds to institutional effectiveness, and it may be questioned accordingly. Most arguments about teacher certification, however, skirt both issues and relate primarily to the question of which groups are to set policy for, and maintain control over, the process of issuing credentials.

Many people have spoken out against the present patterns of teacher certification. Most refer particularly to elementary and secondary school teacher training, but their comments apply equally to the two-year college. Conant, for instance, "would eliminate all course requirements by the state—all adding up of semester hours" and "would have the competence of a future teacher tested by practice teaching under conditions set by the state and subject to state supervision." Beyond that, he "... would put the responsibility squarely on the university or college ..." for determining the prospective instructor's fitness to teach (1963, p. 112).

Other commentators would assign all responsibility to the profession. Schrag (1970) believes certification "is better done by the profession in which the applicant intends to practice than by the institution which trains him." Lieberman (1956) long ago argued for certification through examination, claiming that patterns of preparation do not guarantee any degree of expertise and that other professions have statewide examinations administered under the control of the profession itself. The argument that there are as yet no objective measures that can separate the competent from the incompetent instructor does not hold—Lieberman notes that examinations are given all through the training sequences and that the prospective teachers are passed or failed on the basis of test results. If examination for entry to the teaching profession—administered by the profession itself, as in law, medicine, and accounting—is not valid, then neither are the examinations given in college.

Some critics go beyond suggesting that the profession (rather than the state) should be responsible for certification. They contend not only that certification is outmoded, but also that the entire pattern of requiring diplomas for anything should be abandoned. Goodman argues that students ". . . should sit in at the state capitol until licensing is possible without irrelevant diplomas" (1970, p. 91).

Illich (1970) goes even further, pointing out that legislation should be passed to prohibit discrimination in employment on the basis of degrees, and that just as there are laws prohibiting discrimination on the basis of race and sex, there should be laws stating that an employer may not inquire about an applicant's attained level of schooling. Putting the responsibility squarely on the employer, Illich declares that if a test of fitness to perform on the job is needed, the employer can administer it, but he should not be allowed to require any form of certification based on previous schooling. Drucker (1969) echoes Illich's contentions. These are extreme positions, but they reveal the magnitude of the problem as perceived by significant critics of the educational establishment.

There are other—less comprehensive—issues. In many cases, certification is tied to work in professional education; for decades, people both within and without the profession have doubted the usefulness of such courses. Many satires ridicule the "ed-school prof" who gives lectures on the use of audiovisual aids, describes irrelevant or outmoded experiments in the psychology of children to people who are dealing with them daily, and clouds his discussions with fogs of jargon that is useless at best. However, experiences that are irrelevant to the real world of teaching are not confined to courses in education; most of the criticisms of professional education courses can be applied with equal validity to courses in any subject field. Such arguments miss the more important issues in certification.

The larger questions deal with the instructor's self-image, behavior, and effect. Do professional education courses—or any other courses—bear

on these factors? Teachers in approved pre-service or in-service preparation sequences are supposed to acquire the skills and attitudes that will
lead their students to learn—an obvious statement, but one not honored in
practice. If an instructor fancies himself an expert in his subject matter
and a scintillating lecturer, he will tend to stand before his students and
spin a web of words in and around his chosen field. What effect can an
ed-psych course have on one who would offer lectures, textbooks, mid-
terms, and finals in constantly recurring patterns because "that's what
college is"? Who can tell him that his charges view his spray of words as
irrelevant, perhaps even as a convenient excuse to drop out of formal
education, never to return? For in the two-year college—as in other
educational structures—archaic, unvarying instructional forms may well
contribute in large measure to mass student attrition. Certification requirements or not, these types of instructors need training in sensitivity to others
and, hopefully, preparation so that they tend to hold themselves accountable for their effects.

Regardless of one's position on certification, current requirements
certainly do not point the way toward effective instruction. It may be
that no one document can be submitted as evidence that an instructor can
do everything. Perhaps to be optimally effective, the junior college teacher
needs to be so specialized that his tasks cannot be subsumed under a
single set of requirements. If few people can be expected to be thoroughly
able in all aspects of the profession, a combination of specialists is suggested. Particular certificates should indicate individual talents rather
than generalized superficial abilities.

However, despite calls for junior colleges to do their own teacher
training (Cohen 1969, for example), most of the responsibility for the fore-
seeable future rests with the universities. Their charge is now to produce
subject matter experts who are likewise learning specialists. These experts
are not teachers stuffed with methods of classroom management, a little
psychology of learning, and some philosophy of the junior college movement, but instructors who are aware of the totality of their responsibility
toward student learning and who possess the necessary ability to carry it
out. The certification requirements are incidental. Instructors should gain
positions in junior colleges not because they have completed certain courses,
but because they are willing to be held accountable for student achievement and have demonstrated that they can bring it about.

Certification requirements are anachronistic and, as presently applied, irrelevant to the process of instruction. When training programs
lead instructors to construct and try out courses that include complete sets
of specific measurable objectives, when junior colleges reward instructors
for causing student learning rather than for indulging themselves in a
variety of self-fulfilling activities—from ineffective stage-playing to punish-

ment and voyeurism—the two-year college will be on its way toward true identification as a teaching institution and its instructors on their way toward professional maturity. Changes in certification requirements will follow, or teaching "credentials" will continue to exist without true meaning.

PROFESSIONAL ASSOCIATIONS

Every academic discipline has its own professional association—for example, the American Anthropological Association, the Modern Language Association. Members of these groups are frequently affiliated with institutions of higher education; their disciplinary associations provide them with a forum for the exchange of ideas—usually through annual meetings and research-reporting journals. In addition, the associations establish and maintain codes of professional ethics and serve as clearinghouses for professional interchange with other societies.

The many types of professional organizations with which the junior college instructor may affiliate include disciplinary organizations, unions, professional fraternities, and local, state, and national faculty associations. An individual instructor may belong to one or more of such groups or to none of them. Membership figures fluctuate, depending on the presence or absence of current "burning issues" that tend to bring faculty members together. Nevertheless, the trend has been steadily in the direction of increasing numbers of organizations with ever larger enrollments. And, as the major disciplinary associations are beginning to "discover" the two-year college, this trend seems likely to continue.

Depending on its orientation, an association may be a positive aid to professional identity or a negative force detracting from its members' drive for professional well-being. Even though the associations are supposed to enhance professionalism, their methods and short-term goals do not always fit the purposes they expound. A view of the associations that purport to serve junior college instructors, however, reflects the current status of the profession.

Because junior college instructors tend to orient themselves to their subject matters rather than to their disciplines (Friedman 1967b), they are much more likely to join an organization devoted to the practice of teaching in their particular field—for instance, National Council of Teachers of English—than one that is pointed toward disciplinary research. This lack of disciplinary affiliation is pointed up by the fact that of the 224,000 scientists in the 1964 National Register, fewer than 2,000 indicated staff positions in junior colleges (National Science Foundation 1967). Junior college instructors do form special groups relating to teaching in certain fields—the Community College Social Science Association is an example.

Professional fraternities are usually carry-overs from student days. Since many junior college instructors are working on advanced degrees and thus playing the dual roles of teacher and student, these societies are definite sources of influence. Their purposes are to disseminate information, to present certain conceptual frameworks for consideration, and to alert their members to contemporary issues in education. Phi Delta Kappa for men and Phi Lambda Theta for women are the national professional education organizations. Other disciplines have their own—Phi Alpha Theta in history, Alpha Kappa Delta in sociology, Psi Chi in science, and so forth.

The American Association of Junior Colleges (AAJC) addresses itself exclusively to the junior college field. It is the major professional association for the institutions themselves, serving as a liaison agency between the individual school and the field at large. Nearly every junior college holds an institutional membership, and many administrators, counselors, and instructors maintain individual memberships.

Recent arrivals on the professional association scene are the faculty unions. Addressing themselves primarily—and in some cases exclusively—to wages and working conditions, they frequently pride themselves on their militancy. They borrow terms from the labor movement in their quest for "negotiated collective bargaining contracts," "salary improvement," and "fringe benefits" (Hixson 1968–69). In some areas of the country—especially in the large cities—they are an important force, whereas in others they are scarcely known.

The American Federation of Teachers, an AFL–CIO affiliate, has been the most active faculty union. Building on its post–World War II successes in public school districts, it subsequently moved toward higher education and found the ground more fertile in the community junior colleges than in the universities, primarily because of the two-year college instructor's lack of professional status relative to his colleagues in the senior institutions. In 1969, half its college chapters were in two-year colleges. According to Peterson,

> AFT locals tend to be found in urban areas where they can be in touch with the broader AFL–CIO bureaucracy (which helped get the campus locals started in the first place). Also AFT manages to have networks of chapters working in fairly close coordination. . . . Typically, college AFT locals have been chiefly interested in obtaining a position to bargain with college administrators and trustees . . . regarding salary and other working conditions. Such collective bargaining agreements have been negotiated at about a dozen two-year community colleges, several coming after strikes. (1969, p. 68)

Although state and national faculty associations have been a part of the higher education scene for decades, they have only fitfully taken hold in the junior colleges. In 1969 the American Association of University Professors (AAUP), best known of these groups, claimed 6,500 members in 160 junior colleges—this of a total of 90,000 members in 1,125 chapters (Davis 1968–69). The American Association for Higher Education "has long had several thousand junior college faculty members and administrators in its total membership," according to its executive secretary (G. Kerry Smith 1968–69). And, organized to provide junior college faculty members with their own group, the National Faculty Association of Community and Junior Colleges (NFA) was formed in 1967. A National Education Association affiliate, its 150 chapters had 7,000 members in the spring of 1970. In proportion to their potential constituency, many state groups have far greater enrollments than the national associations.

Such groups form, splinter off, and reform—hence, little is to be gained by citing their specific goals and policies. Their most visible feature is the older groups' response to the union's inroads on their domain by adopting more militant postures that would earlier have been thought inappropriate. The AAUP, for example, "has recognized that in certain situations collective bargaining may achieve some goals of a college or university faculty" (Davis 1968–69), and the NFA is willing to accept the label of "responsible militancy" (Miner 1968–69).

Most junior colleges have faculty senates or faculty associations (sometimes both), and in some cases, state or district policy mandates the formation of these groups. By definition, the local associations do not affiliate with national organizations—although they may have their own statewide associations—but derive their power and support from their own constituencies. In many instances they provide not only forums for faculty exchange but also assume the leadership in salary and working condition negotiations with governing boards; in others, they act as little more than discussion groups. Nevertheless, they are the groups most closely involved with the concerns of the instructors within a single institution.

Each instructor makes his own decision about the extent of his involvement with a faculty group. The reasons for joining vary greatly, ranging from the desire for fraternalism to the need to resolve seemingly crucial issues of salaries or perquisites. Similar variation exists in the degree to which an association can assist faculty members. In the case of the negotiating groups, for example, success depends on the skills of the leaders and on the power and tenacity of countervailing forces. Still, certain general trends and issues regarding faculty organizations may be perceived.

The question of identity looms large. There are many unresolved issues surrounding the role of faculty members in the community college. The instructor is often unsure of himself, of the functions in which he must engage, and of his professional affiliations. As Garrison says, the individual feels his position is particularly different from "his four-year colleagues" regarding his conditions of instruction, his aims, and his professional–philosophical attitudes towards his task. Not simply a post–high school instructor of grades thirteen and fourteen, he is, in his own desire and view, a colleague in a *new* kind of collegiate effort, as yet ill-defined and in furious flux. He is unsure of his status in the educational spectrum, for he fits few traditional categories. He is aware that he is being asked to function professionally in an unprecedented situation, and he is deeply concerned about this professionalism, in the best sense of that term. He is the servant of several demanding masters, and he is groping to bring such demands into a compatibility, a coherence, that will give his work a clear rationale and thrust that will command his loyalty and his long-range commitment. (1967, p. 15)

Thus, perhaps attempting to create a new professional component that stands between high school instructor and university professor, the junior college instructor seeks an appropriate association. He is tied neither to the secondary school teacher organizations nor to a professional discipline.

Alluding to the instructors' desire for a separate status, Friedman's study of midwestern community colleges reported one faculty group's attempt to organize some sort of association that would serve as their official voice.

First, the teachers wanted an association which would be limited to and representative of only junior college teachers in the system—an association which would differentiate them in status and identity from the system's elementary and high school teachers. Second, they wanted an association which did not include administrators in its membership. Third, they wanted an association that would be acceptable to as many faculty members as possible; a local AFT chapter, for instance, would have been unacceptable to many anti–organized labor teachers.

They settled on the AAUP because:

. . . it served to differentiate the status and identity of junior college teachers from other teachers in the system, focused its attention solely upon junior college problems, and served as a vehicle for more united faculty expression and attempted authority. And it did subsequently help to narrow the perceived "authority lag" between traditional public school system authority practices and the more higher-education–oriented authority views of some faculty members. (Friedman 1966, p. 420)

Other groups have also flaunted the issue of distinct identity. The National Faculty Association of Community and Junior Colleges' early promotional literature included such statements as, "Now, for the first time, your *own* organization!" And, although it is certainly far from being a faculty group, the American Association of Junior Colleges echoes the instructors' feelings when it calls for the junior colleges themselves to be viewed as unique structures with problems quite different from those faced by other educational institutions. The individual's movement toward identity is reflected in the pronouncements of his fellows.

PERPETUATING A STATUS QUO

Faculty associations have many targets. They strive to gain greater voice for their members in matters of institutional finance, operations, curriculum planning, and policy, as well as in issues related to salary and working conditions. And in their striving they take on many of the characteristics—even the rhetoric—of labor unions. The National Faculty Association, for example, has taken the position that faculty evaluation and termination procedures should be the exclusive province of faculty members who would arrange appropriate committees and report directly to the district governing boards on these matters, deliberately cutting the administrators out of the process (National Faculty Association 1970). The activities of its recommended "professional practices committees" make them sound just like the shop grievance committees so well known in industrial union shops. So be it.

But despite the commonality of goals between professional associations and labor unions, the crucial issues in the schools are not between labor and management. The major conflict is between two bases of authority, the profession and the bureaucracy. The professional group sets standards and depends on its members to adhere to them—in fact, to internalize them. The bureaucracy has formalized modes of procedure all its own. Although the unions and professional associations claim that they are seeking higher professional status for their members, collective bargaining and similar tactics lead to more rules and more circumscribed behaviors—hence more bureaucratic functioning. The instructor becomes subject to union or association officials as well as to the administrators of his institution. Consequently, as the associations gain power, it is possible that professional status for teachers may become even more elusive than it is now. If teachers are to achieve autonomy and distinct identity through professional status, polarizing the differences between faculty and administration into a labor–management type of conflict is not the way to go. Bureaucracy is bureaucracy and institutionalized procedures have dynamics all their own.

Skirting all questions of professionalism, governance, greater benefits for the people involved, and so on, there is yet one issue that has not been faced by those who argue for or against faculty associations with the characteristics of unions. The more powerful the union, the less likely that alternatives to traditional patterns of schooling will be postulated, much less accepted. Historically, whenever a group has banded together to formalize its conditions of employment, entrance to its ranks, and other factors concerning its stature, a concomitant of this merger has been the lessened likelihood of change. And alternatives to the present pattern of schooling seem more than somewhat desirable.

Some of the issues can be pointed up as they relate to the classroom—the instructor's eminent domain. Here the associations shortsightedly stand in the way of change. Many distinct shifts in instructional functioning would enhance a true professional identity—the thorough acceptance of reproducible media and of paraprofessional aides, to name but two innovations discussed in the chapter on the instructor as manager. However, the pronouncements of the professional association leaders suggest that they do not perceive the long-range concomitants of these "innovations." As some writers have phrased it, "We should not be negotiating for those things that will, in large part in the future, be done by paraprofessionals and programmed instructors" (Phillippi and Childress 1968, p. 408).

If the faculty associations and unions continue to demand smaller classes and to insist that instructors have a direct hand in all classroom teaching responsibilities, they will obstruct the introduction of reproducible media and teacher aides. Call it featherbedding when speaking of railway firemen and airplane flight engineers or a "keen sense of professional responsibility" that allows instructors alone to work closely with individual students—the net effect is the same. Low labor-intensive media are part of the educational scene—and rightfully so. Faculty power that prescribes teacher–student ratios will not enhance their introduction into the two-year college.

The teaching business is sometimes called over-professionalized because of its excessive concern with formal education and certification. It is true that the profession has insisted on rigid training requirements, but this is not tantamount to over-professionalization. It is more accurate to describe a teacher's situation as being one of professional isolation. Janowitz notes, "... in its current organization, teaching is a solo practice profession, in contrast to many other professions which emphasize group practice, or at least close colleague relations" (1969, p. 30). The result is, in fact, under-professionalization in the actual performance of the job, because the professional instructor has few aides of any kind.

Professionalization of the faculty demands the definition of tasks, the ability to transmit the manner of addressing these tasks from one generation of instructors to another, specialization in instructional areas, the acceptance of paraprofessionals within the schools, accountability for results, and an entire scheme of pedagogy that can be examined apart from the person of the instructor. So far, the field has found little knowledge that would fit such a schema; the practicing instructors in the community colleges and elsewhere have accepted even less.

It is not much of an overstatement to say that the only time the professional associations go on the offensive is when they seek higher wages or better working conditions. How much better if the associations addressed themselves to the study of effects? How much better if they set standards for membership that exceed the ability to pay dues? In the short run they would wither, but what might the profession eventually become if its associations were concerned with serious evaluation of new methods and materials (and of its own membership), evaluation on the basis of impact on the client population?

When a "professional" association asserts demands for salary and fringe benefits, it ill-serves its members' drive for professional identity. Salary increases have very short lives as providers of satisfaction; the euphoria they induce is demonstrably transient. The inducements of the true professional person are more likely to be in other spheres—achievement, intrinsic quality of work, professional growth and development, for example, with concomitant reward and recognition for their attainment. Money is nice, but it does not lead to professional status.

What does lead to professional status? Differentiation, for one. Other professions recognize different levels of professional competence. Differences in training and power operate functionally and openly. In education, the artificial unity of teachers who have different levels of training and experience and who perform different tasks leads to weaknesses within the profession as a whole. Some time ago Lieberman noted, "Teachers should not be regarded as belonging to the same profession unless there is substantial equality between their qualifications and training. Otherwise, the educational system should be geared to a frank recognition of the differences in technical proficiency, instead of to spurious and self-defeating equality" (1956, p. 504). Lieberman maintains that the continued existence of a single profession with a professional group organized across specializations is "... a disservice to everyone. Differences between individuals [are] one thing, but substantial and enduring differences between specializations within a profession are danger signs that should not be ignored" (Ibid., p. 506). Developments in the years since that warning was issued suggest that it has been ignored.

The present professional associations could do much that they now do not do. Rather than functioning almost exclusively as salary committees, they could attempt to get tenure regulations revised—perhaps providing for renewable tenure on a five- or seven-year basis. They could establish their own requirements for renewing membership in their national, state, and local organizations. They could arrange procedures so that parents or students could file complaints about alleged teacher incompetence directly with the local association for investigation. However, the trend is in the other direction, with the professional associations serving as protective groups insisting on tenure and common standards for all. "In other words, they want power without accountability . . ." (Brenton 1970, p. 255). They want to protect their own unselected membership from being called to account; concomitantly, they want lifetime tenure protection.

Nevertheless, the basis of true professionalism is the individual in charge of his own activities. Associations may provide a structure for exerting autonomy, but in the final analysis, the instructor is his own man. The usual definition of professionalism includes the notion that the professional association must be responsible for policing the profession, setting standards for admission to it, and so forth. However, the mature profession needs more. Its members must have their own internalized justification for their work. This means not only that the profession as a whole must be accountable to itself, but also that each person practicing within it must be accountable to himself.

Perhaps the teaching profession must be forever different from other professions in that it is regulated by laws, lay boards, and administrators and is therefore not autonomous. But this need not be a hindrance to the individual. Although his profession is not self-controlling, the individual practitioner can become accountable to himself for his own actions through his own sense of purpose. This is true individual professionalism; the mature instructor need not wait for the profession to catch up.

The goal of the professional association should be the development of the aware, self-directed, professional person—the individual who specializes in his area of professional competence, assesses the effects of his efforts, and engages in similar matters relating to true professional responsibility. These associations would set standards for their membership, identify the practices they alone can do best, provide and interpret data regarding the effects of their own efforts, reward their membership for truly professional activities, impose sanctions, and work toward building the professional image. Unfortunately, this type of professional leadership is rarely seen among junior college instructors' groups. Speaking of leaders of higher education faculty associations in general, Livingston said, ". . . there are few who combine a readiness to assume administrative position with a willingness to rely on the persuasive power of their ideas rather than the coercive or manipulative power of their positions" (1968, p. 189).

Can a faculty group assume charge of its own affairs and remain truly democratic? Can a faculty association president who wants to negotiate for better conditions let his achievements rest on the merits of his case rather than on the coercive power he can bring to bear on the administration or board? Can an individual supersede the present status of his profession? These are the crucial issues. The essential non-professional status of the teacher "... has been created by decades of lay control over matters that any other professional group would consider its own affair" (Anderson 1968, p. 191). It will not be easily overturned.

Legislation that controls entrance to the profession—and associations that speak for it—impinge on every instructor's sense of professionalism—hence, on his own well-being. If the laws governing teacher certification and the rules guiding professional faculty associations do not enhance this dimension, the instructor must go it alone. Present practices of certifying teachers, and the goals and methods of his professional associations, suggest that he well might.

13

Preparation

Why teacher preparation programs at all? Isn't it true that anyone who knows anything can teach it to someone else? Aren't teacher preparation programs irrelevant? What bearing do these programs have on the teacher's professional identity?

To a marked degree, identity depends on purpose—knowing what one's goals and directions are. For an individual to develop the sense of directedness and integration that we refer to as identity, he must make a conscious effort to prepare himself for the several roles he will assume. His preparation sequence is important because, as Lidz notes, "In the process of learning a trade or a profession, ... [one] learns a way of life along with the knowledge and skills of the occupation. It will shape or help shape many facets of his personality" (1968, p. 380). Adequate and appropriate training puts the person in a position to focus on tasks rather than on self, and it reduces the element of self-conscious wondering about the appropriate adoption of particular skills and attitudes. It also hastens the transition from student to professional perspective.

A preparation program is, in fact, an extension of the self-selection process. Although entry into a preparation program suggests that the individual has already made a commitment to a field, the program itself allows him to solidify his choice—or to reject it. It gives him a choice to practice his trade before assuming a contractual obligation. It allows him to narrow down the details of the profession. Whereas he may have made his initial choice on the basis of fairly vague notions, the program makes him confront the specifics of his work. It offers a degree and/or a credential. But most important, it allows him to test resources and weigh liabilities, to amplify his talents and question his directions.

Self-knowledge is prerequisite to effective functioning as a socially aware professional being. The experiences of a deliberately designed preparation sequence can help the instructor understand both self and profession, because the program in which he engages decidedly influences the attitudes and approaches he uses in addressing his work. Although these effects may be either positive or negative, they are fairly lasting.

In addition to their immediate effect on the people they prepare, preparatory programs also influence indirectly the development of programs and long-range institutional goals within the junior college. Hence, they continually bear on the instructor's status and well-being. This extended effect can be deep as well as broad. Preparation programs are actually fundamental to any educational organization. They act as core instruments for the system, and any changes in the system may depend on concomitant—or preceding—changes in the preparatory sequences.

This chapter reviews certain junior college teacher preparation patterns, presenting their major program components, discussing obstacles to the development of new patterns, and establishing directions that preparation programs might assume in coming years. All these factors influence the person's integration of self and profession. The organizational components of the program noted here are probably of minimal interest to the instructor. However, an examination of them will reveal the emphases placed by program planners and professional leaders on certain aspects of junior college teaching—emphases that mirror the belief systems and underlying values of the profession. Merely reflecting on these can be instructive.

BACKGROUNDS

Historically, the development of a profession has been accompanied by demands for increased training of its members. It is not certain which comes first—the group's recognition that it is a profession and thus deserves a training sequence for its initiates, or the need for increased training to perform the requisite tasks of the profession. In either event, the phenomenon known as professionalism includes a demand for particularized preparation sequences.

The preparation of junior college instructors is the function of liberal arts colleges, state colleges, and comprehensive universities. Normal schools for teacher training had arrived on and left the American scene long before the junior college movement got under way. Even teachers' colleges, the successors to normal schools, had lapsed into minor roles in the preparation of teachers before the junior college came into its own. Twentieth-century phenomenon that it is, the community college has been able to select its academic instructors almost exclusively from the ranks of the university– and liberal arts college–trained applicants. In addition, it has been able to demand that its vocational faculty accept training offered by higher education institutions.

Around the country, the academic preparation of incoming junior college teachers varies but slightly. Whether required for state certification or merely recommended for employment in local districts, the master's degree is preferred. Somewhat more than two-thirds of all junior college instructors hold this degree (Thornton 1966), while only seven percent hold doctorates (Blocker 1965–66). Both these figures have remained steady for several years. Teachers of non-academic subjects (trade, technical, and vocational) do not typically hold graduate degrees; equivalent work experience in specialty areas usually serves as requisite preparation.

During the 1960s, programs designed especially to prepare junior college teachers increased markedly. Whereas in 1954 only 23 universities or four-year colleges offered so much as one course on the junior college, by 1968 approximately 75 institutions had not only courses but whole sequences for junior college staff preparation. Under the impetus provided by the Education Professions Development Act (EPDA) of 1968, these programs received a marked boost; by 1970, more than 200 colleges and universities indicated interest in establishing programs to prepare junior college instructors. In many cases, new in-service programs were developed with funds provided by EPDA; these might be considered transient. Nevertheless, it appears clear that the special sequence to prepare people for junior college instruction is to be a lasting phenomenon.

Many of these programs, similar in format, have been the outgrowth of plans formulated by state agencies or by consortia of colleges working in association with universities. Since 1967, for example, several specialized programs have been constructed to serve particular geographical areas. Among these are the Midwest Technical Education Program, funded by the Ford Foundation, for which both graduate credit and financial aid may be obtained (Midwest 1967). The program includes intern teaching, observation of master teaching methods, orientation to student personnel services, field experiences, course work, case studies, and seminars. Eastern Washington State College has developed a method of inter-institutional exchange with on-campus internships and summer workshops that provide training and guidelines for its participants. The stress is on the development of "competence in the use of varied instructional techniques and media for dealing with diverse student abilities and for effective communication" (Gordon and Whitfield 1967). Other programs have been implemented elsewhere with special training efforts in Florida and North Carolina and recommendations for the preparation of teachers for junior colleges in Oregon (Loomis 1964) and Kansas (Good et al. 1968).

Reports of several special subject area preparatory sequences—tentative or actual—are included in *Research in Education,* the monthly abstract journal published by the Educational Resources Information Center (ERIC). Among these are programs for teachers of business education

(Birkholz 1969), chemistry (Mooney and Brasted 1969), and psychology–guidance (Williams 1966). At the University of California (Berkeley), a leadership program has been designed to attract members of minority groups into college teaching.

With slight variation, all these programs have similar course and practice components—a remarkable unanimity of format. Using a list provided by the American Association of Junior Colleges, Prihoda surveyed a large number of colleges and universities offering junior college teacher preparation courses or course sequences. All responding institutions presented courses or units on the history of the junior college, learning theory, curriculum development, student guidance and counseling, and administrative organization. All but two offered some form of practice teaching or internship in the junior college. Some training programs also included work in programmed instruction, the use of other reproducible media, the specification of instructional goals and objectives, the sociological characteristics of junior college communities, and/or interdisciplinary curriculum construction. Most of these sequences either led to the master of arts in college teaching or built on subject area master of arts requirements. In all cases, academic subject course work formed the core of the programs; the professional education components were adjuncts.

The same kind of thinking, then, that built training sequences for elementary and secondary school teachers is reflected in most junior college teacher preparation programs. Nearly all have courses leading to some type of graduate degree and nearly all have a practice teaching or teaching internship requisite. Calls for uniquely tailored programs have been plentiful, but these have been answered by minimal revisions in content and sequence and few, if any, drastic breaks with traditional forms. Arrowsmith overstates the case only slightly when he says, "As far as I know, not a single major graduate university has undertaken to provide [bold and experimental] programs and training to staff the community colleges, and, simply because such programs are not 'professionally' respectable, it is very unlikely that any of them will do so" (1970, p. 55).

CONCERNS AND OBSTACLES

In recent years, the standard degree requirements for two-year college teachers—or, for that matter, for teachers at all levels of education—have come under attack by representatives of many groups. Most writers concerned with the community college agree that these institutions need and deserve "teachers who can combine a strong academic background with a sensitivity to special student needs" (Howe 1969); they argue that programs leading to graduate degrees do not nurture personal qualities and competences in teachers. As Taylor states,

There is a huge circular effect at work in the system, by which the boy or girl who is going to be a teacher, and thus be in a position to break the cycle of intellectual and political apathy, is taught to accept the competitive academic and social system through twelve years of schooling, then given another four years of the same kind of thing in college, a little practice in teaching at the same kind of school the student attended for twelve years, and is fed back into the machine at the age of twenty-two to keep it going as before. (1969, p. 9)

Taylor's words are echoed by Silberman in the monumental work, *Crisis in the Classroom* (1970, p. 459). Both argue for faculty members who are able to convey themselves to students as part of the humanizing process. They fear that the typical graduate degree program does nothing to enhance this quality.

Sensitivity to student needs, of course, implies sensitivity to the needs of *all* students. It follows, then, that teachers must be prepared to reach all students—those whose previous academic performances ranged from A's to F's, the academically and the vocationally oriented, part-time and full-time, rich and poor, students from all cultures. To foster such awareness, it is important that teacher training programs solicit participants who represent all groups in our society, the assumption being that the community college's diversity of students requires a comparable variety of teachers.

Some people have reacted against existing preparation sequences, maintaining that the degree requirements for teaching are but part of the subterfuge that keeps members of certain ethnic groups from moving into the professions. They argue that the lower schools in ghetto areas do not adequately prepare their students for college; further, since these students are denied higher education, they are barred from eventually becoming members of the teaching profession. It follows, they say, that degree requirements should be abolished and that people should be employed on their merits—merits which, in the case of minority group members, include the abilities to understand and communicate with young people who come from ghetto areas.

Other criticisms of preparation programs have been raised. One group of concerned educators insists that "the senior colleges have done an inadequate job in instructing lower division students, so many people think the job should be turned over to junior colleges. Yet they still want to let the senior colleges who do a bad job . . . train the junior college teachers" (Riess 1968, p. 13). The executive director of the American Association of Junior Colleges expresses his own skepticism regarding the ability or tendency of graduate degree-granting institutions to build satisfactory junior college teacher preparation sequences. He fears that "programs of this kind may turn out to be only thin overlays on substantially unchanged graduate offerings" (Gleazer 1967).

Other junior college leaders seem to want the schools themselves (together with their professional associations) to directly control preparation in order that novitiates be properly imbued with a junior college point of view. They sometimes claim that university-directed programs stress matters irrelevant to the practices of junior college instruction and to the uniqueness of junior college students. However, certain maverick teacher groups interpret this contention on the part of college administrators to be a thinly disguised plea to "send us acquiescent faculty members who will not cause trouble."

Faculty associations have a different set of concerns. Although the master's degree remains the basic acceptable degree for junior college instructors, associations recognize that status and emolument of a higher degree go with the title "Doctor." The then president of the California Junior College Faculty Association exclaimed, "We want status and money" (Riess 1968, p. 13), and suggested that the way of obtaining both was through gaining doctor's degrees. But some faculty association spokesmen realize that Ph.D. training does not lead people toward expertise in teaching—or that the graduate school hurdles are too high—and frequently propose different types of doctor's degrees. They endorse, in particular, the "Doctor of Arts in College Teaching," a degree that would include a "residency of full time teaching in a two-year college" in lieu of a dissertation (Stratton 1969).

It is apparent that everyone looks at programs from his own viewpoint, posing his own solutions. Administrators, students, and university professors are among those who have commented on the inadequacies of existent teacher preparation sequences and have suggested alternatives.

The junior college administrator wants a program that will be selective in the extreme, producing instructors who are at once docile and dynamic. The docility is to manifest itself when the administrator suggests changed practices or curricula; at that point, the instructor is expected to acquiesce. The dynamism is to manifest itself in the classroom and in community activities of a socially acceptable nature. The implication is that the training program that does not screen its candidates to provide these types of people is not quite doing its job. But how many program directors could—or would—deliberately choose Jekylls and Hydes?

The student undergoing a teacher preparation program has other concerns. He wants to know how it really is—the working conditions, the chances for self-satisfaction, and especially whether he will survive as an individual when he is faced with the demands of a new role. All matters included in a training program apart from those contributing to his immediate concerns are considered somehow irrelevant or peripheral. Most students submit to the formal requirements, however, because of their long prior apprenticeships as student-acceptors. Few elements in other courses have been relevant to their lives, they reason. Why should this program be different?

The university professors who operate the teacher preparation programs have their own concerns. Their criticisms are frequently directed not to their own programs but to the types of people who are attracted to them. Trent and Medsker, for example, found that students entering teacher preparation programs were considerably less intellectually oriented than liberal arts students, and that they were least interested in education "for the sake of knowledge, ideas, and creative development" (1968, p. 104). However, this implies a problem related to recruitment and to students' perceptions of the profession, not one that can be solved by changed preparation sequences alone.

Despite these concerns about preparation programs, the same people who criticize them are often those who block their development. They may not be aware of how they hamper the introduction of alternatives, but they do maintain subtle barricades. One obstacle to program development has been that most junior college leaders are much less concerned with the preparation of prospective teachers than they are with other matters. The colleges have been expanding so rapidly that their administrators are preoccupied with buildings, finances, and people who in some fashion would handle the floods of students descending on them. Employing teachers who have gained experience in classrooms at other levels of education is frequently seen as the quickest, surest way to build a faculty.

A survey of California junior college presidents revealed their attitudes toward teacher preparation (Rio Hondo Junior College 1966). Of 52 presidents responding to questions regarding standards for new faculty, only seven indicated that they had thought through criteria for employment "over and above minimum state requirements"—requirements which, at that time, included a master's degree in the teaching subject or "equivalent experience" for teachers of vocational subjects. Those administrators who had established their own criteria indicated "successful teaching experience at the college or high school level" as being of prime importance.

The tendency to prefer instructors with prior teaching experience rather than those trained in programs particularly addressed to teaching in the junior college is further reflected in institutional staffing patterns. Nationwide, more than 64 percent of 3,283 junior college teachers surveyed in 1960 recorded previous secondary or elementary school experience (Medsker 1960, p. 172). In California—with the nation's largest and most comprehensive system of higher education—300 of the 681 new teachers of academic subjects who entered junior colleges in 1963 had moved in from high school positions; only 98 had come directly from graduate schools (California State Department of Education 1963–64). In 1968 a similar study reported that the pattern had not changed in the direction of more specialized junior college teacher training. On the contrary, as the teacher shortage had been alleviated during the 1960s, junior college administrators were even more likely to seek instructors with prior experience at other levels of education (Phair 1969). And, in states where community college systems were less well developed, administrators similarly tended to staff their institutions with people who had been prepared to teach in other kinds of institutions. As Lombardi (personal communication, 1970) notes, "The conventional wisdom predicates experience above inexperience." This bodes a lack of support for training programs as points of initial entry into the profession.

The paucity of new ideas in pre-service teacher preparation may be a result of the lack of clear-cut responsibility. Who is supposed to do the training? The universities? The colleges themselves? Other agencies? That there is no distinct allocation of tasks further hampers the development of programs for training junior college teachers. Graduate schools have not been particularly concerned with the preparation of any type of college teacher—junior or senior. Typically, this function has been seen as a total university commitment—a shibboleth which, in practice, suggests that it is no one's charge.

Most graduate school professors pay little attention to the preparation of teachers. Busily filling their students' time with specialized courses, they frequently assume that if a person can earn a master's degree or a doctorate, he can teach. Accordingly, there is now in American education a marked gap between the preparation sequences experienced by elementary and secondary school teachers, on the one hand, and by college teachers, on the other. Certification requirements for the former group demand immersion in several courses dealing with pedagogical theory and practice. For the latter, there is no credential required other than the possession of a graduate degree in an academic discipline. Yet differences in teaching at the various levels of education cannot be so great that the one calls for a year or more of deliberate training to teach while the other requires none. The difficulties experienced by students moving from high school to college may result in part from the fact that teachers at the two levels of education are selected differently, think of themselves as members of different professions, are trained differently, and (perhaps consequently) communicate little with each other. One preparation sequence or the other is out of phase.

ORGANIZATIONAL ALTERNATIVES

The concerns of the various people who express dissatisfaction with teacher preparation sequences are far ranging. The programs, they say, are ill-conceived, fail to address the junior college as a unique institution, do not enhance the teachers' feeling for—or humanitarian treatment of—students, bar members of certain groups from entering the profession, and so on. All these contentions have some validity, and they have lead to several alternative proposals.

The move toward a doctor of arts degree has many proponents. In 1970, more than 75 graduate institutions offered, were developing, or were considering programs leading to this degree. Supporters of the new degree offer a variety of reasons. The *Carnegie Quarterly* foresees "an oversupply of Ph.D.'s" in the 1970s but points out that "if large numbers of potential Ph.D. candidates could be redirected into [doctor of arts] programs, a new market would open up in the community colleges..." (1970). Hechinger feels that "an unprecedented number of Ph.D.'s" will be available to teach in community colleges, but that the "traditional preparation of Ph.D.'s, with its stress on research, makes them questionable assets...." He fears "a massive infusion of the wrong kind of teaching staff..." (1970). Dunham (1969) insists that the state colleges should move quickly into the establishment of doctor of arts programs to prepare people for service at all levels of higher education except graduate divisions of universities. "The research-oriented Ph.D. is highly inappropriate for the community college teacher," says the Carnegie Commission, adding that "Considerable emphasis should be placed on the... Doctor of Arts degree as the degree to be attained by those who will assume leadership roles..." (1970, p. 43). Backing up its contention with cash, in the summer of 1970 the Commission awarded $935,000 to ten universities to establish doctor of arts degree programs.

Thus the doctor of arts degree, a special teaching degree emphasizing inter-disciplinary courses—and playing down any specialized training leading to research in the field—is seen as a worthy solution to questions of teacher preparation. Most junior college administrators would accept it, but would it make a difference to individual instructors? To the profession?

Other alternatives have been proposed. A separate institute organized and staffed by junior college personnel has been suggested (Singer 1968). In this institute, the "West Point" of the community college movement, instructors would be prepared to understand the unique role of the junior college. The institute would "provide a spiritual home for career junior college teachers." In addition to the doctor of arts, the degrees offered might include the "candidate" or "master" in philosophy, master of arts in teaching, and a variety of titles that suggest preparation sequences other than those found in the typical master's degree program.

In reporting the results of a nationwide study of junior college teacher preparation, E. Cohen (1970) suggests a related pattern—the establishment of "Masters College units" within existing institutions. These would be semi-autonomous programs operated under the direction of—and staffed by—personnel experienced in junior college instruction. Their graduates would be prepared to teach general studies, academic disciplines, or occupational subjects, singly or in combination with each other. The masters college would have distinctive features of its own, serving the community colleges in its locale with ideas and consultants, as well as with especially prepared instructors.

These patterns seem to offer little that would change the present situation. Altering the degree titles or the course sequences is of minimal value as long as the basic premises remain the same. When the doctor of education (Ed.D.) degree was introduced, it held the same promise that the doctor of arts has now. It was to involve a practice-oriented preparation sequence, avoiding the stress on research. Perhaps because it was housed in schools of education, perhaps because of other reasons, it never became the preferred teaching degree. It seems quixotic to hope that the doctor of arts degree will perforce do what the doctor of education could not. In fact, the degree bodes to perpetuate the presently felt teacher–administrator split—the "us versus them" that the professional associations capitalize on.

Nor is the profession likely to be enhanced by the abandonment of all training requirements. Alternative patterns must be found, sequences that build on an awareness of the diverse characteristics (cognitive and affective) of both teachers and students, an understanding of the ways junior colleges are presently functioning, and an ideal vision of effectively functioning institutions. As Cremin argues,

> ... education is too significant and dynamic an enterprise to be left to mere technicians; and we might as well begin now the prodigious task of preparing men and women who understand not only the substance of what they are teaching but also the theories behind the particular strategies they employ to convey that substance. (1965, p. 59)

Who will undertake the task? Some combination of institutions with the delegation of certain tasks to each seems to be one potentially fruitful variation on the existing pattern. Junior colleges have already begun to work with four-year institutions in preparing people for new careers. The training of professional teacher aides has been undertaken as a joint effort. This, then, may foreshadow "a new partner in the teacher education enterprise as junior and community colleges enter heavily into the training of para-professionals for education, health, and social services" (Engbretson 1968, p. 229).

Such a joint arrangement seems conceptually sound. To train people exclusively in one institution—with its peculiar mores, ethos, emphases—for work in another is to run the continual risk of lag, of mistaken perceptions of conditions in the place of employment, and of attempting to train personnel for all institutions and thus, in fact, to train for none. Similarly, for the junior college to turn its back on the university and do its own preparation exclusively is to return to a form of laboratory experience or apprenticeship comparable to that in which the normal school of the early part of this century was engaged. This would seem to argue that teacher preparation is not academically respectable, that reliance on abstract learning patterns is less worthy than dependence on direct experience, and that the university has nothing to offer. Both positions are too extreme to be worthy of much consideration.

A natural division of the responsibility to be assumed by the junior college, on the one hand, and by the senior institution, on the other, is between those tasks that are parochial in nature and those that may be universally applied to processes of instruction. It seems inappropriate that a teacher training institution should devote its efforts to helping its candidates learn how to serve on campus committees or to understand the financial bases and internal organizational arrangements within the junior college. Those considerations vary from institution to institution and may well be handled through in-service orientation during the instructor's first year (Kelly and Connolly 1970). The senior institutions' charge can include the teacher's disciplinary expertise, gained in a master's degree program. Curriculum construction, course structuring, and measurement procedures, as well as the appropriate uses of reproducible media, can also be learned in the senior institutions' courses.

ALTERNATIVES IN CONTENT

A point frequently overlooked in any discussion of alternative arrangements is that, whatever the organizational pattern, all preparation programs are built on certain value positions regarding appropriate functioning within a certain type of educational institution. The key terms here are "appropriate functioning" and "certain type of institution."

What is "appropriate functioning"? The entire graduate school experience for prospective teachers is an exercise designed to lead them toward the proper mixture of deferent and assertive behaviors. No one expects them to discover new knowledge. Few program planners even anticipate that they will gain a repertoire of teaching skills. Instead, one demonstrates that he can follow through—begin and end a program. In addition, he shows his tendency to maintain the social skills that enable him to move in a school environment without unduly distressing his peers. Look as though you won't cause trouble for the organization and you are a success!

The "certain type of educational institution" that is held as a model by most program planners is an image of the junior college as it is now. That is, the college is an institution that accepts a wide variety of students, sorts them according to vague criteria, causes some learning but attends little to instruction as a discipline, and provides a social environment that is, in fact, a microcosm of the community in which it is located. What these planners do not recognize is that, if the intent of a program is to prepare good people to serve in present day junior colleges, selection—not training —is the key. Find the people who work well with other people, who are content to accept the college and its community as they are, and all will be well. As for the preparation sequence itself, exhortation on moral virtue and training in how to thread film projectors and fill out grade reports seem to be prime program components.

Some educators take different views. Although credential requirements do not specify courses in human relations and although few preparation sequences include them, deans of instruction and others responsible for selecting and supervising community college faculty members might well take the lead in suggesting that instructors enroll in such courses. Sensitivity training workshops, group interactions, and even individual therapy can help instructors become better sensitized to their own needs and to the needs of others. For some, on-the-job group counseling is also appropriate. Under the auspices of the employing institution, human relations laboratories could be arranged to encourage the expression of thought and feeling in group discussion. A variety of approaches should be evaluated in terms of the degree to which they enhance or decrease the potential for individual growth among members of the instructional staff. These are institutional aids to personal and professional integration that do exist, regardless of the establishment requirements.

There are other views as well. Heist and Wilson are among those who believe that the college faculty must move from "amateur to professional status" as teachers. They suggest that "standard preparation programs, such as they exist, do not result in a set of pedagogical skills, let alone in a comprehensive understanding of what good teaching entails" (1968, p. 196). Other critics of teacher preparation have reached similar conclusions.

Whether or not there exists a body of pedagogical skills that are effectual as tools for transmitting information is not the question at issue here. We believe that there are, but we also believe that these skills can be learned in a short period of on-the-job practice. Our own position regarding teacher preparation programs is that there can be only one real reason for them—that is, to force the prospective instructor to lay himself on the line, to face up to his real motives for entering the profession and to his feelings about it, to make him examine his discipline and determine what in it is worth knowing. Once he does that, he can find his own communication skills and repertoire of teaching techniques. The content of the program can put him in a position to assess his own effects. And in our view, judging self on the basis of effects not only enhances personal maturity but is the ultimate in professional integration.

14

A Focus
on Learning

No one suddenly becomes a teacher. The process is one of development. Its roots are in the home where the child's relationships with his first teachers—his parents, siblings, and other significant adults—represent his initial exposures to teaching–learning situations. From there the incipient teacher gathers impressions from other sources—primarily teachers, the school environment, peers, and authority figures—the general setting in which the maturing child develops. The personality traits that define the teacher's life are very likely firmly embedded long before he decides to enter the teaching profession.

When the potential instructor finally enters a college or university to "learn the ways of teaching," he already has an armament of impressions and a mass of apperceptions. Several teachers-to-be in the same classroom with the same professor, similar in measurable respects (age, sex, previous academic achievement, and so on) will still learn in different ways and will still communicate different impressions to others. Teachers are people—variable, unique, and dependent on past experiences as well as on contemporary exposures.

Can a single teacher preparation sequence allow for these differences? Can it enhance an instructor's identity? What direction might such a program take?

In constructing any program, several factors must be considered. Some experiences and characteristics are shared by all people; many are different. Since recognized divergence can indeed be a sign of strength, it is important to be aware of, to respect, and even to capitalize on differences as well as similarities. Just as an individual must learn to reconcile the conflicts within himself, teacher preparation programs must coordinate the experiences of many different people, consider varied personalities, and encourage individual autonomy.

Just as it must consider variations among people, a training program must also attend to the distinctive characteristics of individual junior colleges. Most colleges appear similar, but teaching conditions actually vary markedly. Organization, divisional structure, evaluation procedures, types of students enrolled, institutional commitment to reproducible media—all have a bearing on the teacher's situation. A preparation sequence must transcend these differences. By adhering to a fundamental philosophy and establishing directions according to that philosophy, the program will not be threatened by differences but will see them as strengths on which to build. It can do so only by holding to a central thrust of its own.

This chapter presents a distinct rationale for a teacher preparation program, outlines a preparatory sequence built on such a structure, and discusses some of the various effects that preparation programs have on the person. It is our thesis that a precisely designed preparation sequence can aid the individual by directing him toward a process wherein he tends to appraise the affects he has on his students. This is a move not only toward personal maturity and professional integration, but also in the long run to a distinct identity for the two-year college.

A PROGRAM FOCUS

A program of teacher education must have a focus, a reason for being. Preparing teachers is not the sole end of the enterprise. As Bode (1927) pointed out decades ago, teacher preparation programs that in effect train "mechanics" by teaching "tricks of the trade" have little lasting impact. By their very modes of organization, the programs should raise questions of ideals instead of directing their efforts toward minimal refinements of prevailing practices.

If the program's purpose is merely to supply bodies to staff the schools, almost any pattern will suffice. But if its purpose is to have a lasting impact on the people it serves and on the institutions in which they will teach, it must have a clear vision of the behavior desired from those who pass through it. Further, the program must deliberately attempt to influence the practices employed by the instructors in the institutions it serves.

Along with Silberman (1970), we see the problems of the schools—hence, of the instructors—as having "less to do with incompetence or indifference or venality than with mindlessness." Accordingly, the solutions are related to an infusion of purpose—"more important, with thought about purpose . . ." (Ibid., p. 379). It is not necessary that everyone associated with the schools have the same goals, but it is essential they *have* educational goals that can be articulated into some coherent structure. A preparation program that itself has a distinct focus is uniquely qualified to foster this sense of purpose in each of its students. As for content, it is important to recognize that a teacher preparation program cannot do everything. It cannot, for example, restructure the personalities of the people who participate in it, nor can it teach its clients all possible procedures to be followed in the various institutions in which they will be employed. It can, however, focus attention on those things each instructor must know and do in order to make his particular contribution.

The community college's commitment to teaching and learning overrides all supplementary goals and functions, broad and narrow. Whatever else the instructor is expected to do, whoever he may be, he must above all cause learning. A sound rationale for guiding a teacher preparation program must be founded on learning—both the process and the product of instruction. These are the concerns that affect all teachers, all administrators, and all students in all institutions. A focus on learning can well be the guiding theme for a junior college teacher preparation program.

Such a focus demands particularized definitions of teaching and learning. To be most useful, the definition of teaching must encompass much more than the teacher's activities. Lecturing, conducting discussions, selecting media, and so on define the teaching task, but they do not relate to teaching in its success sense. Merging both the task and the success uses of the term, *teaching* or *instruction* is best defined as "the deliberate sequencing of events so that learning occurs." Teaching must cause learning.

Learning is then, by definition, a necessary condition of teaching. But what is learning? Hilgard suggests that learning is "the process by which an activity originates or is changed through reacting to an encountered situation . . ." (1956, p. 3), while Gagné identifies it as "a change in human disposition or capability which can be retained. . . ." Both definitions characterize learning as human change, one adding the condition of retention. Gagné modifies his definition further by saying, "It exhibits itself as a change in behavior and the inference of learning is made by comparing what behavior was possible before and what after treatment" (1965, p. 5).

Learning may thus be characterized as a changed capability for, or tendency toward, acting in particular ways. Learning is retainable and not ascribable merely to normal growth, to maturation, or to temporary states caused by drugs or fatigue. We don't know how it occurs—exactly what happens in the mind to allow change is still a challenging but unanswered question—but we do know that it occurs. We don't know all the ways that it can be measured, but certainly it is assessable through observable behavior, changed activities, and the products of such actions. Although it would be nice if we could measure learning reliably by hunch, feel, or a glint in the learner's eyes, at the present time we are forced to depend primarily on his manifest operations.

As learning can be inferred by observing changed learner actions or products of actions, teaching can be inferred by determining what learning has occurred as a result of certain experiences. The "success" use of the term demands that such inferences be limited to situations in which evidence of learning is produced. Thus, although learning may occur without teaching, teaching depends on learning.

The teaching–learning paradigm is a sound basis on which to construct a program. Such a focus allows for differences among people in the program and enhances individual development by turning the incipient instructor's attention away from himself, toward the results he obtains. Attention to task and product emphasizes the development of both personal integrity and professional identity.

THE PROGRAM

An example of one sequence built on this teaching–learning paradigm is the UCLA Junior College Teacher Preparation Program. The program's effects have extended well beyond California; it has prepared people who have become junior college instructional leaders in many parts of the country. More important, it has served as a model for several other university-based junior college teacher preparation schemes. Thus, although at first glance the description might appear parochial, it actually describes a program that, because of its distinct focus, has some important implications.

Under the impetus of a Ford Foundation grant, UCLA revised its teacher training procedures between 1962 and 1967. Teacher preparation was individualized and explicitly pointed toward creating teachers who would themselves be hypothesis makers and testers, not merely classroom methodologists. Teachers were to be prepared to cause learning, to consciously and deliberately arrange their professional practices so that they could predict, gather, and submit evidence of learning achieved by their students.

At the core of the program resulting from this changed thrust is the requirement that prospective instructors teach; that is, that their students learn under their direction. All facets of the program are designed to help teachers gain the ability to specify objectives, select appropriate media, and gather evidence of learning. Instructors are taught to manage student learning in the most precise sense, and to evaluate themselves accordingly. Other aspects of the teacher's position are viewed as peripheral to this major thrust. Matters parochial to the institutions in which teachers will work—committee service, text selection procedures, report filing, faculty organizations, and so forth—are relegated to a distinctly secondary position.

The program includes only a core course and a year of internship in a junior college. The core course is the essential component; through it the program's values are articulated. Although student teaching is available for those who want it, the paid teaching internship is the preferred sequence of preparation because internships blend theory with practice and incorporate rationale with valued techniques.

The internship approach differs from the student-teaching mode of training in several ways. An intern may be considered an advanced student teacher, but he is paid by the district in which he teaches; the student teacher is not. The intern is considered a member of the school faculty; the student teacher is an apprentice. The intern has completed his academic course work. He prepares and conducts his own classes. And, most important, he is not under the often untoward domination of a supervising teacher who is, as Silberman points out, "perhaps the weakest link in the chain of practice teaching, and the one that is most difficult to correct . . ." (1970, p. 458). The intern is actually a teacher with one foot still in the university, whereas the student teacher is more like a graduate student with one foot in the schoolroom.

Candidates for internships are recruited from the ranks of graduate students who are completing master's degrees in academic specialties. In addition, junior college deans and presidents often send inexperienced applicants for positions in their institutions to the training program. The selection of candidates usually occurs during the winter preceding the intern year. It is not a rigorous process—the candidate need only possess a master's degree in a subject normally taught in the junior college and be admissible to the UCLA Graduate Division.

An intern's placement in a junior college is facilitated by a career services placement officer who attempts to determine particular junior colleges for which the intern is suited—on the basis of his own preferences and characteristics as well as of the school's size, location, salary schedule, and types of curricular offerings. The placement officer then assists the candidate in applying to these colleges and in arranging for interviews with employing administrators. A candidate may apply for either a full-time or a part-time position with commensurate pay. The final determination of placement remains with the junior college to which the intern applies.

Since an intern is paid at the same rate and works under the same conditions as any other beginning teacher, he must often compete with several candidates for employment. That the prospective intern has the support of the program is often a help in convincing the employing administrator that he is especially qualified for the available position. Many area deans, in fact, prefer to employ one or two interns each year and accordingly hold positions especially for them.

Most employment contracts are negotiated between March and June of the year in which the intern is to begin teaching. If accepted for a position, he enrolls in the core course for his pre-internship training. No intern is allowed to assume responsibilities in the junior college until he has had this course, designed especially for the internship program.

The students' major project in the course is to construct outlines for the courses they plan to teach in the junior college. These outlines are not lesson plans; they are complete listings of the way actual learning takes place and of how it will be demonstrated by junior college students whom the interns will teach. Each outline includes a complete set of goals and specific objectives. The course is described in detail in the appendix.

The Intern Year

After completing the core course and before assuming his teaching position, the intern meets with his supervisors in order to plan jointly the evaluation of his first year of teaching. Present at the conference are the community college dean of instruction, the department or division chairman, and a representative of the program. The intern presents the courses he proposes to teach and receives final approval for them. College representatives spell out their expectations in the areas of professional involvement, college duties, and community service, and explain procedures for evaluating the intern's work at the college.

At the beginning of the first semester of employment, most interns meet students for the first time. Although they may have had a term of practice teaching concurrent with the pre-service course, such experience is optional. In some cases, interns who so desire are put in contact with regular junior college faculty members who allow them to conduct a few lectures or discussion sessions. Thus some of them may have served previously as unofficial practice teachers in junior colleges, but for most, their own classes are the first they face.

Although the degree and type of supervision provided the intern by the junior college varies, it is usually limited. On occasion, an intern is put under the surveillance of an experienced faculty member who may tell him about the ways of the college and provide tips on teaching. Typically, however, interns do not officially affiliate with other instructors and in no case are they treated as practicing or "cadet" teachers. Their status is that of regular, first-time instructors obligated to conform to college policies. Their orientation to the college is rarely more formal than an occasional group meeting with other beginning teachers and the dean of instruction or a division chairman.

To help interns in their first semester of teaching, the program offers bi-weekly seminars in which the new teachers sample class presentations, discuss results achieved, and share ideas on why students have or have not learned according to their predictions. They gain ideas on procedures and methods from each other and from their professor. They modify their objectives and change their emphases according to the results they attain and the suggestions they receive.

The intern's teaching is thus supervised by indirection. By submitting scores made by his students on pre- and post-measures and by bringing in copies of materials he has used, the intern and his fellows in the seminar are able to plot together the best means of moving students toward his objectives. Predictions regarding the number of students who will achieve certain scores on particular assessment devices are made and adjusted periodically. The merits of the intern's procedures are considered by the seminar and suggestions are frequently made.

The first-semester seminar—along with the experience of teaching— is seen as a time of trial. Just as interns are encouraged to modify procedures in light of results obtained, they are also expected to alter objectives on the basis of ideas gained after confronting their students. As they realize the futility of attempting to move great numbers of students as far as they had anticipated during the first term, most interns reduce the number, scope, and complexity of their objectives. And as they cast about for key ways to secure achievement on the part of their students, they try varied methods and techniques. Each intern makes new plans with the help of the seminar, and at the close of the semester he prepares revised course outlines to fit the realities of his position.

During the second semester, the interns meet formally only two or three times. They continue to submit tests, scores, and written reports of their teaching. And they meet individually with the program director for help in revising objectives or media.

During the second semester, the intern attends faculty meetings at the community college, serves on committees, and generally finds his place as a member of the staff. He has revised his objectives and methods and is increasingly more able to predict accurately and to achieve success in learning. His continued tie with the program helps insure that his attention is centered on the primary task—that of causing learning. At the close of the year, he once more submits to his university professor outlines for the courses he teaches, revised for the last time as far as the university program is concerned. By this time, each intern has completed his obligations to the teacher preparation program at the university and has been launched in his particular teaching situation.

The intern thus begins his teaching experience in a junior college. He is not under direct supervision by a master teacher. Free to find his own best way of causing learning, he selects and uses those methods that are most comfortable for him. In his seminar sessions, he and other interns are helped to sharpen skills and encouraged to try various techniques. This pattern allows him to gain specific requisite abilities (survival skills) first and then to learn more of the broad generalities associated with his position.

In essence, the program attempts to change the emphasis in teaching from teachers' activities to students' changed behaviors. It moves from the practice of viewing a teacher as one playing an ascribed role to a focus on the results obtained. The training sequence is designed to avoid suggesting imitation of other teachers; instead, it allows each instructor to find his own best way of bringing about learning. No one method of instruction is sacred. The teacher is seen as an empiricist and is encouraged to change procedures whenever necessary to achieve specified results. He moves from looking at his own activities to assessing attainment of objectives and to introducing self-correction on the basis of feedback. He goes beyond the generally prevalent notion that he must *sort* students to the realization that he must measure their learning according to criteria other than norm group achievement. The teacher is seen not as one who draws precise portions from a pool of knowledge for his students to taste, but as one who prepares learning paths that lead to deliberate ends.

*The Person
and the Program*

The UCLA program attempts to influence junior college student learning by turning the attention of teachers-in-preparation toward defining the nature of that learning, predicting its extent, bringing about and assessing it. This philosophical focal point aids the instructor in his process of becoming, and indirectly, it helps his students and his college. Other programs have different focuses, but however they are arranged, there are some interesting questions common to all: How is the instructor affected as a person? What changes occur in the individuals during training?

One way the effects of a preparation program may be determined is through the examination of trainees' responses to open-ended questions about their training experiences. Accordingly, several UCLA junior college teaching interns were asked to react to the program described in this chapter and to their first-year teaching experiences. One intern wrote:

> Objectives afford a teacher a constant direction, purpose and perspective. He may change and alter his local or immediate . . . objectives but his broader objectives lend him substance and keep him always within a valid framework. . . . It is difficult, at best, to formulate the "perfect" program. [The student comes] seeking answers (for one is easily perplexed, never having taught before), and he gets rather questions. This approach is unsettling and somewhat disenchanting, but I think it assumes a greater validity *after* the intern starts his actual teaching. For then he realizes . . . he must ultimately turn to his own creative resources and energies with a consistent awareness of objectives underlying his direction.

Thus in a final sense, I think the most conspicuous value within the program lay in the attempts to encourage the intern to question and examine and investigate his own latent resources within an objective framework, rather than to cling to the more immediate comforts of answers, for there is no common manner which all teachers can share other than the desire to evolve in the student a state of consciousness larger than that which he entered the class with, and the manner in which this is done can be as diverse as the personalities of the teachers who do it.

Another responded,

. . . Fifteen hours a week is a heavy load for a new teacher. Long hours were spent every night in preparation for the next day's classes. Teaching took all my strength and concentration . . . planning something special for one class would not allow enough time for preparation for the others . . . I didn't have a very good idea of how much the students could learn and how fast. . . . My first year of teaching . . . was an exciting, rewarding and happy year for me. Teaching is more strenuous than I thought it could possibly be. . . .

The universities do not consider teaching as the primary function of their staff and this demoralizing attitude has communicated itself to all higher education. Lower division students suffer the most since these students need good teachers. The Universities do not realize the importance of training teachers at all except, of course, in the Education Department. . . . What do junior college teachers need? They need mental stimulation in their own field of interest. They need to discuss new ideas in education. They need to be encouraged and supported in attempting to bring about worthwhile changes.

. . . Perhaps you can't "train" a college teacher. Why is it that some colleges are outstanding in lower division education and others are poor? The immediate reply is: "The students are better." What nonsense! The teachers are better. A program to prepare lower division teachers for their new responsibilities and to make them aware of what the superior teacher is doing in his classroom is an important need in our system and a need the internship program is trying to fill.

And from one of the more expressive interns, apparently enjoying her own "soul searching":

Being myself a product of the lecture system, I assumed that teaching meant primarily lecturing. What knowledge I had gained with sweat and pleasure, I would impart with fervor to roomsful [sic] of eager students. When I had fantasies about myself as a teacher, I heard myself deliver lectures that were a composite of all the most brilliant lectures I had ever listened to.

That seems comical now, but I might have stumbled along that worn-out path for a long time if the Junior College Internship Program had not made me aware that there is a difference between teaching and learning. The shift in my attitude from "How can I best express what I have learned?" to "How can I help the student learn this?" had changed my whole concept of what school, at any level, is all about. I have discovered that if you want learning to be accomplished by students, you must use every device, every aid, every last scrap of attention and insight and imagination that you have.

Last semester I tried a mixture of specific objectives and Socratic-type dialogue; next semester I'm going to try for even more involvement on the part of each student. I already know there is no straight, royal road that leads to helping someone to learn, but I am everlastingly grateful to the internship program for jarring me off that narrow dead-end I was prepared to travel. I still blush and cringe a little when I remember those brilliant-lecture fantasies. (quoted in Cohen and Brawer 1968, pp. 45–46)

Such comments suggest that one of the values of a program focusing on learning outcomes rather than on teaching methods lies in its forcing each prospective instructor to face his own intent, a type of self-confrontation that can act as a definite input to identity. It would seem that a most important cause of ineffective teaching—of frustration in all educational efforts—is the tendency of teacher training programs not to establish definite criteria for their students. Yet knowledge of self is as important as knowledge of subject matter. Teachers cannot be prepared only to know certain subject fields or to communicate in one or another fashion. If we fail to help the individual develop in a worthy fashion, we cannot say that the goal of education is personal growth and development. What the teacher is and what he lacks will be conveyed to the students.

Except for the insistence on the prospective instructors' specifying their objectives, no "methods" are taught in the UCLA program because no one knows which teaching techniques would be best for the trainees. Few teaching methods in use have developed on the basis of empirical study. Few have distinct rationales. As Wallen and Travers point out,

... little has been done to develop teaching methods on the basis of scientific knowledge of learning. Most widely advocated teaching methods are based either on a philosophical tradition or on the personal needs of teachers. ... Little effort has been made to design teaching methods in terms of established principles of learning. (1963, pp. 465–66)

Hence, while numerous studies compare the effects of various teaching methods, most of them fail to develop a perceptual foundation on which an instructor can base his own teaching activities. At present, definitive relationships between singular instructional techniques and student learning are impossible to discern. And since each instructor must find his own best way of communicating, his own style, a teacher preparation program should deal very little with tips on teaching.

What should it focus on? Many writers have lamented the lack of teacher training programs designed to enhance self-awareness. It is unfortunate that "prospective teachers who lack self-actualizing qualities," says Will, "are not provided [with] the appropriate guidance and experiences to help them confront themselves as persons who need to grow in the direction of greater commitment and responsibility and involvement" (1967, p. 472). And Sanford (1966) points out the need to provide opportunities for students to accept responsibility for their personal growth and for the development of sensitivity to and acceptance of self and others. But to move in these directions, we must know much more about how these qualities are developed. Some people, of course, can develop on their own. Others need a great deal of help because they

> . . . find the transition from the passivity of being a student to the act of involvement of being a teacher too demanding. They feel that it is unrealistic to be asked to take the responsibility for their actions, to exhibit genuine feelings, and to become actors in rather than reactors to life. (Will 1967, p. 473)

Teacher education programs should attend to qualities of personal growth. For each individual, however, the development of these qualities is a long-term project that cannot be accomplished completely in a school of education, or in any college. The search for integration and self-actualization is a tedious, continuing project. The individual who attempts to use a teacher preparation program as the basis for this search is on his own. Integration and self-actualization should be developed, but whether they can be taught is unknown. Certainly they cannot be left to the training institution.

The prospective teacher—like all other people—should have opportunities for expression, but if he thinks that he can find his answers solely in academic relationships with others, his search is leading in the wrong direction. He must first look within himself, especially since development is a highly private concern, dependent on all one's experiences. In any case, there must be a shift from the "methods" curriculum found in many preparation programs to one that enhances self-discovery. Any program that leads the individual toward identity within the profession is valuable and successful to the extent that it aids in his development of self.

Whether teacher education programs in general are indeed designing curricula conducive to the development of personal qualities is another question. If the qualities of a "good teacher" are fixed relatively early in life, any attempt to help prospective teachers develop them during their training periods would be futile. Moreover, if this were the case, a clinician could train prospective teachers during their freshman year and save both student and staff considerable trouble in the ensuing years. If, on the other hand, these qualities are not fixed, if they can be encouraged in the prospective teacher, and if they are considered of prime importance in the development of competent teachers, experiences conducive to personal growth must be made a vital part of the teacher education curriculum. A focus on ends achieved, on the prospective instructor's own effects, enhances this growth.

A Combination of Forces

This section has reviewed some of the external forces that operate within the person's environment and play a dominant part in shaping his behavior. These forces include the preparation for his occupational role, the professional associations, and the certification requirements—all of which seem to be apart from him, but in fact tend to influence his orientation to his work and his students.

Much of this book deals with the person in terms of intrinsic factors—his personality traits, how he selects his teaching role, the functions he chooses to perform in that role. It is slanted to the individual and to the way that he operates, rather than toward the extrinsic forces in his environment. Consistently, we have said that for the person to have a real sense of identity, he must understand himself—his various behaviors, his goals and desires, his conflicts, and even the feelings, motives, and thoughts that he attempts to guard from others and often from himself. Such understanding is personal. Yet it is also dependent on his awareness of the extrinsic forces that influence him and with which he must interact.

part six

Inputs
to
Professionalism

The instructor's move toward maturity is revealed in his work and the way he and his fellows view it. All that he has become—his securities and doubts, hopes and fears, strengths and weaknesses, whether or not he is conscious of his inner dynamics—manifests itself in his professional role. A person can erect temporary screens and engage in all kinds of defense maneuvers. He relates to different people and different situations in seemingly inconsistent ways. But behind everything stands the individual.

When the person has finally resolved many questions about his own identity, when his search for self-knowledge turns into a search for integrity, actualization and individuation, he has moved toward maturity. Included in such a transition must be a consciousness of goals, an awareness of directions, and a concentration on the tasks to be performed. The mature person thus merges his own awareness of self with a recognition of his professional functions. He is able to look to his occupation for much of his satisfaction in life. He prefers to be judged on his work, not on his face, his personal characteristics, or the number of times people say he is a good lecturer or a good guy. Instead of focusing primarily on self, he focuses on his task and on the resulting effects. The mature instructor

171

merges his personal identity with his professional identity, knowing well what he is about.

In this last section, the instructor is viewed in terms of his work. We are concerned specifically with the evaluation of instruction as this ubiquitous practice relates to the individual instructor. Chapter 15 reviews common procedures of assessment by supervisors, colleagues, and students that almost invariably affect the instructor's performances. Potentially, at least, these practices act as control agents. Appraisal by others cannot be ignored—whether or not it is considered desirable. Nor can we ignore self-evaluation. Indeed, what better control exists than a strict internalized sense of direction?

The second chapter in this section is concerned with faculty evaluation procedures, particularly in terms of the institutional and professional values they reveal. Speaking metaphorically, we use the rating schemes as a net that we dip into the junior college pool to catch the real values concealed in the murky waters of professional rhetoric and institutional bombast. New criteria for assessing instruction—particularly instructional effects—are proposed in chapter 17, along with some suggestions for changing procedures and purposes.

We maintain the thesis that teaching cannot usefully be considered apart from learning. If instruction is to be evaluated, the assumption is that there exists an acceptable definition of teaching. If teaching is defined as "causing learning," we must assume that learning can be appraised in some objective fashion. Thus, the instructor who accepts the definition of teaching as "causing learning" has taken an important step toward the type of professional integration that comes with wanting to be judged by one's effects. He defines ends and measures outcomes. This is a giant step on the road from identity to maturity.

DEFINITIONS

Throughout this section, and indeed, throughout the book, we have used several terms that demand explanation. Definitions indicate more than distinctions among words. They also point to perceptions and expectations—hence, to values. How words are typically used reveals much about the way the profession views the scope of its work. Much can be understood about educational structures simply by reviewing how certain key words are used in the context of the schools.

Rating schemes and the terms employed therein—*measuring, evaluating, faculty, teaching, performance,* and *effect*—offer examples. Although some of these words are used interchangeably, they really should carry different meanings. Measuring is not the same as evaluating; the role of the instructor is primarily teaching, but he performs many functions under that rubric; and any real relationships between performance and effect are as yet thoroughly unclear.

In the language of the schools, "measuring" is often used for "evaluating"; however, precision demands that the distinctions be considered. Measuring means using a device to gain a referent for any variable. According to Webster, to measure is "to estimate or appraise by a criterion." Evaluation implies a judgment; the term *value* is within it. But even though the terms are not really the same, they are related—and here the confusion begins.

In the sense that measuring suggests selectivity, it is not possible to measure without evaluating. By selecting one variable to observe, one measuring device or set of standards against which to assess something, value is ascribed. The collection of data costs money and consumes time. Data can be collected without stating the use to which they are to be put, but a value is present none the less. Choosing to collect certain information and to ignore other data involves a value judgment. To select one criterion to measure, and thus to abandon others that might possibly have been selected, implies a choice of goals, a dominance of one value over others.

Other words that should be paired are "faculty" and "teaching." A faculty includes members of a staff holding academic rank in an educational institution. A faculty member is a person employed by a school district to fill certain functions within the teaching role. But assigning activities to him is one thing; measuring his performance is quite another matter. To the profession, teaching is a number of things: lecturing to a large audience; sitting with a small group of young people in a room and conducting a discussion; preparing and presenting films, tapes, or other materials that display lectures and demonstrations—in short, playing an active part in reifying and communicating subject matter. The concept of teaching as "causing learning" is frequently ignored.

Faculty members are presumably evaluated on the basis of their teaching. However, a fair amount of insoluble confusion and difficulty is built into that practice. If teaching is giving lectures and so on, it can be evaluated only by comparing the "goodness" of one performance with another. If teaching is "doing that which a teacher typically does," teaching is not that which is being evaluated. Rather, it is the teacher who is under surveillance because his teaching is not thereby divorced from his body. What standards shall be applied to a good teacher, and why? Agreement can never be attained as long as the process of teaching is interwoven with the person. That makes it impossible to isolate one from the other, to separate instruc*tion* from instruc*tor*.

Performance and effect also demand examination. Many faculty members seem to have a compelling need to perform. Indeed, performing goes along with the role they implicitly adopt when they begin their careers, and it may well be one of the chief reasons they entered the profession in the first place. Thus it follows that any measure of a faculty member that fails to include an assessment of his performance is doomed because of attitudes held by present staff members. Performance, not effect.

Performance is typically assessed by observation. Those who observe may be students, colleagues, or administrators—for the purposes of this discussion, it matters little. Faculty performance is measured by an observer's applying his own criteria or the vague criteria listed on an observation scale. The observer compares one instructor's performance against another or against a standard—often cloudy—in his own mind. Good ratings are given when there is congruence between the criteria and the observations.

But such determinants of teacher evaluation do not assess teaching effect. What is effectiveness? Effect on people; impact. What people? The purpose of all education is to cause changes in students. College spokesmen state that students are to be led to the ability to think critically, to gain a sense of spiritual and moral values, and so on. It follows, then, that effect must be measured as it relates to students' thinking critically, gaining values—in short, to their *learning*. But unless teaching is defined as "causing learning," performance, not effect, will continue to be measured.

Measuring faculty performance (with the stress on performance) is, in fact, the current condition of teacher evaluation and of most of the research being conducted on teacher effectiveness. But the terms are not synonymous. These distinctions are crucial to understanding the following chapters. They also reveal our own biases.

15

Measuring
Faculty
Performance

Scene: A hardware store.

Clerk: *May I help you?*
Customer: *I'd like to buy a tool.*
Clerk: *Yes, sir. What kind?*
Customer: *Something to measure with.*
Clerk: *Yes. What do you want to measure?*
Customer: *I'm not sure.*
Clerk: *Well, what kind of tool did you have in mind?*
Customer: *Oh, the kind of thing my friends use. A micrometer; perhaps a yardstick. One fellow I know uses a surveyor's level. One of those maybe.*
Clerk: *It would really help if you could tell me what you intend to measure.*
Customer: *I don't know. I can't define it.*
Clerk: *Well, why do you want to measure it?*
Customer: *Can't say, but other people have been measuring it for years.* (Cohen and Brawer 1969, p. 49)

Systematic studies of teachers and teaching for evaluation purposes may be almost the last things that interest the instructor. Perhaps he views evaluation by outsiders as an intrusion, frequently feeling that he alone knows what he is trying to do and how well he is doing it. Nevertheless, every educational institution employs some type of instructor evaluation scheme and every faculty member must eventually be involved in the process. This chapter describes faculty rating schemes and various modes of assessing instruction in the schools. In addition, it discusses some of the measures employed by researchers who study teachers and teaching.

Formal or informal practices for rating faculty members are used in every college. Some institutions evaluate only new or non-tenured instructors, while others continue annual ratings throughout the instructor's career. Questions have been raised regarding the usefulness, practicality, and in some instances the ethics of such schemes. But many educators, administrators, and student and faculty groups suggest that

175

rating instructors improves instructional practices. In fact, tenure recommendations are frequently dependent on administrators' ratings of faculty members, and pay scales are sometimes regulated by them. Their usefulness in improving instruction is somewhat more equivocal. Whatever their ostensible purposes, however, we want to make it clear that although we are discussing faculty rating schemes, we are not ascribing a worth to them. We address the rating schemes as they are and point up some of the disparities between intent and purpose in all of them.

BACKGROUNDS

That students discuss teachers, that parents question them, and that administrators judge them is not new. Just as employers in business and industry evaluate their personnel, so teachers are rated by supervisors and administrators. Indeed, teacher assessment has a long history, much of which occurred well before evaluation procedures had become even remotely related to theory. Educational literature describing investigations that evaluate teacher performance and predict effectiveness is filled with reports of procedures for rating instructors. Yet only recently have attempts been made to build actual study on firm rationale and theory.

In many institutions, the appraisal of teachers and teaching centers around an activity called "evaluation of instructors." District policies often mandate evaluation of one form or another but just as often, staff members question—and even protest—the techniques employed, the potential use of findings, even the entire process. Acceptance or rejection of the methods often appears to be related to the degree of acceptance or rejection of the purposes of instructor evaluation. And the explicit purposes for conducting such studies vary as much as do the techniques for gathering data. Despite questions and protests, formal rating or evaluation practices (in the schools, the difference is actually one of terminology) have a long history. They stem from efficiency movements of the early 1900s and they have continued in operation. In 1907 the tendency of school officials to give high marks to teachers was noted, and in 1910 a popular provisional plan for measuring teachers' "merits" was released. This plan consisted of a score card with several specified areas, each containing sub-items that were assigned values and then totaled to arrive at a teacher's score—a form that is still used in many school districts!

Yet, notwithstanding their prevalence, rating scales are not universally appreciated. As early as 1915, the National Education Association adopted a resolution opposing ratings that "unnecessarily disturbed the teacher's peace" (NEA 1945, p. 63). Recognizing, however, that the teaching profession—like other professions—should evaluate the quality of its services, it insisted that evaluation be done specifically *not* for the purpose of setting salaries. Several decades later, the profession had not yet determined how to advance professionalism without tying evaluation to extrinsic reward systems. Distinguished teaching citations, merit pay, and other such testimonies of approbation attest to the perpetuation of old systems.

Whatever their purposes and acceptance, over the years many different measurement devices have been used to evaluate instructors. So-called subjective ratings compete with objective scales for popularity. Unfortunately, the selection of a procedure may be based on little more than vogue ("The way they do it in the next district is good enough for us"). However, the fault is not with the institutions alone. Countless investigators have conducted innumerable studies of "good" teachers and teaching situations and have failed to come up with an evaluation scheme that is at once standardized, reproducible, and fully reflective of the desires of more than one group.

THE STUDY OF EVALUATION

Which type of faculty rating scheme is best? The answer to this question depends on the uses to which the ratings are to be put, the reliability of the devices or methods employed, and the degree to which the concerned parties accept the schemes. The interaction among these three important considerations makes the question difficult to resolve.

We know little about the factors in "good" evaluation of junior college instructors. One reason for the dearth of information is that in the extensive material devoted to assessment, the evaluation of college teaching has not received the critical attention it deserves and needs. In fact, although much lip service is paid to the importance of the good instructor, few criteria for appraising the quality of college teaching have been established. This may be in part because it is difficult to find out very much about what goes on in the college teacher's classroom. Traditionally, that place has been sacrosanct; what transpires there has remained exclusively the teacher's business. However, although most research on rating instructors has concentrated on the elementary and secondary levels of education, the protests of many groups—particularly students—is forcing a change. And, whether he likes it or not, the college instructor is going to be assessed.

A more general reason for the lack of criteria is that although early studies of teachers and teaching employed techniques for collecting and reporting various types of data, they typically viewed the teacher as an isolated entity, functioning independently of his environment. And while some studies were built on an a priori approach and others were conducted on experimental bases that mandated the application of requisite controls, most investigations of teachers have been concerned with normative data, personality characteristics, and teacher performance as they relate to success in practice. The researchers keep looking for the "good" instructor; the schools continue to "evaluate."

RATINGS BY SUPERVISORS AND COLLEAGUES

The methods employed to rate teachers are instructive in themselves. Perhaps the oldest and most popular approach is through supervisor ratings. For some purposes, it is the best approach, as well. Indeed, despite the many studies based on ratings made by students, colleagues, or independent researchers, evaluations by campus supervisors consistently prove to be the most valid yardstick for predicting the success of neophyte teachers, as measured by administration ratings (Ort 1964). In other words, one supervisor's rating best predicts another supervisor's rating of the same person. Surprised?

Another method to rate instructors is based on faculty members' appraisal of their associates. On the surface this procedure seems to contain much merit, but where the process is informal, its value is undocumented. An instructor may invite colleagues to sit in on his classes and to provide criticism, and the feedback that is offered is conceivably valuable. Like the round robin exchanges that typify certain adolescent searches for self-understanding, however, such information is also likely to be fraught with subjective, non-directive assessments. Although sharing ideas may have limited value, in some cases they may prove harmful to the teacher and his teaching situation. The profession will not develop out of tips and unvalidated techniques.

Even when peer evaluation procedures are highly systematized, as detailed in faculty association recommendations, their value is open to question. These formalized collegial evaluations, in use in many districts, usually include teams of faculty members who visit classes and report on the instructor's performance. Frequently the committee meets with the instructor who is being evaluated, discusses his strengths and deficiencies, and in some cases recommends tenure or dismissal. However, although these procedures can be useful selective devices, they do not directly enhance the process of instruction. In any case, formal or informal evaluation by colleagues has one advantage—it is the scheme least likely to meet with resistance from the faculty.

Evaluation by Grants and Degrees

The examination of publications and government awards attributable to faculty members offers a unique approach to teacher evaluation. The report of an investigation at Tufts University suggests that publications and awards do relate to ability in teaching undergraduate students (Bresler 1968). Although many statements in both the popular literature and professional journals suggest that publication efforts and government support for research activities detract from classroom teaching effectiveness, the Tufts data do not support these conclusions. Instead, students rated as their best instructors those faculty members who had published articles and received government grants and/or other support. Whether this is true of the faculty in other higher education institutions is a topic certainly worthy of further investigation. For example, faculty members in community colleges are becoming more and more involved in various community service projects. Is there a relationship between leadership in such endeavors and "good" teaching?

Many evaluation attempts have been concerned with instructors' attained degrees and the sizes and types of their degree-granting institutions. In the section on the junior college in the *Encyclopedia of Educational Research* (Harris and Liba 1960), much attention is given to the question of academic degrees, and in one issue of the *Junior College Journal* (Blocker 1965–66), faculty competence has been dismissed almost solely in terms of earned degrees. However, the question of how much a degree contributes to one's teaching ability is still very much open. The degree itself is only one part of the issue of faculty competence—probably not even an important part. It yields little information useful for understanding individuals or for appraising faculty. Nevertheless, the colleges frequently equate competence with degrees and point proudly to the number of people on their staff holding the doctorate.

Self-Evaluation

For any mature person, perhaps the most difficult—but eventually the most rewarding—kind of evaluation is evaluation of self. This requires a degree of maturity and a concomitant need for objectivity—difficult for all to attain and for some, impossible.

The American Association of Colleges for Teacher Education attempted to further efforts at self-evaluation by publishing a list of "teacher self-evaluation tools" (Simpson and Seidman 1966). These items were listed in order by 5,303 college and university instructors who had found such procedures as planned meetings with colleagues and the taping of regular class sessions to be particularly helpful. The list includes many illustrative check forms, rating scales, and open-ended questions from which a teacher may select and create his own forms. More important than the items in the list, however, was a statement of the uses to which they could be put. Although ratings were to be made by colleagues, by students, by administrators, or by self, the instructor alone could decide what he would do with the findings. Unfortunately, no attempts were made to follow up the effect of this list by determining whether anyone had changed his teaching practices as a result of what he learned about himself.

Brown and Thornton (1963) take the position that college teachers can evaluate themselves through various procedures: by introspection; by asking colleagues and student committee members to sit in on classes and comment; by tape-recording their own classes and noting the extent of student participation, the quality of student comments, and the types and quality of the teacher's own comments; and finally, by collecting student ratings. They further suggest that the instructor should not average the ratings submitted by students, but rather should note patterns of responses clustering about particular strengths and weaknesses. Their advice is eminently sound, but some vision of desired ends is still necessary.

Our position is that the instructor can truly assess his work only if he knows exactly what he is trying to do—or better still, what his students should be able to do subsequent to his efforts. Self-examination becomes a circular route to nowhere if it includes only such questions as "How am I handling the students? Was the lecture well-paced? Am I in a rut?" The instructor needs to establish specific goals that subsequently act as criteria against which he can assess his processes.

STUDENT EVALUATIONS

For a number of years, evaluation of instructors by their students has been a popular practice. In fact, in spite of the somewhat cynical opinions of some teachers that very little value can be placed on student judgments, greater attention than ever before is now given to student ratings. Questionnaires, checklists, and rating forms are used extensively by students at different levels of education and in hundreds of school settings. However, ratings by students are subject to many of the same criticisms that relate to other measures of judgment based on nebulous criteria.

In practice, the dimensions on which students rate instructors vary widely. Students at St. John's River Junior College evaluated their instructors in 500 class sections on the basis of four measures: positive personal traits (appearance, attitude); scholarship; skill of presentation; and accuracy in evaluating students (understanding, fairness) (Overturf and Price

1966). And ratings of college instructors by former students were collected by Knapp and Goodrich (1952), who factor-analyzed qualities that
correlated with high effectiveness in motivating students. Three general
characteristics were isolated: masterfulness (shown by severe grading
standards, leadership in departmental entrepreneurship); humor; and intellectual distinction.

In a study by Cooper and Lewis (1951), the *Rorschach* was used to
assess teachers previously given checklist ratings by their students. Those
teachers who were considered to have good student relationships tended
to possess such personality traits as a sense of humor, courtesy, tact, fairness, flexibility, self-control, ability to create interest, sympathy, friendliness—and so on. These general qualities of "goodness" only emphasize
again that good teachers are good people—and this type of research offers
little more to what we already know.

The use of student ratings has been well studied. Some researchers
report that there are stable and reliable means of assessment, while others
point out that many factors other than the instructor himself significantly
influence the students' opinions of him. But many gaps in knowledge must
be filled before teaching effectiveness can be assessed on any scale worthy
of mention. These voids relate to students' ratings as well as to other forms
of assessment.

When student ratings are used as a way of bringing order into communication processes among students, faculty, and administration, a serious gap in knowledge becomes apparent. We do not yet know how
accurately students can rate teaching effectiveness. The role concept of the
student—that is, the image he holds of what a teacher ideally should be—
undoubtedly clouds the picture drawn by the ratings. Another problem
is that even if we can validly and reliably measure some aspects of teacher
behavior, we do not know the relationship of that behavior to student
learning. This is, of course, the crux of the matter. However the students
rate the teacher, the relationship of teacher behavior to student learning
is still not known. We have not yet begun to understand the factors
accounting for the instructor's impact.

There are problems in the use of student ratings themselves. Such
ratings seem to be affected by course size and other variables. Some anal-
yses of student ratings have found that teachers in courses with 30 to 39
students consistently receive lower ratings than do those in courses having
either more or less students. Also, teachers of on-campus courses have
received poorer ratings than those of off-campus courses, and teachers of
electives have been rated more favorably than have teachers of required
courses.

The argument against using a single standard may be raised here.
Why are instructors in very small and very large classes rated higher?

Are such sections easier to teach? Or are the students more lenient in their ratings? Are teachers more effective in elective courses, or are the students easier to please because they are better motivated? If student ratings are the only ones available, such questions are unanswerable.

One way around this difficulty would be to present separate norm tables, interpret student ratings in all course categories, and then compare each instructor's rating against the norm. Student ratings could then be used for teachers' self-improvement in the sense that each instructor would establish his own norms over the years. Student biases and other problems might still be operative. However, if the instructor interpreted the ratings for himself, he would gain valuable information.

With student ratings, as with other forms of evaluation, the questions of who is to be served—and how—reappear. Knapp has concluded that of the three functions of college teachers that he had designated (research, information, and character-development),

> . . . professors tend to esteem and respect themselves primarily on the basis of their research function. Students and administrators, however, especially in smaller institutions, tend to value most the informational and character-developing functions. [And] . . . the public at large is probably inclined to attach great significance to what we have called the character-building function. Thus, different segments of the population, to whom the college professor must in some degree answer, apparently expect different kinds of performances. (1962, p. 306)

To which drummer does the junior college instructor march?

SCALES AND BIASES

Beyond the questions of sampling size, appropriateness of techniques, rationale, and relevance, there are other difficulties in measurement. These include the problems inherent in rating scales and the common practice of relying on untrained, biased observers.

Rating scales themselves have been the subject of study. Several decades ago, Barr and Emans (1930) analyzed 209 scales used in the 1920s and categorized them by the teacher qualities they purported to assess: classroom management, instructional skills, personal fitness, and so on. Not only are the major divisions that were isolated by these investigators the same as those on which rating forms are still built, but the very wording of many old forms is exactly that used today! (See Boyce [1915], Monroe [1924], along with Barr and Emans, and compare the scales with those in present use in any college.) Forty years of research on teaching has had little effect even on the rating scales used in public school and junior college districts. In fact, the number of scale values normally used in checklists is still five—curiously approximating the A to F grading scale!

Although classroom ratings may have much to offer, all variables must be considered before one can really understand what is being said and by whom. In this context, the question of rater bias is of particular concern. There is, of course, the possibility of personal bias in any situation where individuals are being assessed, but when untrained people assess others, the likelihood of warped perception is compounded. People see different people in various lights. One may project his values and problems to the person being assessed without being aware that they are his own projections.

Few studies point to the potential effects of the observer and the validity of his interpretation. Yet in any situation where subjective judgments are called for, the characteristics of the person doing the evaluating must be considered. Descriptions vary and ratings are established on different scales, but all are equally dependent on the particular needs, expectations, and projections of the rater; his own personality and values; and his background. Therefore, any individual who examines evaluations of performance (often based on unspecified criteria) must also look at the rater to decide from what viewpoint he has assessed his subjects. The dean who rates an instructor high in classroom management skills may be revealing less about the instructor than he is about himself. Another instructor, rated low on the same dimension, may manage his classroom in exactly the same way, but the rater is unaware that he is influenced by the instructor's flamboyant necktie. Consequently, a poor rating is given.

Response tendencies—seeing all individuals in a particular light—and the attitude known as the "halo effect" must also be considered. It is easy to rate individuals in the same way they have been assessed in the past, thus perpetuating failures or successes. The instructor who for years has received consistently high ratings simply cannot be seen by his supervisor as being anything but good. Past assessments carry over to influence present judgments. For anyone who has gone beyond elementary school, it cannot be anything new that different teachers—using the powerful tools that are grades—rate students on the basis of varying measures. Johnny may receive an "A" for a paper that is ostensibly like the one for which Mary was given a "C". Miss Jones and Mr. Brown may consistently give discrepant marks to the same students who submit similar work. This same kind of variance also appears in the grading of teachers by supervisors and training specialists. Here, too, the concepts of projection, individual differences, personal biases—even whether the rater slept well the night before—enter the picture.

In general, the field is plagued by untrained raters. Students and supervisors alike allow irrelevancies to influence their assessments of good teaching. The instructor's mannerisms are invariably given undue emphasis, to the detriment of more pertinent dimensions. Rater training—one way around the problem—at least leads to reliable measurement. However, only a rare dean or department chairman would bother to concern himself with this type of functional training.

GENERAL STATUS

Most of the data in the preceding sections have been drawn from the literature pertaining to elementary and secondary school teaching and extended to the community college. However, even the university, the foremost bastion of the non-teacher in the realm of education, has become concerned over questions of teaching and teacher effect. Unhappily for the profession, it is student disaffection that has triggered the wave of examination of teaching in the university. But whatever the instigator, if better teaching is the result, it has served a particularly positive function.

At any level of education, the situation regarding teacher examination reflects the instability of teacher evaluation in the profession at large. Educational researchers have not been able to isolate dimensions of teachers or of the teaching situation that correlate significantly with measures of effect on students or institutions. Hence it is not surprising that administrators in most schools despair of finding effectual means of evaluating teachers and thus merely accept or maintain practices that are least likely to stimulate controversy.

Surveys conducted by the American Council on Education in 1960 and 1966 studied existent practices in the evaluation of faculty members in higher education. The first survey obtained responses from 584 institutions, including 25 junior colleges; the second from 1,110, including 128 junior colleges. These inquiries found much similarity in procedures for evaluating instructors in liberal arts colleges, private universities, state universities, state colleges, teachers' colleges, technical–professional colleges, and junior colleges. All these types of institutions were similar along at least one dimension. They all shared equal confusion regarding the purposes of evaluation and a consistent lack of concern about the use of apparently invalid methods for gathering data on faculty members. As Gustad noted,

> It was not assumed, when this study was planned, that the situation with respect to faculty evaluation would be found to be good. It was no great surprise, therefore, to find it as it was. What was somewhat surprising was the extent and depth of the chaos. . . . It is apparent that little is done to obtain anything that even approaches sound data on the basis of which reasonably good evaluations of classroom teaching can be made. . . . In

general, to call what is typically collected or adduced to support evaluative decisions "evidence" is to stretch the meaning of this honored word
beyond reason. (1961, pp. 208–10)

Astin and Lee's 1966 follow-up of Gustad's survey found little that
was different. In evaluating teachers, all or most departments and institutions used chairman evaluation and dean evaluation—in other words, forms
of supervisor rating. Some also collected colleagues' opinions and informal
student opinions. The universities and four-year colleges relied heavily on
evidence of scholarly research and publication as a measure of teaching.
Few institutions of any type reported the use of systematic student ratings, enrollment in elective courses, long-term follow-up of students, or
alumni opinions as measures of teacher effect.

In both surveys, the junior colleges as a sub-sample of the group
deviated little from the total findings. However, classroom visits were used
by approximately half the junior colleges, whereas in the total group,
which included all units of higher education, visits were used to a much
lesser degree. Other discrepancies between junior colleges and four-year
institutions were noted: junior colleges relied somewhat more heavily on
grade mark distributions and follow-up of students and they rarely collected information about the instructors' scholarly publications. Astin and
Lee concluded,

> If the ultimate measure of the teacher's effectiveness is his impact on the
> student—a view which few educators would dispute—it is unfortunate that
> those sources of information most likely to yield information about this
> influence are least likely to be used. (1966, p. 4)

Evaluation of instructors, then, is often an inconsistent exercise,
archaic and in large measure unrelated to apparent purpose. An extensive
survey of evaluation practices in California junior colleges revealed
nothing to refute that contention (Fitch 1965). Classroom visits; committee
consultations in association with deans, colleagues, and division chairmen;
and ratings provided by students were the chief methods of appraisal. In
common with elementary and secondary schools as well as with universities, most junior colleges apparently use the same media to assess the same
variables in the same old inconsistent ways.

What Is Being Rated?

The use of superficial assessment techniques, the absence of rater training,
and the frequent refusal of many instructors to accept ratings as a necessary
concomitant of professionalism all contribute to the present low state of

the art of teacher evaluation. Measures that are more objective than classroom observation systems (for example, degrees attained, years of experience) also fall short of desirability. Rating forms filled out by supervisors, colleagues, pupils, or administrators seem to provide a more objective approach to assessment; however these, too, are subject to many of the problems already designated and are compounded by ambiguity in definition of concepts and criteria. Indicative of the magnitude of the problem is Barr's statement that the safest approach to the appraisal of teaching is a multiple one "employing more than one theoretical orientation, a variety of data gathering devices, and . . . a number of persons studying teachers and teaching under a variety of conditions" (1959, p. 28).

After well over a half century of efforts, we are still at the most rudimentary empirical stage of assessing instructors. Because many studies have indicated low correlations among such variables as supervisory ratings and student learning, the field might better concentrate on the *products* of learning and teaching rather than on isolated or irrelevant dimensions.

Tests, rating forms, observational techniques, and similar measures for evaluating teaching performance have been cited in this chapter along with the attendant difficulties in obtaining valid, reliable, and consistent measures of instructors. Many of the problems can be traced to the failure of researchers and administrators to build their evaluation programs on coherent conceptual frameworks. A group of variables (for instance, "classroom techniques") is isolated; measurements (for example, "students fill out checklists") are taken; the results are tallied; and the instructor is rated.

Is change feasible? One pervasive barrier to change is that postulates assumed to underlie behavior are mentioned as though they were the behavior itself. Theoretical constructs are confused with observational descriptions. Teacher competence, for example, is a quality dependent on interpretation. It cannot be observed directly, but can only be inferred from descriptions of teacher actions. Yet the term is often used as though the construct were being observed. Similarly, most studies and practices of faculty evaluation ignore the fact that all "good" people are not necessarily good teachers—a problem that could be erased in part if an operational definition of "good" were universally accepted.

But the most persistent difficulty in assessment is that in almost all measurement of teaching, the teacher's *performance*—not his effect—is assessed. This distinction must be borne in mind when any study of faculty is being discussed or reviewed. The connections, if any, between performance and effect are as yet thoroughly unclear. Nevertheless, performance is measured, examined, and evaluated as assiduously as though it were the end goal of every formal educational structure!

A more meaningful definition of teaching and a tendency to speak of constructs in operational terms are necessary first steps to building new schemes of faculty evaluation. Until the effects desired of a teacher are decided on and clearly spelled out, no comprehensive definition of teacher worth is possible. The evaluation of faculty members can have a definite impact on schools only if there is agreement on even more basic premises—namely, the purposes for which the evaluation is being made, the clear definition of terms and of variables for which the concepts stand, the criteria against which evaluation is applied. The following chapter discusses some of these underlying premises in an effort to build a bridge toward change.

16

From
Performance
to Effect

Should the instructor concern himself with rating schemes and with the sundry ways in which he is evaluated? And if so, why? How do his own needs for feedback compare with institutional needs for information about him? More basically, why assess instructors at all?

Answers to questions of why faculty members should be rated run the gamut from superficiality to laborious specificity. Responses may reveal a sincere belief that evaluation aids in making personnel decisions. Or perhaps everyone in the institution assumes that evaluation is somehow related to the improvement of instruction. Almost anyone can articulate at least one reason for justifying the college's evaluation system. More specific reasons than those noted here might be cited, but they would probably relate to one or the other of these two general purposes.

The existing practices of evaluation were discussed in chapter 15. This chapter deals with the ostensible and actual purposes behind the rating of faculty members, the types of values the rating practices represent, and finally, the need for effecting change. New directions for faculty evaluation are described in chapter 17.

REASON AND PURPOSE:
OSTENSIBLE VERSUS ACTUAL

Although rating schemes are commonly employed to assess instructors, the purposes behind their use are often nebulous. Indeed, because it is difficult to differentiate between the reality and the rhetoric, ostensible reasons may mask the actual ones. While the expressed purposes of appraisal are to improve instruction and to provide a basis for making personnel decisions, the methods typically used relate seldom to instructional practices and even less often to instructional effects. And, as Fishman asks, "If improved evaluation cannot lead to improved effectiveness, then what do you need it for? It's kind of an expensive game" (1967–68, p. 31). Or, put another way, ". . . if teaching is so mysterious that criteria for teacher effectiveness can't be set up . . . then either education is in worse trouble than one suspects or the old canard—'Anybody can teach'—really holds true" (Brenton 1970, p. 244).

Then why evaluate? One reason is suggested by the tendency of some administrators to display their power by standing in judgment of instructors. Power is a heady thing. The administrator may actually enjoy passing on—or withholding—tenure recommendations. But lest we berate administrators unduly, we might point out that their tendencies to demonstrate authority only parallel similar practices on the part of the instructors who insist on standing in judgment of their students. A personnel dossier that includes negative comments about instructors is little different from a transcript full of failing grades.

Another reason for evaluation is institutional self-enhancement. The desire to proclaim loudly, "We are good" is revealed in numerous articles on junior college teaching, especially those that proudly declare faculty competence. "Our instructors are as good as those anywhere!" say the spokesmen for the colleges. So it may be, but this kind of defense maneuver leads nowhere but to superficial and temporary satisfaction with self.

Simple inertia may be fundamental to faculty appraisal. Most public school districts evaluate their teachers; many four-year institutions engage in similar practices. Why shouldn't the community college join the parade—especially when it is frequently easier to continue a practice than to justify a change? Evaluation is only one of many archaisms. And so stagnation is perpetuated.

Is evaluation to be used to determine which instructors should be given continuing contracts? In some states, once an instructor is employed he cannot be dismissed unless sufficient cause is proved. Although interpretations of specific cause for dismissal are not clear, they include such matters as incompetence and moral turpitude. Gathering evidence on which to dismiss instructors is an unfortunate reason for introducing and maintaining a faculty evaluation scheme. It puts the evaluators in the position of doing the investigative work—a task performed much more efficiently by an outside agency! Still, it exists.

Should evaluation be used to build a case for the worth of junior college instructors? Who must be convinced? The university will believe that junior college faculties are competent if students who transfer are well prepared. As it is typically practiced, however, evaluation is far from enhancing student learning—no one has brought evidence to show that students learn less in institutions where faculty evaluation is not practiced. The public can be better convinced of the worth of a junior college faculty by a skillful public relations officer who writes a variety of glowing tributes than by reports written by evaluators. And if the purpose for appraisal is only to convince one's colleagues and oneself of competence, the practice should best remain haphazard and voluntary, awaiting each instructor's need for a particular type of approbation—or disapproval, if masochism is his thing.

These reasons alone could not justify evaluation. Some of the blame for present appraisal procedures must be ascribed to the nature of the profession itself. Despite teachers' longings to be identified as professionals, few of them are oriented toward causing learning and concomitantly examining the results of their efforts—both inputs to professionalism. Most teach for other reasons. As Lieberman (1956) notes, many instructors may be in the business to win affection; their desire to win respect through professional attainments may be very limited.

If purposes, criteria, and reasons for conducting appraisal are ambiguous, why bother to evaluate at all? Is the purpose to allow administrators to stand in judgment of their faculty? Then little wonder that instructors categorically reject the process! Development of a profession cannot be enhanced, they argue, if members of the profession are subject to external judgment because, by definition, a profession must be self-policing. A corollary argument against judging faculty is that administrators, removed from the teaching situation itself, are not qualified to assess teachers. Both contentions have some merit. However, if the teaching profession is to counter external judgment, it must begin to police itself, to find ways of evaluating its members rather than merely to counter others who try.

Merit Pay

Intentions are often mistaken for the realities of life. In the schools there is much whistling in the dark to the effect that "We are one big, happy family of dedicated, competent professionals." Faculty evaluation schemes frequently perpetuate that illusion. The administrators visit the classes and the instructors respectfully attend to their reports. All is in the spirit of a better school. Unfortunately, an attitude of betrayal is fostered when judgments are tied to tangible rewards. Thus, when merit pay or tenure recommendations become dependent on evaluation, the entire process becomes an occasion for despair.

Is evaluation to be used for the purpose of awarding merit pay? Nothing can cause as much uproar among a faculty! Statements made by four authors in a single issue of *The Educational Forum* demonstrate how the lines are drawn. Teilhet points out that

> Whatever the theoretical virtues of merit pay may be, the special conditions of our profession deny justice in its application. Consider first the

impossibility of applying an objective yardstick to the creative process of teaching. It cannot be measured as a salesman's sales for a given period can be measured, nor weighed as the amount of sand a hod-carrier shovels in one day can be weighed, nor even calculated as box-office receipts for an opera can be calculated. (Teilhet 1968, p. 413)

The argument is that because the teaching process *cannot* be measured, it *should not* be measured.

Conversely, "The failure of the education profession to advance beyond the landmark of an equitable salary schedule to the provision of widely accepted criteria and methods of rewarding good teachers for their excellence no doubt contributes to the shortage of talented people who become and remain classroom teachers" (Peltier 1968, p. 421). And, "If new methods of evaluating teacher effort must be created, let's get on with the task of creating them rather than continuing to perpetuate excuses for not doing so" (Phillippi and Childress 1968, p. 406).

On the one side, then, are those who say that as presently defined, teaching cannot be measured. On the other side are those who argue that unless provision is made for differentially rewarding teachers, the profession is doomed to mediocrity.

What is the present status of merit pay in the junior college? With rare exception, quality of teaching is not recognized in apportioning salaries; instead, the measures are years of service and earned academic credits. By failing to give a "satisfactory" rating to an instructor each year, an administrator may, of course, hold him back from step increases on the salary schedule, but to do so is tantamount to an institutional scandal.

Rather than trying to decide directly on merit, most community college districts prefer to assume that years of experience and university courses taken are equivalent to effectiveness. Arguments against merit pay are usually formulated on the fact that where such schemes have been tried, the merit committee has based its determination of worth on observation of the teacher's performance and on general impressions gained through conversations with the instructor, his colleagues, and his students. Empirical assessment of merit is practically unknown. Thus, the preparation and experience components remain dominant on the salary schedules.

People who argue against merit pay frequently say that teacher proficiency cannot be measured, that the true value of a teacher manifests itself in ways unknown. To accept this argument, however, is to call into question the matter of initial employment and the awarding of tenure for continuing contract. If it is not possible to determine a teacher's merit for purposes of salary advancement, it is not possible to determine his potential at the time of initial employment, either. Further, most instructors seem to refuse to acknowledge openly that their fellows operate at varying levels of competence and effectiveness. Only if the existence of the varia-

tions is freely recognized can the development of valid measures for awarding merit pay follow.

VALUES AND IDENTITY

It is not our purpose, however, to argue the usefulness of faculty rating
schemes, either as aids to instruction or as factors in administrative decision making. The instructor's main concerns should be the kinds of teachers or teaching practices the institution holds as models—the criteria against
which assessment is made.

Whether the instructor tends to ignore his institution's patterns of
faculty evaluation, feeling them beneath his dignity, or whether he accepts
them—nervously or with equanimity—failing to question their premises,
there is one key reason why he should consciously concern himself with
them. Rating schemes offer a true reflection of institutional values. Sometimes customs perpetuate themselves even when their reasons for being
become extinct, but rating schemes—however outmoded in form—actually
mirror the values of the college. They reveal much that affects the instructor.

The values of an institution are its core. They reflect the mores of
the community in which the college is located and the thinking of the
people instrumental in its development. Even more important, they are an
aggregate of the belief systems of the people actually working within the
institution. Hence they offer a picture of the instructors, counselors, and
administrators that might otherwise be unobtainable. Whether or not the
instructor subscribes to the basic belief systems of his institution, they
affect his work and sense of well-being. If his own values counter those of
his institution and his colleagues, he tends toward either fight or flight—
finding himself in frequent overt conflict with his peers or in a shell of
his own making.

The values that give rise to patterns of institutional functioning—
to faculty evaluation schemes, in this case—also point up the status of the
teaching profession. They relate to what instructors as a group accept or
reject, believe or disbelieve about their own work. The values of both the
individual college and the teaching profession at large demand the instructor's attention because they impinge on the way he and his fellows perceive
their role and address their several functions.

Faculty rating schemes themselves, then, are not at issue here. For
purposes of illustrating institutional values, we could have selected in-
service teacher preparation, instructional program accreditation, or the
methods used to decide whether to build a new building or to buy new
instructional equipment. Any of these offer insights into institutional and
professional value systems. However, faculty rating schemes seem to be

the best indicators because they are fairly consistent throughout the country. In addition, they directly affect every instructor. The teacher may or may not be involved in decisions to purchase equipment, may or may not serve on a committee that aids in preparing a report for accreditation, but he is always the object of formal or informal judgments of his person and his works.

The major theme of this book is the integration of the individual's personal identity with his sense of professionalism. Awareness of one's identity is invariably built on many dimensions—his own modes of functioning, his sense of goal and direction, and his perception of how he is viewed by others. When these factors are integrated, the person has carved out a firm awareness of self which is, in fact, a hallmark of the mature individual who tends to judge himself by his works.

A major consideration in achieving identity is the individual's interaction with his institution and his profession. Institutional and professional values affect this interaction. Indirectly, but importantly, then, they play a major part in the person's own move toward maturity.

We see rating schemes as two sides of a coin. From one viewpoint, they are screens through which institutional and professional belief systems may be viewed. By examining systems of instructor and instructional assessment, some rather fascinating pictures of institutional values can be drawn. Obversely, those values are a matrix in which rating schemes are embedded; any attempt to change evaluation practices must accommodate the implicit value systems. Accordingly, both the rating schemes and the values they reveal affect the individual instructor.

THE REFLECTION OF VALUES

What institutional values are reflected in the faculty rating schemes presently in use? Several are apparent. First, the institution reflects the community which has created it, its mores and preferred modes of individual life styles. To perpetuate these patterns, the institution—as exemplified by the board of trustees and the administration—sets codes of conduct for the faculty members and oversees their conduct. It criticizes, imposes sanctions on, and otherwise attempts to control the behavior of those who function within it, students and instructors alike. The faculty member may be given a poor rating if he dresses "inappropriately" or otherwise behaves at variance with the customs and belief systems of the community. College officials accept as a necessary function the policing of instructors' conduct in accordance with these mores.

Another institutional value, one that stems from the most basic need of every individual and every society, is self-survival. The ethic of Western civilization insists that individual human life must be preserved. Only in the most extreme cases will Judeo–Christian thought tolerate suicide. Self-preservation is a prime value.

Like individuals, institutions tend to cherish self-preservation. In this sense they reflect the ethics of their founders, workers, and apologists—in short, of nearly all the people who are associated with them. Trustees, administrators, and, indeed, most faculty members, sincerely wish to maintain the institution's viability. The need for continuity may, in fact, supersede all other questions of institutional purpose or function. Since a tenet of American education is that there must be an institution called "school" in which teaching and learning occur, education can survive only if the institution survives—according to those who subscribe to that tenet.

To the extent that the individuals within the institution deviate from social norms, the life of the institution is threatened. When dollars count, the community must be pleased with the people in the schools. Failing bond issues and unsuccessful tax-override elections are more frequently a result of community dissatisfaction with student and/or faculty behavior than of any other single cause. The rating schemes attempt to prevent the instructors from embarrassing the college by policing their behavior just as the rules governing student conduct try to control student behavior (or at least to divorce the college from responsibility for their actions). Thus the schemes are tied to institutional survival.

In addition to their involvement with community mores and institutional perpetuation—and with the relationships between them—rating schemes also reflect what the teaching profession thinks of itself. A pattern of faculty rating that judges the instructor through assessment of traits or presumed *competence* suggests the importance the profession attributes to these qualities.

The rating schemes presently in use indicate that the profession is willing to be judged by what the people within it *seem* to be or by what they *apparently* do, rather than on the basis of the *effects* of their efforts. Making an analogy with the medical profession, it is as though doctors would be judged by their bedside manner and their skill in handling surgical instruments rather than by whether or not their patients recovered. That faculty members are judged by their classroom mannerisms and their skill in presenting information bespeaks an immature profession—one that seeks judgments of quality on the basis of superficial, perhaps irrelevant, characteristics rather than of effects. If one concomitant of maturity is the desire to be judged by one's works, the person, the profession, and the institution grow to the extent they accept this criterion. Their effects are demonstrated in the magnitude and direction of their students' learning.

Faculty rating schemes are important to the individual instructor for other reasons as well. The rating schemes reflect an institution, a profession, and indeed, a type of thinking that by choice deal in intangibles; that is, the people in the profession prefer not to assess tangible outcomes. The premises underlying their evaluation practices reflect this looking away from visible products.

At best, the rating schemes serve as second- or even third-order inferences of what should be the true purposes of the institution. An educational structure must by definition cause change in individuals. However, a rating scheme that exclusively assesses characteristics of its faculty members is far from providing an accurate view of institutional effects.

The point deserves elaboration. The use of interviews or personal rating forms in which other people judge the teacher's own characteristics is an example of third-order inference. The *person* is rated. On the basis of this holistic view, the prediction of how well he will *perform* in class is made. And on that basis, we assume his *effects* on his students. Viewing the person is presumed to offer insight into his performance, which in turn is presumed to affect his students in positive ways. Thus effect, presumably the ultimate purpose of the profession and of the institution, is three orders of inference removed from present rating practices.

Another example of second- and third-order inference in the assessment of faculty members is the examination of graduate school transcripts presented by applicants for employment. The instructor who has made "A's" in history is presumed to know more about that subject than the instructor who presents a transcript filled with "C's." This is second-order inference—giving the applicant a history test or viewing his written work would penetrate closer to the truth. More to the point, it is assumed that one who knows history well can explain it well. This is another inference that may not be warranted. And even assuming that both these inferences are in order, the further assumption is made that the instructor's students will learn history. Thus the examination of transcripts becomes a third-order inference far removed from the ostensible intent of the institution. Yet the practice persists.

Thinking at some distance from the true issues gives rise to many of the difficulties in communication encountered by instructors in different fields. Some deal with tangibles—the building must stand, the theorem must prove out. Others tend toward metaphor—to the poet, the third-order inference is reality. For corroboration of this point, ask the same question of two instructors—one in humanities, the other in construction technology.

The values implicit in rating schemes, then, are important to the instructor because of what they reveal about his profession. And his profession is very important to him as a human being, because although the individual's personality influences his choice of an occupation, his occupation in turn is a major influence on the sort of person he becomes. A person's identity is enhanced through his association with a group of people pursuing similar objectives. Ideally the instructor would be in accord with peer values, but short of Utopia, he must at least be aware of them.

Group values and the demands of group leaders may solidify a person's own belief systems or they may create strains and conflicts that delay growth and in fact, warp personal development. Therefore, institutional and professional value structures impinge directly on the individual's sense of identity. Membership in a profession with ambiguous standards of conduct, association with an institution whose rating schemes apparently reflect less concern with ostensible purpose than with self-survival, can retard the individual's movement toward integrity of self and professional maturity. The rhetoric of the profession ("You are entering a noble calling") may serve superficially, but the actual institutional and professional values have more pervasive and permanent effects. Might the dissatisfaction, unease, and stricture of many instructors be related to the fact that the values of their institution and profession have delayed their self-development?

The mature instructor, if he must be judged, wants the judgment to be made on the basis of his effects, not his efforts. He is concerned with outcomes. These are his raison d'être. He is secure enough within himself not to need external corroboration of his modes of functioning. He studies instruction and people—himself included. He knows how to achieve the results he seeks.

The teaching profession needs this type of maturity. To the extent that it polices its ranks and judges its members on the basis of their own effects, it will gain maturity. The individual will develop to the extent that he gains an awareness of self, functioning within an institution and a professon that are themselves mature. Faculty rating schemes can enhance the process only if they aid the instructor to focus on instructional effects.

17

Measuring
Instructional
Effects

Suppose that:

—a college's primary value were self-preservation;
—a profession had not yet achieved maturity;
—conceptualizations of both institutional and professional purposes were indistinct.

How would instructors working within that college and profession be evaluated?

To satisfy the institution's primary value of self-preservation, rating procedures would have to screen out, or at least isolate from view, people who might embarrass the college. Institutions seldom—and never openly—acknowledge their predominant motive. Instead, they talk about generalized and extremely ambiguous goals: to serve the community, to provide free access to higher education to all students, to encourage high ideals of good citizenship. But they assess faculty members on the basis of their tendencies to support the organization. Most of the approaches to faculty assessment described in the last two chapters give the lie to this institutional belief in self-perpetuation.

The profession reveals its lack of maturity by rating practitioners on the basis of their own apparent competences rather than on their effects, by accepting rating systems that judge instructors rather than the effects of instruction. Only an immature profession would allow—and indeed, encourage—its members to be judged on their efforts, their presumed competence. Years ago Lieberman said, "The fact that a profession of teaching would render teachers personally and directly responsible for their teaching . . . is not yet appreciated by either teachers or administrators as a group" (1956, p. 485). Responsibility for teaching means responsibility for causing learning.

The indistinct conceptualizations of both institutional and professional purposes are reflected in the ambiguous criteria for faculty evaluation. Applicants for positions are judged according to whether an interviewer feels they will "attain rapport" with their students, "fit in" with their colleagues, and not cause trouble between the college and its constituent community. Assessment of classroom functioning is made by a visitation or by a conference in which the instructor's supervisors, colleagues, and in some cases, students, discuss his apparent competence. If his effects are mentioned at all, it is in commentary on the pattern of grade marks he distributes. The criteria shift, the purposes are nebulous, and the relationships between faculty evaluation and faculty effects are vague.

The reasons for faculty evaluation in its current form, then, are invalid. The practice fails to differentiate between the teacher as a social being and the teacher as one who causes learning. It serves no useful purpose. If the profession is to gain a true identity, it must abandon evaluation as it is presently conducted and replace it with something of value.

Suppose that:

—a college's primary values centered around student learning;
—a profession had achieved maturity;
—conceptualizations of institutional and professional purpose were distinct.

How, then, would instructors working within that institution and profession be evaluated?

Instructors would be assessed according to the extent that their students learned. The profession would evaluate its own members on the basis of their demonstrated effects, attesting to its maturity. And distinct conceptualizations of institutional and professional purpose would lead to direct measurement of changes in the individuals and in the community that the institution and the profession purport to serve.

The integrated person, the viable institution, and the mature profession go hand in hand—the basic assumption of this book. The instructor who is certain of himself and of his direction wants to cause learning. He recognizes that his own worth depends on his successful effects. Evaluation practices that scrutinize him rather than his works are anathema—the mature person will not abide a situation that fails to enhance personal and professional growth. He welcomes evaluation of his effects, not of his smile, his blue eyes, or the number of failing marks he doles out to his students.

The person who has successfully passed through the phases of development basic to the formation of a strong sense of self is able to integrate his personal and professional identity. At this stage, he merges his own being with the demands of his occupational and social roles. He can state positively, "Don't come and look at me"—not because he fears being judged, but because his sense of professionalism demands that if he *is* to be judged, it must be on the basis of his effects.

By the time the person is considered capable of handling groups of students, he must be allowed to exercise his autonomy as he sees fit. This does not mean that evaluation must be discarded. It means that evaluation must be tied to the criterion of learning achievement, rather than to such measures as individual personality descriptors or any other singular, limited behavioral trait. Evaluation practices that are based on views of classroom performance or of the ways instructors conduct themselves are frequently little more than forms of voyeurism—a type of regression the schools can no longer tolerate. The mature person scorns evaluations that merely satisfy curiosities.

Building our theme of evaluation of mature people operating within a mature profession on the basis of demonstrable effects, this chapter discusses a set of defined purposes for faculty evaluation, explains what should be the ultimate criteria for faculty evaluation, and suggests new directions for the supervision of instruction.

FACULTY EVALUATION: ALTERNATIVE PURPOSES

Present difficulties in assessing instructors can generally be traced to ambiguity of purpose, misplaced values, and indeterminate criteria. Until these issues are resolved, all rating schemes are doomed to severe and legitimate criticism if not to abject failure.

Conscious intent should undergird all faculty evaluation procedures. Only when purposes have been carefully defined can an institution design a useful scheme of appraisal. The common disparity between purposes and current practices can be reconciled and practices can have meaning only if faculty evaluation schemes are based on valid institutional goals that give rise to reasonable criteria. What are these valid purposes?

Evaluation schemes can be used to direct faculty efforts. Assessment techniques and procedures are powerful forces in determining what goes on within schools and classrooms. If, for example, evidence of student learning is to be gathered, instructors are more likely to direct their efforts toward causing learning than they would be if their performance alone were accepted as the major criterion of teaching worth. For that reason, the practice of making sound or sight recordings of instructors' performances, whether in training or in actual teaching situations, seems to have little effect on directing efforts toward causing learning. Rather, it tends to focus attention once again on quality of performance, and it encourages instructors to continue assuming a connection between their performance and the achievement of their students.

Faculty evaluation can be used to improve instruction. But if the evaluation practice is to be effectual, it must be related to instruction as a discipline. Instruction is a process that shapes the student's environment so that meanings are easier to grasp. It is a way of ordering experiences so that learning occurs. Without measuring the resultant learning, there is no way of telling whether a student's environment and perceptions have been so ordered. Thus, if instruction is to be appraised, the parallel assumptions must be made both that students can learn and that this internal process can be deliberately shaped by external forces.

A measurement of instruction views total instructional sequences, implying that instruction can be measured independently of the person of the instructor—despite the belief that continuing investigations may eventually establish the relationships between personality characteristics and instructor effectiveness. It assumes that the person of the instructor is a force—but only one force—in the total learning environment, and it puts a negative value on limited observations of instructors. Measuring instruction means that if the instructor is to be observed or rated as one portion of a total learning environment, methods other than those typically in use must be employed. And, most important, effects of the instructional process must be included in the paradigm. This discussion assumes, of course, that the purpose of schooling is to provide instruction to the students, not merely to offer them custodial care and both positive and negative adult models.

Instructional specialization can be enhanced by changed modes of faculty evaluation. Presently an instructor must be competent in all aspects of the instructional process. He must be a scintillating lecturer, a stimulating discussion leader, an omniscient setter of objectives, a warmhearted counselor, a skilled media producer, and a careful writer of examinations. To expect all persons working in the schools to be thoroughly competent in all facets of the discipline of instruction is to doom the teaching profession to mediocrity.

The self-evaluating instructional team can mitigate this untoward effect of continued reliance on the "compleat teacher." If specialization were encouraged, the institution might be staffed by a corps of people who collectively, but not necessarily individually, display excellence in all matters relating to teaching. The instructional team might have one of its members write objectives, another give lectures, a third select and produce reproducible media, a fourth construct and continually analyze test items. Each team member would carry his share of the load or else he would adversely affect his immediate colleagues. If one instructor were not doing his part, the team members could apply necessary sanctions to cause him to change or to remove him.

In such a schema, each teacher learns to do what he can do best. Each adds something of value to the group. Evaluation then becomes a process by means of which one's fellows directly influence his activities. Even now, whether or not instructors work together in teams, evaluation different from that typically practiced would encourage them to build on their special strengths.

Evaluation can enhance communication. Instruction today has changed little from instruction 100 years ago. On many campuses, instructors still do everything as it was done by their nineteenth century counterparts, short of shaking down the coal stove. It is not stretching a point to picture a modern junior college as a collection of little red schoolhouses—boxes of isolation, one for each instructor who operates within a self-contained classroom. To what extent is the long established—and cherished—right of privacy of the classroom used indiscriminately as a shield of academic freedom to block all possible approaches to change?

In keeping with the vociferous demands of the people who seek meaning and relevance, evaluation can serve a useful purpose. It can help break down isolation and compartmentalization by creating situations in which faculty members communicate with each other regarding instructional processes. A design built on such a rationale would have instructors evaluating each other *solely* on the basis of their teaching effectiveness. Joint consultations and visiting—practices that occur informally now—could be used more widely. They might even act as a communications bridge between faculty members and administrators who hold common goals but perceive different avenues to attainment.

EVALUATION AND MATURITY

Such goals are fine for the profession as a whole, but the instructor can be excused for not accepting them as his own. The new faculty member, especially, might tend to ignore general aims and practices and, if he is to be evaluated at all, he might prefer that it be done for the purpose of helping him come to grips with his own move into the teaching profession. He wants neither his professional activities nor his effects on his students to be the main areas of concern. He often tends to guard himself from such intrusion, preferring to work everything out in his own way.

> But when it came to the job, each teacher preferred to close his door to the rest of the world and exercise unlimited and uncriticized authority in his own classroom. . . . And it really didn't matter much anyway, so long as nobody noticed, I thought. As long as I kept my door and my mouth shut as much as possible and polished up a set of "good" answers for any official questions likely to be asked. (Ryan 1970, pp. 108–10)

If he maintains this posture, however, he may well be accused of arrested development or, at best, of immaturity. The instructor in process of becoming is willing—perhaps eager—to have his performance judged. He invites criticism of his classroom procedures, his lectures, and the way he interacts with his students. He is able to have his performance reviewed because he perceives these functions as the sum total of his professional role.

The mature person, however—the true professional—wants his *works* reviewed. In the case of the professional instructor, his works are his effects on his students. The mature instructor has integrated his profession with his personal sense of self. He recognizes that affecting the students' cognitive and emotional development is his proper role, and he wants to assess himself—or to be assessed—on no other basis. A faculty evaluation scheme that enhances this posture serves institution, profession, and individual.

STUDENT CHANGE
AS A CRITERION

If it is necessary for students, colleagues, or administrators to evaluate instructors, then specific criteria must be established before assessment can be undertaken. Just as every person needs a sense of direction, every institution needs to be aware of its own purposes. However, because there is no universal agreement on the goals of education, the people in the college must spell out these purposes, decide on its objectives, and translate them into operational terms. These objectives then become the criteria on which practices are adopted, policy is projected, people are selected, and evaluation is made.

Throughout this section we have alluded to the desirability of using measurable change in students as the main criterion on which faculty evaluation and other institutional practices should be based. This criterion counteracts many questions of purposiveness and validity. Simply establishing criteria, however, does not mean that selection and evaluation of instructors can be undertaken. Criteria must not only be valid, they must also be amenable to measurement. For example, a valid criterion for evaluating an educational system might well be institutional ability to effect community transformation. Nevertheless, it would be an understatement to say that it is difficult to create reliable measures of community change and to relate change to the efforts of a school—much less to a single person.

Compounding this difficulty are the problems of reliably determining student development. Indeed, the question of how students change under the impact of college is related to the more fundamental concern about the general conditions of personality change. Young people do change and personalities do develop, but tying that development to life experiences in general (let alone to the effects of a college or of an individual instructor) is a puzzle that psychological, sociological, and educational research has not begun to solve.

Individual and institutional effects must be assessed along several dimensions. Strategies for measuring long-range community transformations and effects on students' personal development are serious issues to which people in the junior college can well address themselves. But assessing effects on even less far-reaching criteria must be undertaken as well. Because we have no reliable ways of assessing long-term impact does not mean that we should fail to seek ways to measure the effects of a single instructor (along with the media he employs) on his students.

Student achievement of specific learning objectives is a valid and feasible criterion—probably the most useful presently available. Many instructors already accept this criterion as being valid for self-evaluation. Whether the objectives center on student growth or on subject matter learning, all involve measurement of change in student behaviors, actions, or abilities. Failure to attempt to measure student gain on the tangibles, simply because long-range human development does not lend itself to reliable measurement, is futile and shortsighted. Perhaps, as Marland points out, "The pupil test is a shabby and unworthy alternative to the assessment of teachers. But we have never faced up to systematic and objective teacher evaluation (1969, pp. 107–8)." We must begin somewhere.

For assessing instructors, then, manifest student learning can be viewed as the ultimate criterion primarily because it enhances the instructor's awareness of his own effects. Using student progress toward specific objectives as if it were the ultimate purpose of the institution has the additional value of being methodologically related to assessing the personal growth of students; that is, as tools are developed to assess student gain, measurement of broad student change may be furthered. The two seem related. There is certainly face validity to the contention that measuring student gain toward specific objectives is more closely akin to measuring student change in general than is assessing an instructor on the basis of his methods or his efforts.

Student gain as a criterion for measuring instructor effectiveness has had much support among educational researchers as well as among instructors and theoreticians. It is generally acknowledged to be a more valid criterion than, for example, the various perceptions of classroom observers. Orleans and others suggest:

As the ultimate criteria of the effectiveness of the teacher's performance, we posit *the changes which take place in the behavior of pupils.* If the overall function of the educational process is to produce changes in the individuals, then the effectiveness of the teacher's performance must be measured by the extent to which it produces such changes. (1952, p. 642)

A committee of the American Educational Research Association (AERA), set up to define problems in establishing criteria of teaching effectiveness, reported that "... a teacher's effect on the pupil's achievement of the immediate objectives of the given curriculum segment for which each teacher is responsible is somewhat less ultimate ... than the teacher's effect on the student's total life, yet, it must be considered as essential in measurement" (Barr et al. 1952). McKeachie (1963) insists that "the ultimate criteria of effective teaching are changes in students in the direction of goals of higher education." And Anderson concludes, "Teacher evaluation experts are almost universally agreed that the measure of true effectiveness as a teacher is the change that is produced in the pupils taught by that teacher" (1954, p. 44).

The list of educators who insist that student change must be considered the ultimate criterion of teacher effectiveness could be extended. In fact, the recent demands for "accountability" are based on this premise. However, the issue cannot be settled merely by establishing the validity of an arbitrary standard. Reliable measures for assessing student change and teacher effects must still be produced. The effort needed to find them and the problems of establishing them should not detract from the fact that assessing instructors on the basis of student change moves the entire issue of evaluation closer to the ultimate purpose of education.

ISSUES IN MEASUREMENT OF EFFECTS

There are many difficulties in using student gain as a measure of teacher effectiveness. Most problems are related to two broad issues: the kind of change (gain, learning) that shall be measured; and the way that student learning reflects the efforts of an individual instructor.

What types of gain shall be measured—general or specific? A case can be made for assessing learning by general achievement tests, but such techniques may be far removed from the instructor who teaches a particular subject area and makes no direct effort to affect his students' broad abilities. The determination to assess instructional effects only on the basis of each instructor's specific objectives could resolve this issue. However, the concept of specifying measurable objectives is far from being universally accepted. Many instructors still insist, "The things *I* teach, you can't measure." (Perhaps they should be glad.)

Another problem is establishing the comparative worth of objectives. Students who are led to memorize and to show gains on measures of factual recall must be viewed as having learned in a different sphere from those showing gain on measures devised by the instructors who encourage them to analyze and to synthesize information. It is futile to consider using student gain on measures other than those that assess learning toward the instructors' own objectives. If all instructors would specify clearly what they are trying to teach and what measures they intend to use to assess learning, arrangements could then be made to assess their effects. But the teaching field is a long way from such an arrangement.

The second set of difficulties in assessing effect through student change involves the problems of contamination. Are changes due solely to the influence of a particular instructor? Students learn as a result of many things besides one instructor's efforts. Learning is influenced by general ability, past educational experiences, available instructional materials, influence of family and peers, socioeconomic backgrounds, types of extracurricular activities, quality of instruction in other areas of the curriculum, effects of mass media, and dozens of other variables.

In addition, any teacher in a classroom is himself an image whose effect may be altered by his students' perceptions of the total environment—perceptions that are often built on prior experience. The permissive teacher who has a positive effect on one student may have the opposite effect on another, simply because his permissiveness reminds the student of a previous instructor who had exhibited those characteristics and then failed him. The implication, of course, is that the effective teacher is one who can alter his procedures to fit individual students—a concept explored by the studies reported in chapter 10.

A different type of problem relates to the tautological, yet commonly accepted definition of teaching as "that which a teacher does." Any successful scheme for assessing instructors demands the active cooperation of the faculty. If instructors feel they have entered the profession to lecture and conduct discussions—that which a teacher "typically does"—assessment on the basis of what their students learn represents an alien dimension. When a student-gain assessment scheme is at variance with the instructor's frame of reference, it is unfeasible. When the word "learning" is left out of the instructor's definition of teaching, resistance to evaluation on the basis of student gain inevitably follows.

Some instructors possess a genuine belief in their long-range effects. Their definition of learning is not "changed capability for, or tendency toward, acting in particular ways," but "something mysterious that will manifest itself at some unknown time." If measures of student gain are to be related to the influence of any single instructor, the duration of time between pre- and post-testing must be short. If, these instructors reason, their effects may not be realized until years have passed, how can they be rated on any short-range basis? Therefore, they doubt the efficacy of any form of rating.

Still other difficulties in using student gain as a criterion to assess instructors enter the picture. Does the instructor have the ability to cause learning in any and all situations, or only in particular situations—for example, with certain types of teaching objectives or with certain types of students? This question is clearly important. The teacher who stimulates consistently high gain scores among low-achieving students is not the same as the one whose students learn—or could learn—without his intervention. Who is more valuable? The analogy is to the doctor who treats only healthy patients. Is he to be considered as useful to society as the one who takes sick people and makes them well? Again, the purpose for which the assessment is conducted must be considered.

Another difficulty in using student gain as a criterion of effectiveness is that in order to control for extraneous influences, the measure must be based primarily on classroom activities. It must exclude the instructor's advising, participating in extracurricular activities, and otherwise inter- acting with—hence influencing—his students. It correspondingly fails to consider students' contacts with people other than the teacher. How can the effects of librarians, parents, and peers be isolated?

Test validity also affects the feasibility of employing a student-gain criterion. The instructor who uses tests that assess his students' abilities to analyze is at a disadvantage compared to the instructor whose tests measure simple recall (Bloom et al. 1956). If tests built by outsiders are used, the instructor may feel that they do not properly reflect his own objectives. These problems are well summarized by Dressel, who argues,

> The growth and development of students in regard to course objectives as measured by pre- and post-testing is one of the most attractive and logical means of evaluating teaching. Lack of adequate measures and the sheer work of collecting and analyzing the results limit the actual utility of the approach. (1959, p. 12)

Nevertheless, if the teacher *must* be judged—and the reasons for judging him vary almost as much as the schemes that are used—let him be evaluated on the effects of his efforts, not on the perceived worth of the efforts themselves. The apparent difficulty of using student gain as a criterion should not encourage members of the profession to fall back exclusively on the use of proximate criteria.

TEASING OUT THE EFFECTS

No adequate definition of teacher competence can be set until the precise effects desired of a teacher are established.

Those words should be written in letters of fire across all schemes of faculty evaluation currently employed in junior colleges. As Richmond has said, "To declare that we have no way of assessing these effects is tantamount to saying that we do not know what we are trying to do" (1969, p. 61). Yet no two people fully agree on what the competent teacher is, because before beginning to judge competence, we must reach agreement on outcomes.

The difficulties of selecting media and theoretical frameworks on which to build valid instructor evaluation practices appear at first glance to present insurmountable problems. But certainly they cannot be so great that junior colleges must surrender to other schemes considerably less potent. Efforts must now be devoted to defining the kinds of effects desired and to assessing them accurately. Until the major task of identifying the specific dimensions of the ultimate criterion—learning—has been undertaken, the attempt to define and assess the competence of an individual instructor or total faculty will suffer. Initially it may be difficult to drop old procedures and create new ones, but the usefulness of changed techniques makes the effort worthwhile.

Some attempts to stabilize procedures for assessing teachers' proclivities to cause student learning have been reported. Interestingly, some of these efforts are rather old. As long ago as the early 1930s, the results of examinations given to all high school students in Minnesota were reviewed and absolutely no difference in scores attained by students who were in any particular instructors' courses was found. Similar attempts have since been made with similarly inconclusive results—perhaps reflecting slipshod methodology.

Educational researchers are attempting to find designs that more accurately assess individual instructors' effects. One technique, developed for use in Air Force schools, has become the prototype for more recent studies that use student gain as a measure of instructor effort (Morsh, Burgess, Smith 1955). Experimenters using this design selected instructors who were teaching identical subject matter to certain students in similar classrooms, using the same training aids. Pre-tests that served as a basis for assessing learning were administered to all subjects. The chief results of these investigations indicate that when adequate experimental controls are employed, student gains can be reliably measured and related to individual instructors. They also suggest that although students seem to know when they are being well taught, an instructor's supervisors and peers alone cannot accurately identify the effective instructor.

> The high relationship . . . between ratings and rankings by fellow instructors and supervisors, together with the fact that these measures appear unrelated to student gains, suggest that *fellow instructors and supervisors judge instructor effectiveness on the basis of factors other than what students learn.* One of these factors appears to be the instructor's knowl-

edge of subject matter. To obtain a completely adequate evaluation of an instructor it may be that a multiple criterion composed of supervisor ratings, student ratings, and student gains should be used. (Ibid., p. iv)

The Air Force studies were able to isolate individual teacher effects because they controlled certain important variables. All instructors worked toward identical learning objectives, and common examinations were administered. Both these procedures at least are necessary if teacher effects are to be identified without contamination.

Who are the "good teachers"? Using student gain as the criterion, Popham (1967) employed a design in which common objectives and test items were given to two groups—secondary school teachers and graduate students with no prior teaching experience. Each instructor prepared and presented his lessons in any manner he considered appropriate. The result: no significant differences were found in mean scores on the criterion examination between pupils taught by inexperienced teachers and those taught by the experienced group. It was concluded that because experienced teachers are not typically "set" to effect student learning toward specific objectives, they could do no better in a situation requiring such a task than could a group of people who had never taught before! (This is fine from a methodological viewpoint, but what would the experienced teacher say to these findings? "They failed to measure truth and beauty," that's what!)

When knowledge of subject area and of students is isolated and controlled along with extraneous influences, some teachers can consistently prepare and present lessons better than others. To test this contention, Justiz (1968) prepared objectives and validated tests for a group of teachers in several high schools. Each instructor, working from common sets of objectives in an unfamiliar field and with limited time for lesson preparation, was free to select content from a list of suggestions and to structure his lesson in any way he chose. Each teacher's class was composed of students selected at random—their prior abilities or tendencies unknown. He was thus required to present a lesson to unfamiliar students, but he was free to reveal his objectives to the students, to provide practice exercises, and to give students information about the accuracy of their responses. In short, he could select any teaching technique, but learning was determined by tests provided by the investigator.

The variable tested was narrowed from the teacher as a total person to the instructor engaging in just those activities that conveyed the preparation and presentation of lessons. Accordingly, the evidence gained was that of pure classroom teaching. Each "good" teacher found his own best way of presenting his lessons; there was no consistent teaching style. It was found, however, that those who could teach one subject well could also teach the other. The design thus seemed to yield an index of generalized teaching ability, with some instructors consistently more effective than others.

A useful model developed on the basis of these studies was presented by O'Connor and Justiz (1970), who separated from all possible and potential teacher activities just those that have direct effects on students. This design controls for teachers' overall knowledge of subject area and for their knowledge about students with whom they are confronted. It seeks only evidence of teaching ability—and in this case, even "teaching" is narrowed to include only teachers' abilities to prepare and present classroom lessons that teach toward predetermined objectives and test items.

Designs that assess ability to prepare and present lessons effectually view only one part of the total instructional process; hence they seem to have limited applicability. However, the part they *reliably* measure is that which is *supposedly* being observed by a rater who sits in a classroom and watches the instructor. These types of procedures, then, might potentially replace classroom observers who view instructor performance and assume connections between such performance and student learning. The assumption is somewhat less valid, and certainly less reliable, than the actual test. The test represents a move in the direction of first-order inference—toward measurement of equivalents rather than of analogues.

INSTRUCTIONAL SUPERVISION

Genuine supervision of instruction is rarely applied consistently in junior colleges. It is a spotty enterprise, too often subordinate to evaluation and frequently confused with that wearisome endeavor. Repelled by the idea that any facet of their instruction might be supervised by outsiders, many instructors see no reason for supervision and view the entire process as somehow resembling "public school."

Yet the junior college is by its own admission a teaching institution. Some type of instructional supervision seems warranted—with the proviso, however, that it be designed to lead to instructional improvement. A supervision process can be the coordinating mechanism for causing particular changes in instructional practices, fostering communication between faculty and administration, and placing both the college and the mature instructor in a better position to answer the key question in all education, "Is anyone learning anything here?"

Communication between administration and faculty frequently suffers from misunderstanding and faulty perceptions. The supervisor who attempts to use evaluation as a means of communication often fails because evaluation is a judgmental—hence, usually anxiety-provoking—process. But the junior college dean or division chairman who must write faculty evaluations can make this process a true communication device by subordinating evaluation to instructional supervision. He can make supervision positive by offering specific help to instructors, rather than by standing in judgment of them. However, much depends on the instructors' perceiving the supervisor's suggestions as helpful in attaining common goals. That is, instructors must themselves sincerely seek to cause student learning. Otherwise, all supervisor suggestions are perceived as being praise or blame—ends in themselves, and inadequate at best.

A supervisory scheme that seems to hold particular promise both for enhancing communication and for assessing instructional effects was introduced in 1967 at Golden West College in California (Cohen and Shawl 1970). Designed particularly to gain information so that resources could be properly allocated and institutional effects assessed, it was also intended as a curriculum-planning aid and as a way of leading instructors to specify their objectives—a worthy enterprise in its own right.

The Golden West College scheme of instructional supervision begins at the initial employment interview. At that time, instructors are informed about the college's move toward the definition of specific objectives in all courses and curricula and are encouraged to specify objectives in their own work. Because most new instructors have not had previous training in writing objectives, arrangements are made for them to study the process. Help is provided by an experienced colleague, a department chairman, or an outside expert.

A continuing series of interviews is scheduled for both new and experienced instructors. At these meetings, the division chairman and the dean of instruction review the instructor's objectives and the student learning he has effected. Tests are examined and criticized; objectives and media in use are reviewed. The situation is not one of threat, but of aid. For example, an instructor who has sound objectives and testing devices but whose students are learning little may be given help in the form of suggestions about various media and techniques that he might employ. Meetings between department chairman, dean, and individual instructors thus represent a continuing process of instructional supervision. Time allocated for the individual meetings is that which would ordinarily be used by the dean and the chairman to visit and observe classrooms.

The Golden West College instructional supervision scheme brings the process of supervision into meaningful perspective. It allows the administration to apportion resources in the form of aides and secretarial assistance; thus, in a sense, faculty members are rewarded for participating in the voluntary plan. In reality, however, the process of instruction is being rewarded. The program allows for in-service professional upgrading, for the introduction of new techniques of teaching, and for the development of experimental curricula and instructional designs. It is actually supervision by the objectives of instruction rather than supervision of instructors. And as McNeil (1966) points out, there is a marked distinction between the two.

Evaluation practices that depend on singular variables independent of theory have given way in the Golden West scheme to instructional supervision based on the extent to which students learn what their instructors attempt to teach. It is felt that evaluation on the basis of what is happening to the learners is more appropriate than evaluation of teachers' activities. Similar plans have recently been introduced at junior colleges in many areas of the country.

NEXT STEPS

We have taken the position that student gain toward specific learning objectives should be recognized as the ultimate criterion in assessing effects of teachers and teaching situations. Because it relates directly to the acknowledged purposes of all educational endeavors, it seems to be a most defensible variable. Student gain is also a desirable dimension because it can help education as a whole move into a sphere in which educators can predict, manipulate, and accept accountability for their actions—in short, become an aware, mature profession.

Teaching is the acknowledged main purpose of the junior college. It follows that precise study of instruction must be undertaken. Teacher evaluation along unspecified dimensions can and should give way to merged procedures and practices of much greater potential. The evaluation of instructors and the study of instruction must be integrated.

Epilogue: Toward Maturity

Throughout this book we have addressed ourselves to people, practices, and issues related to instructors and instruction in the two-year college. Rather than attempting to hide under a guise of false objectivity, we have openly projected our own attitudes toward schools, instructors, and the teaching profession. For example, unlike many other writers, we do not feel that the two-year college is a unique enterprise. Instead, we see it as a form of school that has taken on a plethora of functions and, accordingly, has found it difficult to achieve any of them fully. We feel that the institution's shortcomings must be faced realistically, that little is to be gained by pretending that the college has accomplished all it set out to do.

In addition, we have attempted to conceptualize the many functions associated with teaching and to talk about how instruction might be conducted to be most effective for the student and most satisfying for the instructor. Our position has been that junior college instructors may gain identity and serve their students and communities best by being aware of themselves, of their strengths and weaknesses, and of their actions, and by holding themselves accountable for the effects of their efforts. It is time to return to the instructor the responsibility for seeing that learning occurs.

We also believe that the two-year college instructor has more control over his practices, more autonomy, than he typically uses. Still, he does not function in isolation, practicing his craft apart from others. He is a member of an institutional organization that has its own ethos and he is subject to various influences from peers, supervisors, and clientele. Just as the institution influences him, he influences the institution. Indeed, the instructor *is* the institution—without him there is nothing but buildings and grounds and statements of vague intent. He has a responsibility to grow, to become a mature professional person.

For college, for profession, and for person, the movement toward maturity has many dimensions. Each individual is responsible for integrating his personal and professional being with the purposes of the institution and the people he serves. He is a member of a profession that is still groping for self-definition but one that concurrently can be markedly enhanced by the purposiveness exhibited by each of its members. And he works within an institution that is itself striving for a form of maturity as a respected and potent entity in the milieu of American higher education.

We see, then, a three-way drive toward maturity—exhibited simultaneously by the two-year college, the teaching profession, and the instructor himself. Each makes its separate move toward maturity, but since each interacts with the others, the progress made has mutual effect. In this last chapter we summarize some of the present phenomena that presage maturity, we recount a few of the drawbacks, and we plot trends for each of the three entities.

TOWARD MATURITY
FOR THE COMMUNITY COLLEGE

The junior college was organized in the early twentieth century to provide certain kinds of services to people who were not being served by existing institutions. As the junior college became a community college and adopted a multiplicity of functions, the numbers of institutions and their enrollments mushroomed. By 1970, the more than 1,000 institutions enrolled approximately 2,400,000 students.

This type of growth suggests a well functioning, viable institution, appropriately serving its constituency. And the community college has served well. Nevertheless, there are some indications that things could be better—high student drop-out rate, community disaffection expressed in the form of lessened tax support, and the growing militancy of faculty members are but a few of these indicators. In addition, the institution's indistinctly conceptualized purposes suggest that it presently occupies a twilight zone between the secondary school and the liberal arts college or university. The mature institution would not have to wonder what it is about. The junior college still does.

What does maturity mean to an institution? It means that the institution has a high degree of autonomy, that it does not have to adopt outmoded forms just because other schools use them. Simultaneously, the institution has distinct purpose and value. For appropriate decisions to be made, all who are involved with the institution—both directly and less obviously—must know clearly where it is going, what it is trying to do, how well it is doing. This means that the lay citizenry of the district must have a clear perception of the institution; more particularly, it means that the college's staff holds this sense of institutional purpose as its own.

The two-year college could assume—and indeed, has assumed—several purposes. As presently operated, it is a safety valve that allows the state universities to maintain high admissions standards. It is a training agency operated for the benefit of the community's industries. It is a place for young people to be as they await their own growth, experiencing, in Erikson's term, a "moratorium." And it is a sorting and certifying agency that dips its net into the pool of youth, catching various types of individuals, giving them one more chance to succeed in school.

Study Instruction

But there is much more the junior college could do as an institution. In particular, it could enhance its own identity to a greater extent. For one thing, it could take the lead among educational institutions in the study of instruction. Despite the magnitude of the American educational enterprise, surprisingly little is known about the process of instruction and few agencies are systematically studying the matter. The two-year college does not presently have the skilled personnel to carry on full-blown studies of instruction, but changed patterns of staffing, coupled with appropriate liaisons with neighboring research centers, could equip it to take on the task.

If the community college does assume the task of studying instruction, what kinds of questions might be asked? Several come immediately to mind. Exactly what is being learned in the junior college? By whom? Are curricular and instructional practices as effectual as they might be? For whom? And if not, why not? What forms of student achievement should be accepted as evidence that learning has occurred? If students were provided with sets of specific objectives at the time of their entrance to the college, would their learning be enhanced? Would the drop-out rate be reduced? What else could be done to facilitate the process and guarantee the product?

The people who are actively involved in the teaching—learning enterprise must be considered in connection with any issue. How can particular types of instructors be prepared to cause learning? Should students be placed with instructors whose cognitive styles match their own? Or must "tracking" be done solely on the basis of prior achievement? Can everyone teach all types of learning objectives with equal facility? Or are some instructors better at causing recall, others at stimulating students to continue learning on their own? Why so? Is it the result of discernible actions or of basic personality characteristics that can be measured only indirectly?

We know little about such matters and about others that we might name. There is so much that must be learned about people, developmental styles, the special traits and characteristics that both enhance and impede learning. One of the thorniest problems is the need to discover who can teach whom. Interactions among teachers and students and among dimensions of instructional situations must be identified. Prerequisite to the identification of effects is the specification of forms of learning to be accepted as evidence of attainment.

Such variables represent directions for potentially fruitful study in which junior colleges can profitably engage by turning themselves into experimental colleges or learning laboratories wherein these types of questions are constantly raised, disputed, answered, and finally communicated to the field of education at large. When studies of instructors and of instruction merge, a step will have been taken toward institutional maturity. No one else is going to study instruction for the colleges. They must do it themselves.

Prepare Instructors

Another type of service that would augment professional instruction—and hence, maturity for the junior college—is active participation by the institution in preparation of instructors. Many colleges have student teaching arrangements with neighboring universities through which cadet instructors are allowed to practice their craft with rooms full of students. However, most of these arrangements are apprenticeships with single students working under the direction of individual supervising teachers. More could be done.

Every two-year college should establish at least one "training chair." This would be a faculty position at full pay, held for a beginning instructor, with the proviso that the contract run for one year only. At the beginning of each school year a totally inexperienced person who wanted to become a teacher would be given a contract. Whether or not he was properly certified, he would receive the same pay as the beginning certificated instructor. For its part, the college would provide a deliberate set of sequences, a full range of experiences for the instructor. He would be encouraged to gain experience in every facet of the instructional act and to share his experiences with his counterparts at neighboring institutions. A university-based teacher training division might or might not be brought into the process, depending on whether the college staff saw a value in doing so.

This type of arrangement would have several positive effects. In the case of the larger institutions where a training chair might be established in each division, the steady influx of new instructors with fresh ideas would act as a catalyst, forcing the older instructors to defend—or to change—their ideas as they are required to explain them to the new teachers. This type of situation may not seem important while the institutions are expanding in staff and enrollments, but as they reach maximum size, and as new staff appointments must await the exodus of older staff members, the influx of fresh ideas looms important for institutional viability.

In addition, the training chair idea would resolve many of the preparation and orientation problems now plaguing the field. Junior college administrators frequently complain that new instructors are not properly imbued with a "junior college point of view." By preparing carefully drawn sequences for training their own instructors, they would not only take a part in the teacher training enterprise, they would also be forced to examine periodically just what the phrase "junior college point of view" means to them. This type of self-examination is one of the many inputs to identity because it encourages a look inward. Even if certification requirements and/or institutional policy militate against the college's preparing full-fledged instructors, it can still train paraprofessional educators. There is a growing demand for people to staff child-care centers, nursery schools, community youth centers, senior citizens' educational groups, and other quasi-institutional endeavors. The universities—with rare exception—are not interested in preparing people to serve in these types of educational situations; hence, the field is open for the junior college to provide an important service.

The overriding purpose for the junior college's involvement in the preparation of instructors is that the organization of appropriate curriculum and experiences for these people would force a continuing redefinition of institutional role. The more the institution is required to seek out appropriate experiences for its teacher candidates, the more it must face up to its own educational program responsibilities. As the college becomes the educational training center for its community, it finds alternative modes of functioning in its own right.

Alternatives

A third avenue that might lead the two-year college toward maturity is for it to seek alternative organizational and functional patterns, both for itself and for the other educational segments of its community. The need to find alternative structures is pointed up by the recent vociferous criticisms of educational institutions in general. The college that is built on a model originally developed in the Middle Ages simply cannot be the best of all possible forms to assume the total task of educating the diverse groups in contemporary America.

Preservation of the community college in its present form is unlikely. The colleges will continue to grow in scope, importance, and enrollments, but diversity of form must accompany changing functions. Different configurations must be tried, not only in administration and curriculum but also in total institutional structures. The impending high level of involvement with the local community alone demands alternative forms of campus planning, student matriculation, curriculum, and staff function.

The two-year colleges are in a unique position to select and try out different modes of functioning. They do not have to remain tied to the standard academic model that is, in fact, a quasi-imitation of the best known graduate schools. As Jerome states,

> Free from the publish-or-perish formula of the national institutions, [the two-year colleges] might create a professional model of good teaching, personal responsiveness, social betterment at the local level, cultural enrichment of the community. Rather than adding to the storehouse of knowledge, they might concentrate on making it publicly available and adapting it to immediate community purposes. (1969, p. 20)

This seeking of alternatives requires a conscious and continuing effort to find relevant patterns of function and structure. The search cannot be based simply on a flurry of innovation or on the "Let's keep everything stirred up" syndrome, which is, in fact, dysfunctional. Simply maintaining a climate of innovation in the hope that sooner or later something useful will appear is like setting an infinite number of monkeys at an equal number of typewriters, hoping that sooner or later one of them will write a work of art.

The individuals who set policies for the colleges need to say, "We pledge to keep working at a specific pattern of functioning until it works or until we have clear-cut evidence that it is an improper way to proceed." Failing this, the technique—pedagogical, curricular, organizational—does not penetrate the thinking of the people within the institution to the level of their own work and total thought. The innovation remains superficial and unrelated, leading to the all too prevalent attitude of laissez-faire, or a feeling of, "Why bother? Something else will be around tomorrow." Much more needed than a climate of innovation are minimum five-year-long commitments to try out certain modes of organization, processes, or institutional objectives.

The study of instruction, the preparation of instructors, and the postulation of alternatives are only three possible lines of distinct involvement that can lead the junior college toward maturity. There are others. The junior college might, for example, focus many of its activities on upgrading the community. As a center for cultural activities—theater, art exhibits, music, dance—and as a locus for research on community problems, the college could be a viable, important interactor. It could serve as a guidance center—engaged in evaluation, vocational placement, and data compilation. Here again, its liaison function becomes apparent. The school would provide information for decision making about vocational, academic, and personal directions and goals. It might even act as a placement steering committee, much as did the Veterans' Guidance Centers of post–World War II days. A further involvement might be as a resource center, disseminating information about various community agencies, educational and otherwise. It would make periodic pronouncements regarding the state of the community's psychic health and would offer consulting services to other educational endeavors—for example, to elementary schools and adult education segments.

Whatever directions such efforts take, the point is the same: clear-cut definition of intent is essential for an institution that purports to be educational. If, for example, custodial care of the young is the junior college's main function—as some have suggested—let this be openly acknowledged and as widely defended. Honest self-examination and public recognition of the function would in themselves be refreshing alternatives to the more frequent grandiloquent statements of ambiguity.

TOWARD THE MATURE PROFESSION

Just as the institution cannot usefully exist primarily to perpetuate itself, the profession must guard against falling into a similar trap of its own making. Some of the problems associated with an institutional focus on self-preservation have been discussed. Tyler (1967) notes that after a school has been in operation a number of years, it begins to believe that it is its own raison d'être. Frequently such an emphasis leads to both sterility and decay—to the institution's becoming an empty shell, preserved for its own sake but no longer viable in terms of its effects. The college that focuses on preservation rather than on purpose is doomed to fail in its service functions, no longer satisfying its professionals and clientele. As Gardner (1963) points out, an institution must be self-renewing and more concerned with changing direction, scope, function, and purpose than with furthering its own life.

The same phenomenon applies to every discipline of organized knowledge and to every profession. Speaking of academic areas, Bevan states that

> . . . as it develops, [every discipline] inevitably turns in on itself, defines
> and redefines its own problems, and continually elaborates its structures
> in terms of these internal concerns. Thus, it may become dissociated, in
> this introverted state, from the problems and phenomena that gave rise to
> it or that others, including the layman, identify with it. (1970, p. 442)

Within the junior college, institutionalism may well be breaking down. The students enter for a semester, drop out to take jobs in the community, drop back into school, drop out to go into the service, and return again in recurring cycles. Short courses and community services become ever more important. Many colleges have greater numbers of part-time students who are *not* working toward academic degrees than they have full-time students. The picture of the college as a housing for an isolate group of instructors who offer singular patterns of classes with certificates to be given at the end of specified periods of attendance is no longer accurate. The college is becoming ever more responsive to its constituency.

This trend toward merging the institution with the community's general education effort has distinct implications for the teaching profession. As the institution develops in the direction of greater involvement with the community, the profession will evolve along with it. The breakdown in the institutionalization of education will tend to foster a move toward a profession that is accountable to itself, not to the agency known as "school." The profession will become responsible for setting its own selection criteria and standards of practice. This will demand a unique form of professionalism that blends teaching, distinct service to the community, and inquiry into the discipline of instruction. In this context, the profession will divorce itself from the institution and become more than "school" as it is known today. As it attains a sense of identity, the teaching profession will take its own form. And as it becomes comfortable with this unique structure, it can focus on evaluating its effort—and thus gain its own maturity.

The profession may split along several lines. One group of instructors will incorporate principles of instruction, assess its own effects, and assume responsibility for deliberately shaping its students and its community. Other instructors will offer casual, short courses on whatever strikes their fancy. Many of the latter group are presently in the experimental or "free" universities that have sprung up around existing institutions. These are part-time instructors who, in fact, owe their allegiance to other disciplines or simply to other employment positions. The casual instructor will drop in and out of the teaching role; the professional instructor will base his position and standing in the community on the learning he brings about. Yet both will be "teachers."

As spokesmen for the occupation, the professional associations have distinct roles to play in the movement toward a teaching profession that is broader than the institutions themselves. While teacher organizations are presently little involved in educational management, choosing instead to address working conditions, salaries, and fringe benefits, some associations—in particular those at the state level—have begun to involve themselves with questions of professional responsibility, functioning, and integrity. The mature profession would require that its associations become involved with these types of questions and move away from the trade union stance.

On the local level, the faculty association can similarly adopt new roles. The time has long passed for it to concern itself only with petitioning for larger light bulbs in the faculty lounge. It could better act as a steering committee to arrange seminars in instruction, set up distinct evaluation criteria, and otherwise move actively toward enhancing professionalism. It is the job of the professional group to translate the findings of research on instruction into the practice of member instructors. The discipline of instruction requires professional disciplinary associations that go far beyond the function of protective and benevolent societies. Unfortunately, most instructors do not now see that their associations, by taking on this kind of leadership, would promote professional survival through maintaining professional relevance.

Toward the Mature Instructor

The junior college as an institution with distinct identity and the mature profession setting criteria and standards for its own people and attending to instruction as a discipline are both important. But the instructor with an integrated sense of self is the person to whom this book has been addressed. The instructor is the focal point. His institution's success, the maturity of his profession, and the learning achieved by the students with whom he interacts are his responsibility. The professional associations, the administrators, and the supervisors are important to the instructor because they affect his life. But in the final analysis, he must take charge of his own affairs.

Who are the mature instructors of tomorrow? The people now entering the profession reveal certain trends. In the early 1970s, more than ever before, people with doctorates were entering the junior colleges. There were fewer available university jobs, and the absolute number of people receiving doctorates had increased dramatically in the late 1960s. In the 1970s, the expansion of doctor of arts programs will tend to increase the number of people with higher degrees who enter junior college teaching.

Other trends are apparent. Many of the instructors who joined the junior college during the rapid expansion in the 1950s and 1960s had long careers in the secondary schools. They tended to overshadow the inexperienced people with newly minted master's degrees. This fact is neither good nor bad in itself; it merely shows that the modes of functioning that had previously been adopted for the secondary school predominated in a majority of two-year colleges. But the number of instructors who come from high school into the junior college may decline as the institution becomes more visible as an employment target in its own right.

One more trend in recruitment is that many people with experience in activities other than schooling are entering the two-year college. The person with twelve years of public school, four years of college, and two years of graduate school who subsequently becomes a teacher is becoming a rarity. Many options are available for the young person who is concerned with other endeavors; the Peace Corps and organized work with neighborhood youth are but two. More people will tend to engage in such activities before they turn to teaching. In that individual growth may depend on experiences outside academe, this may well be a positive factor.

Nevertheless, regardless of varying prior experiences, mature instructors must still be of a certain type. Clear-cut conceptualization of purpose reflects maturity in both institution and profession. The willingness to be judged by one's effects is a primary factor in personal and professional integration. It also reflects maturity by suggesting both autonomous functioning and value congruence between the individual and his environment. We have pointed out repeatedly that for the instructor to function as an independent, mature individual, he must face himself honestly and be very much aware of what he is trying to do. In our view, this self-awareness is a major indicator of an integrated being who is at home with himself and certain of his identity.

How will the mature instructor operate? Throughout the book we have commented on his arranging procedures so that he tends to judge himself—and to be judged—by his effects. Whatever role he plays—model, mediator, or instructional manager—he must be his own mentor. He adopts particular functions because they suit his personality and the needs of the institution and the people he serves. He adjusts his activities to his effects on his students. He becomes a professional instructor—one who causes learning. In his persistent search for consciousness of who he is, he continually asks himself, "Is it important to my students that I *be* what I am?"

The child crawls before it walks. The practicing instructor who would integrate self and profession should first seek small victories—for example, gaining measures of his effect on the basis of pre-tests and post-tests covering single lessons or single courses; or a readiness to ask for help in test construction and interpretation—realizing that each person has something unique to offer and that specialization may be more effective than duplication. His colleagues in the mathematics division, for instance, can explain statistical inference to him, if he needs this type of expertise.

The mature instructor may also move ahead by stepping back. Occasionally he can retreat into himself—searching for answers to some of the questions that constantly confront him. At times he may even manifest substantial primary-process thinking, certain that he can, when necessary, "snap back" to a more "reality-oriented" world. Such "regression in the service of the ego" (Kris 1952) suggests a high degree of ego functioning. For example, although he cannot avoid attending to the discipline of instruction, he can shrink back from the hordes of students with whom he must deal when such a maneuver is necessary to his own survival.

Only the person who is sure of self can afford to *be himself*, allowing expression of the many nuances of his personality, both positive and negative. He knows that meaningful answers to basic questions are never easily come by, and that in order to arrive at some kind of agreement with self, some measure of inner harmony, and some sense of directedness, he may well face considerable conflict between his own values and feelings and those of the significant others with whom he interacts. Some conflicts are not easily resolved; hence, they require a considerable ability to tolerate ambiguity. Such a stance demands a high degree of ego functioning but the mature profession deserves no less.

The flexible person, certain of his identity, fully professional in his work orientation, able to search persistently into himself for greater consciousness of all his processes of being, is the person who manifests a high degree of ego strength. The good teacher is the good person. Indeed, the mature instructor who would enhance institutional and professional maturity must be a decent sort of individual. Beyond that, however, the mature, conscious professional must know well what he is about and accept himself as a many-faceted, ever-developing human being.

Appendix

The rationale for the core course in the UCLA Junior College Teacher Preparation Program has been described in chapter 14. This course was constructed consistently with the program's teaching–learning thrust and is in itself a model for the courses designed by the intern teachers in their own subject fields—that is, the course, its goals, and its objectives epitomize its content. A list of the course units follows, along with explanations of why each unit is included and statements of unit goals.

UNIT I. THE JUNIOR COLLEGE:
FUNCTIONS, FACILITIES, STUDENTS

Rationale: The facilities and services of junior colleges extend far beyond the individual classrooms. The instructor should be aware of the variety of services available to his students and of the many facets of the college which can aid in curriculum construction. He should also consider the types of students who attend junior colleges, because their ages, abilities, and goals vary widely. Understanding the nature and purpose of the institution is prerequisite to the formation of courses and programs.

Goals: The student will understand the functions of junior colleges and the derivation of their goals. He will be able to apply these criteria to junior college practices. He will also understand the extent of facilities and services available in junior colleges and the numbers and types of students who enroll in junior college programs.

UNIT II.
THE JUNIOR COLLEGE CURRICULUM

Rationale: The curriculum is the main force within the junior college. It includes a complex of courses, programs, and subject matter, but all to the end that the students move toward cognitive and affective goals.

Goals: The student will understand the process of curricular development, change, and purpose. He will be able to validate course goals and understand and be able to apply the term *general education* to courses and programs.

UNIT III. GOALS AND OBJECTIVES:
CRITERIA AND CLASSIFICATION

Rationale: Objectives are the basic building blocks of the course, for through their use the instructor communicates specific expectations to his students. This gives direction and facilitates learning. For the sake of clarification and communication within the whole field of education, the Taxonomies (Bloom et al. 1956; Krathwohl et al. 1964) were developed. The terms and concepts embodied in the Taxonomies have been widely adopted.

Goals: The student will be able to write goals that are appropriate for various chronological positions in the curriculum. He will be able to write specific, measurable objectives and to apply taxonomic classifications to educational objectives.

UNIT IV. TESTS AND ASSESSMENTS

Rationale: Assessment of learning serves several purposes. Primarily, it determines the effect of the curriculum on each student. The ability to construct valid testing devices is prerequisite to all assessment procedures.

Goals: The student will know the vocabulary of testing. He will understand the uses of pre-assessments and different types of tests and will understand principles of item analysis. The student will be able to write test items that meet standards of clarity and direction for such items. He will understand the relationships among goals, objectives, and assessment procedures.

UNIT V.
INSTRUCTIONAL MEDIA AND DESIGN

Rationale: All materials and methods are mediators of learning. In fact, any controllable influence intervening between the instructor's communication of objectives and his assessment of their attainment may be considered a medium of instruction. The selection of appropriate media from all that are available is an important task.

Goals: The student will be able to select appropriate instructional media and to apply criteria for selection of media to texts and programs. He will write the specifications for an auto-instructional program in his field.

UNIT VI.
BUILDING THE COURSE

Rationale: Carefully designed courses are essential to curriculum construction. Teacher–student interaction gains meaning when it is pointed toward particular ends.

Goals: The student will design a complete course to be included in a junior college curriculum.

Each intern's course is developed from content and coverage suggested by course outlines on file in the junior college in which the intern will teach. The interns' outlines are based on this format:

1. Title page
   A. Catalog number and title of course
   B. Name of instructor preparing outline
   C. Name of college
   D. Date of preparation
2. Course description; this should include:
   A. Curricular placement: (transfer, terminal—to what specific curriculum is the course assigned)
   B. Time assignment: hours per week, lecture, laboratory, or activity
   C. Description of student population (estimate)
      (1) Ability levels of students
      (2) Institutions to which students transfer or occupation which they enter
      (3) Anticipated student dropout rate
3. Glossary—definitions of terms used in the subject area (if appropriate)
4. Course content
   A. Statement of major course objectives validated in terms of relationship to goals of the college
   B. List of units or areas of instruction
      (1) List of unit titles
      (2) Time allotted for each unit
5. Materials of instruction
   A. Statement of required texts and manuals
   B. Bibliography of library materials
   C. List of audiovisual materials: films, slides, tapes, programmed instruction
6. Organization of each unit of instruction
   A. Statement of major concepts (tied with course on file with junior college dean)

       B. Goals: list of specific measurable objectives
          (1) Type of behavior
          (2) Criterion of performance
          (3) Conditions of performance
       C. Planned activities
          (1) Materials of instruction
          (2) Assignments to be made
       D. Pre- and post-assessment
          (1) Level of achievement intended
          (2) Sample test items
    7. Instructor's evaluation
       A. Procedures for revising course
       B. Provision for students who fail to meet level

Unit VII. Assessment of Curriculum and Instruction

Rationale: The entire curriculum must be assessed periodically in light of changing populations and community needs or it is in danger of losing relevance. Similarly, each course within the curriculum needs regular inspection to insure that it continues to be appropriate. The assessment of curriculum, courses, and instructional achievement is a necessary, continuing process.

Goals: The student will be able to report pupil progress toward specific objectives. He will design appropriate procedures for assessing effects of junior college courses.

Each goal within each unit in the core course includes its own set of specific, measurable objectives. These objectives are arranged sequentially and range from those demanding simplest recall tasks to those that call for complex higher-order behaviors. The objectives logically tie to the goals. Whereas "the student will understand . . . " represents a process of mind, defined objectives state clearly what he will do to indicate his understanding. A set of objectives included in one goal in Unit III will illustrate.

Goal: The student will be able to write specific measurable objectives.

Objectives: He will list and define in ten words or less the three criteria for specific objectives. (100%)

              Given a list of objectives, he will distinguish between those that do and those that do not meet the criteria for specific objectives. (90%)

              Given a list of objectives, he will note the reasons why they fail to meet the criteria for specific objectives. (80%)

              Given a goal, he will restate it in terms of objectives which meet the criteria for specific objectives. (80%)

Outside class, he will write one to three specific objectives that
stem from each of the goals he has previously submitted.
(100%)

In this example, the student is led from the simple task of defining
criteria for objectives through restating objectives to writing his own
objectives. Each task carries its own minimum achievement standard that
must be fulfilled before he moves on to the next task. Goals and objectives
are not simply content that must be covered. They are clear statements
of abilities that must be demonstrated. As such, they lend precise direction to course assignments and activities. Copies of the entire course are
available from the ERIC Document Reproduction Service (ED 015 760).
For further details, see Cohen, *Objectives for College Courses* (1970b).

Further
Readings

The major concepts discussed in each of the sections of this book are given detailed treatment in the following works:

INTRODUCTION: A QUESTION OF IDENTITY

Erik Erikson has developed the concept of identity in several of his books, particularly *Childhood and Society* (1950). A readable interpretation of the concept may also be found in Theodore Lidz's *The Person* (1968). Abraham H. Maslow's *Motivation and Personality* (1954) examines the actualization process of the individual, a concept that is very closely tied with the search for identity. More general but also related is *Maturity in High School Teaching*, by Gail Inlow (2nd ed., 1970).

PART ONE: WHO AM I?

The history of higher education in America is covered in many sources, particularly in Frederick Rudolph's *The American College and University* (Vintage Books edition, 1965), while the concept of general education is well described in Lewis B. Mayhew's *General Education: An Account and Appraisal* (1960).

The development of the individual in higher education has been recounted by Nevitt Sanford in *The American College* (1962) and in *Where Colleges Fail* (1967). Joseph Katz's *No Time For Youth* (1968) offers another comprehensive account of the developing college student.

A good basic text on the development and functions of the junior college is James Thornton's *The Community Junior College* (2nd ed., 1966). *The Two Year College: A Social Synthesis*, by Blocker, Plummer, and Richardson (1965), offers another view.

PART TWO: TRAITS AND TYPOLOGIES

Many studies of teacher traits are reviewed by Getzels and Jackson in their chapter on "The Teacher's Personality and Characteristics" in *Handbook of Research on Teaching* (1963). Accounts of various types of teachers may be found in the familiar "how to teach" textbooks. However, for a conceptual approach to typology, see C. G. Jung, *Psychological Types* (1923), and E. Spranger, *Types of Man* (1928).

The concepts of creativity, flexibility, and authoritarianism have been discussed by numerous psychological and sociological researchers. For creativity in college, see *The Creative College Student: an Unmet Challenge* by Paul Heist (1968), and D. W. MacKinnon, *Selection and Educational Differentiation* (1960). Arthur Koestler's *The Act of Creation* (1964) is a monumental treatment of the concept in general.

The flexible teacher has long been sought. Postman and Weingartner's *Teaching as a Subversive Activity* (1969) and many of John Holt's books (for example, *How Children Learn* [1967]) call for teachers who can shift directions as indicated by the classroom situation. Jones's *Fantasy and Feeling in Education* (1968) is another in the genre. Authoritarianism is documented in the definitive work, *The Authoritarian Personality* (1950), by Adorno, Frenkel-Brunswik, Levinson, and Sanford.

PART THREE: ROLES AND IMAGES

T. R. Sarbin's chapter on role theory (in G. Lindzey's *Handbook of Social Psychology*, 1954) is a particularly useful treatise on the subject. The function or sub-role of "model" is implicit in Gilbert Highet's *The Art of Teaching* (1950); of "mediator," in Carl Rogers's *Freedom to Learn* (1969); and of "manager," in W. Kenneth Richmond's *The Education Industry* (1969) as well as in the various volumes of *Educational Technology* magazine. Certain chapters in Nevitt Sanford's *The American College* (1962) are also applicable to these concepts.

PART FOUR: INSTRUCTOR AND STUDENT

The many dimensions of teaching have been explored in a number of general works addressed to professional instructors and teachers in training. One particularly useful collection of articles is included in K. Yamamoto's *Teaching: Essays and Readings* (1969). Bandman and Guttchen's *Philosophical Essays on Teachings* (1969) is another worthy collection.

The study of teacher–student interaction has been summarized in the *Handbook of Research on Teaching* (1963), particularly in the chapters entitled "Measuring Classroom Behavior by Systematic Observation," by Medley and Mitzel; "Social Interaction in the Classroom," by Withall and Lewis; and "Research on Teaching at the College and University Level," by McKeachie.

Much of the research on junior college students has been summarized by K. Patricia Cross in *The Junior College Student: A Research Description* (1968).

PART FIVE: ON BECOMING A TEACHER

The professional associations that address themselves particularly to community college instructors disseminate much literature detailing their own activities. The National Faculty Association for Community and Junior Colleges, the American Association of University Professors, and the American Federation of Teachers publish numerous pamphlets and articles. The American Association of Junior Colleges also can provide information about certification requirements and related matters. The *Junior College Journal* and other specialized publications are available from the Association.

Various teacher preparation programs are described in *Focus on Learning: Preparing Teachers for the Two Year College* (1968), by Arthur Cohen and Florence Brawer. New directions for teacher preparation have been summarized by E. Cohen in *Faculty for Teaching–Learning* (1970), available from ERIC Document Reproduction Service (ED 038 133).

PART SIX: INPUTS TO PROFESSIONALISM

The evaluation of teachers and teaching is a thoroughly documented topic. *Measuring Faculty Performance* (1969), by A. Cohen and F. Brawer, summarizes much of the research on the topic. *Current Research on Instruction* (1969), edited by Richard C. Anderson and others, is a useful collection of articles. The yearbooks of the National Society for the Study of Education are a mine of information on the topic.

EPILOGUE: TOWARD MATURITY

Except for an occasional article, detailed schemes for alternatives to the present patterns of community college education are difficult to find. William Birenbaum's *A College in the City* (1969) is useful, as is *Campus 1980* (1968), edited by Alvin C. Eurich. Ivan Illich and Everett Reimer of CIDOC in Cuernavaca, Mexico, frequently propose alternatives. Their work has appeared in *Saturday Review, New York Review of Books*, and elsewhere. Arthur Cohen's *Dateline '79: Heretical Concepts for the Community College* (1969) offers a model for a college built on a defined outcomes format.

Bibliography

Adelson, Joseph. "The Teacher as a Model." In *The American College*, edited by N. Sanford. New York: John Wiley, 1962.

Adorno, T. W.; Frenkel-Brunswik, Else; Levinson, D. J.; and Sanford, N. *The Authoritarian Personality*. New York: Harper, 1950.

Allen, James E., Jr. "Does Anybody Hear?" Address given at commencement exercises, University of Notre Dame, Notre Dame, Indiana, 7 June 1970.

Allen, Lucille A., and Sutherland, Robert L. *Role Conflicts and Congruences Experienced by New Faculty Members as They Enter the Culture of a College Community*. Austin, Texas: University of Texas, Hogg Foundation for Mental Health, 1963.

American Association of Junior Colleges. *To Work in a Junior College*. Washington, D.C.: American Association of Junior Colleges, 1966. (ED 032 886)*

Amidon, Edmund, and Flanders, Ned A. *The Role of the Teacher in the Classroom: A Manual for Understanding and Improving Teachers' Classroom Behavior*. Minneapolis, Minnesota: Paul S. Amidon and Associates, 1963.

Anderson, Harold M. "A Study of Certain Criteria of Teaching Effectiveness." *Journal of Experimental Education* 23(1954):41–71.

*ED numbers refer to documents available from ERIC Document Reproduction Service, P.O. Drawer O, Bethesda, Maryland 20014.

Anderson, James G. *Bureaucracy in Education.* Baltimore: Johns Hopkins Press, 1968.

Arrowsmith, William. "Idea of a New University." *The Center Magazine* 3 (1970):47–60.

Astin, Alexander W. "Personal and Environmental Factors Associated With College Dropouts Among High Aptitude Students." *Journal of Educational Psychology* 55(1964):219–27.

————, and Holland, John L. "The Environmental Assessment Technique: A Way to Measure College Environments." *Journal of Educational Psychology* 52(1961):308–16.

————, and Lee, Calvin B. T. "Current Practices in the Evaluation and Training of College Teachers." *The Educational Record* 47(1966):361–75.

Axelrod, Joseph; Freedman, Marvin B.; Hatch, Winslow R.; Katz, Joseph; and Sanford, N. *Search for Relevance.* San Francisco: Jossey-Bass, 1969.

Axen, Richard. "Faculty Response to Student Dissent." In *Stress and Campus Response,* edited by G. Kerry Smith. San Francisco: Jossey-Bass, 1968.

Bales, Robert F. *Interaction Process Analysis.* Cambridge, Mass.: Addison-Wesley, 1950.

Barr, A. S. "Appraising Instructor Behavior." In *The Appraisal of Teaching in Large Universities,* edited by W. J. McKeachie. Ann Arbor, Michigan: University of Michigan, 1959.

————, et al. "Report of the Committee on the Criteria of Teacher Effectiveness." *Review of Educational Research* 22(1952):238–63.

————, and Emans, Lester M. "What Qualities are Prerequisite to Success in Teaching?" *Nation's Schools* 6(1930):60–64.

Barr, Stringfellow. *Purely Academic, a Novel.* New York: Simon and Schuster, 1958.

Beardslee, D. C., and O'Dowd, D. D. "College Student Images of Key Occupations." Address given at the annual meeting of the American Psychological Association, Cincinnati, Ohio, September 1959.

Bellack, Arno A., et al. *The Language of the Classroom: Meanings Communicated in High School Teaching.* U. S. Office of Education, Cooperative Research Project No. 1497. New York: Columbia University, Institute of Psychological Research, 1963.

Bevan, William. "Psychology, the University, and the Real World Around Us." *American Psychologist* 25(1970):442–49.

Biddle, Bruce J., and Ellena, William J., eds. *Contemporary Research on Teacher Effectiveness.* New York: Holt, Rinehart & Winston, 1964.

Birkholz, John R. *A Faculty Internship Program for William Rainey Harper College.* Palatine, Illinois: Harper College, 1969. (ED 035 407)

Blocker, Clyde E. "Are Our Faculties Competent?" *Junior College Journal* 36(1965–66):12–17.

————; Plummer, Robert H.; and Richardson, Richard C., Jr. *The Two Year College: A Social Synthesis.* Englewood Cliffs, N.J.: Prentice-Hall, 1965.

Bloom, Benjamin S., ed. *Taxonomy of Educational Objectives I. Cognitive Domain.* New York: David McKay, 1956.

Bode, Boyd H. *Modern Educational Theories.* New York: Macmillan, 1927.

Bousfield, W. A. "Students' Ratings of Qualities Considered Desirable in College Professors." *School and Society* 51(1940):253–56.

Bowman, Claude. "The College Professor in America." Doctoral thesis, University of Pennsylvania, 1938.

Boyce, A. C. *Methods for Measuring Teachers' Efficiency.* Part 2 of the Fourteenth Yearbook, National Society for the Study of Education, edited by S. Chester Parker. Chicago: University of Chicago Press, 1915.

Boyer, L. B.; Klopfer, B.; Brawer, F. B.; and Kawai, H. "Comparisons of the Shamans and Pseudoshamans of the Apaches of the Mescalero Indian Reservation: A Rorschach Study." *Journal of Projective Techniques and Personality Assessment* 28(1964):173–80.

Brawer, Florence B. "The Concept of Ego Strength and Its Measurement Through a Word Association Technique." Doctoral dissertation, University of California, Los Angeles, 1967.

————. *The Person: A Conceptual Synthesis.* ERIC Clearinghouse for Junior Colleges, topical paper no. 11. Los Angeles: University of California, 1970.

————. *Personality Characteristics of College and University Faculty: Implications for the Community College.* ERIC Clearinghouse for Junior Colleges, monograph no. 3. Washington, D.C.: American Association for Junior Colleges, 1968. (ED 026 408)

————. *Values and the Generation Gap: Junior College Freshmen and Faculty.* ERIC Clearinghouse for Junior Colleges, monograph no. 11. Washington, D.C.: American Association of Junior Colleges, 1971.

————, and Cohen, Arthur M. "Global and Sign Approaches to Rorschach Assessment of Beginning Teachers." *Journal of Projective Techniques and Personality Assessment* 30(1966):536–42.

Brenton, Myron. *What's Happened to Teacher?* New York: Coward-McCann, 1970.

Bresler, Jack B. "Teaching Effectiveness and Government Awards." *Science* 169(1968):164–67.

Brown, James W., and Thornton, James W., Jr. *College Teaching.* New York: McGraw-Hill, 1963.

Bush, Robert Nelson. *The Teacher–Pupil Relationship.* New York: Prentice-Hall, 1954.

Buxton, Claude E. *College Teaching: A Psychologist's View.* New York: Harcourt, Brace & Co., 1956.

Cahn, Meyer M. *To My Introductory Psychology Class: A Postlude.* Mimeographed. San Francisco: San Francisco State College, 1968.

California State Department of Education. *Summary of Source and Education Background of New Teachers in California Junior Colleges, 1963–64.* Mimeographed. Sacramento, Calif.: State Department of Education, 1963–64.

Caplow, Theodore, and McGee, Reese. *The Academic Marketplace.* New York: Basic Books, 1958.

Carnegie Commission. *The Open-Door College.* New York: McGraw-Hill, 1970.

Clark, B. R. "Faculty Culture." In *The Study of Campus Cultures,* edited by T. F. Lunsford. New York: Social Science Research Council, 1963.

————. *The Open Door College: A Case Study.* New York: McGraw-Hill, 1960.

Coffman, W. E. "Determining Students' Concepts of Effective Teaching from Their Ratings of Instructors." *Journal of Educational Psychology* 45 (1954):19.

Cohen, Arthur M. *Dateline '79: Heretical Concepts for the Community College.* Beverly Hills, Calif.: Glencoe Press, 1969.

————. "Developing Specialists in Learning." *Junior College Journal* 37 (1966):21–23. (ED 017 269)

————. "A Hierarchy of Disciplinarianism." Mimeographed. Los Angeles: University of California Graduate School of Education, 1970a.

————. *Objectives for College Courses.* Beverly Hills, Calif.: Glencoe Press, 1970b.

————. "Teacher Preparation: Rationale and Practice." *Junior College Journal* 37(1967):21–25. (ED 013 088)

————. "Technology: Thee or Me? Behavioral Objectives and the College Teacher." *Educational Technology* 10(1970c):57–60.

————, and Brawer, Florence B. "Adaptive Potential and First-Year Teaching Success." *Journal of Teacher Education* 43(1967):179–85.

————, and Brawer, Florence B. *Focus on Learning: Preparing Teachers for the Two-Year College.* Los Angeles: University of California Junior College Leadership Program, 1968. (ED 019 939)

————, and Brawer, Florence B. *Measuring Faculty Performance.* ERIC Clearinghouse for Junior Colleges, monograph no. 4. Washington, D.C.: American Association of Junior Colleges, 1969. (ED 031 222)

————, and Brawer, Florence B. *Measuring Student Characteristics: Personality and Dropout Propensity.* ERIC Clearinghouse for Junior Colleges, monograph no. 9. Washington, D.C.: American Association of Junior Colleges, 1970. (ED 038 130)

————, and Shawl, William F. "Coordinating Instruction Through Objectives." *Junior College Journal* 47(1970):17–19.

Cohen, Edward. "Faculty for Teaching–Learning: Proposed New Graduate Centers for the Systematic Preparation of Community College Teachers." Mimeographed. 1970. (ED 038 133)

Colvert, C. C., and Baker, M. L. *The Status of College and University Offerings and Service in the Area of Junior College Education and Professional Upgrading of Junior College Faculty Members.* Austin, Texas: Research Office, American Association of Junior Colleges, 1955.

Conant, James B. *The Education of American Teachers.* New York: McGraw-Hill, 1963.

Cooper, James G., and Lewis, R. B. "Quantitative Rorschach Factors in the Evaluation of Teacher Effectiveness." *Journal of Educational Research* 44(1951):703–7.

Cooper, Russell M. "The College Teaching Crisis." *Journal of Higher Education* 35(1964).

Cottingham, W. Thomas. "A Study of Faculty Departures in Florida Public Junior Colleges, February 1962–February 1964." Doctoral dissertation, Florida State University, 1964. (ED 017 243)

Cottrell, L. S., Jr. "The Adjustment of the Individual to His Age and Sex Roles." *American Sociological Review* 7(1942):618–25.

Cremin, Lawrence. *The Genius of American Education.* Pittsburgh: University of Pittsburgh Press, 1965.

Crispin, David B. "The Technology of Interaction Analysis." *Educational Technology* 10(1970):13–18.

Cross, K. Patricia. *The Junior College Student: A Research Description.* Princeton, New Jersey: Educational Testing Service, 1968. (ED 024 354)

————. "The Quiet Revolution." *The Research Reporter* 4(1969), (Berkeley: Center for Research and Development in Higher Education).

Daniel, Robert S. "Teaching Psychology in the Community and Junior College." *American Psychologist* 25(1970):537.

Darley, J. G., and McNamara, W. J. *Minnesota Personality Scale.* New York: Psychological Corporation, 1961.

Davis, Bertram H. "American Association of University Professors." *Junior College Journal* 39(1968–69):11–16.

Dixon, Robert W., and Morse, William C. "The Prediction of Teaching Performance: Empathic Potential." *Journal of Teacher Education* 12(1961): 322–29.

"The Doctor of Arts: A High Degree of Teaching Competence." *Carnegie Quarterly* 18(1970).

Dressel, Paul. "The Current Status of Research on College and University Teaching." In *The Appraisal of Teaching in Large Universities,* edited by W. J. McKeachie. Ann Arbor, Mich.: University of Michigan Press, 1959.

Drucker, Peter F. *The Age of Discontinuity.* New York: Harper & Row, 1969.

Dubin, Robert, and Taveggia, Thomas C. *The Teaching–Learning Paradox: A Comparative Analysis of College Teaching Methods.* Eugene, Oregon: Center for the Advanced Study of Educational Administration, 1968.

Dunham, E. Alden. *Colleges of the Forgotten Americans.* New York: McGraw-Hill, 1969.

Dutton, Wilbur H. "Attitude Change of Elementary School Teachers and Anxiety." *Journal of Educational Research* 55(1962):380–82.

Eckert, R. E., and Stecklein, J. E. *An Exploratory Study of Factors Influencing the Choice of College Teaching as a Career.* Minneapolis: University of Minnesota, 1958.

Educational Technology 11 (January 1971).

Eiduson, Bernice T. *Scientists—Their Psychological World.* New York: Basic Books, 1962.

Engbretson, William E. "Curriculum Relevance in Teacher Education." In *Stress and Campus Response,* edited by G. Kerry Smith. San Francisco: Jossey-Bass, 1968.

Erikson, Erik H. *Childhood and Society,* 2nd ed. New York: Norton, 1963.

Evans, Richard Isadore, and Leppman, Peter K. *Resistance to Innovation in Higher Education.* San Francisco: Jossey-Bass, 1967.

Eysenck, H. J., ed. *Handbook of Abnormal Psychology.* New York: Basic Books, 1961.

Farley, Delbert Ray. "The Image of the College Professor as Disclosed in General Magazines, 1938–1963." Doctoral dissertation, Florida State University, 1964.

Feldman, Kenneth D., and Newcomb, Theodore M. *The Impact of College on Students*, vol. 1. San Francisco: Jossey-Bass, 1969.

Fiedler, Fred E. "The Concept of an Ideal Therapeutic Relationship." *Journal of Counseling Psychology* 14(1950):239–45.

Fischer, John H. "Who Needs Schools?" *Saturday Review* 53(1970):78–79; 90–91.

Fishburn, C. E. "Teacher Role Perception in the Secondary Schools of One Community." Doctoral dissertation, Stanford University, 1955.

Fishman, Joshua. "The Pains and Pleasures of Evaluation." *Educational Horizons* 46(1967–68):25–34.

Fitch, Naomi. *Evaluation of Instructors in California Junior Colleges*. Berkeley: University of California, School of Education, 1965. (ED 014 959)

Foster, Florence P. "The Human Relationships of Creative Individuals." *Journal of Creative Behavior* 2(1968):111–18.

Friedlander, Bernard Z. "Today's Innovations in Teaching." *NEA Journal* 55(1966):11–14.

Friedman, Linda, et al. *Community College*. Chicago: New University Conference, 1970.

Friedman, Norman L. "Career Stages and Organizational Role Decisions of Teachers in Two Public Junior Colleges." *Sociology of Education* 40(1967a):231–45.

————. "Comprehensiveness and Higher Education: A Sociologist's View of Public Junior College Trends." *AAUP Bulletin* 52(1966):417–23.

————. "The Public Junior College Teacher in Unified Public School System Junior Colleges: A Study in the Sociology of Educational Work." Doctoral dissertation, University of Missouri, 1965.

————. "The Subject Matterist's Orientation Toward Field of Academic Specialization." *The American Sociologist* 2(1967b):12–15.

Gaddy, Dale. "Faculty Recruitment." *Junior College Research Review* 4(1969).

Gage, N. L., ed. *Handbook of Research on Teaching*. Chicago: Rand McNally, 1963.

Gagné, Robert M. *The Conditions of Learning*. New York: Holt, Rinehart & Winston, 1965.

Gardner, John. *Self-Renewal*. New York: Harper & Row, 1963.

Garrison, Roger. *Junior College Faculty: Issues and Problems*. Washington, D.C.: American Association of Junior Colleges, 1967. (ED 012 177)

Getzels, J. W., and Jackson, P. W. "The Teacher's Personality and Characteristics." In *Handbook of Research on Teaching*, edited by N. Gage. Chicago: Rand McNally, 1963.

Gleazer, Edmund J., Jr. "Concerns and Cautions for Community Colleges." *Junior College Journal*, 38(1968):18–21.

————. "Preparation of Junior College Teachers." *Educational Record* 48 (1967):147–52. (ED 016 489)

Goldberg, I., and Dailey, J. T. "Research on Academic Degree Projections: The Identification and Development of Talents of 1960 High School Graduates." Unpublished report. Palo Alto, Calif.: Project Talent, 1963.

Good, Wallace E., et al. "Faculty Profile: Kansas Community Junior Colleges." 1968. (ED 023 392)

Goodman, Paul. *New Reformation: Notes of a Neolithic Conservative.* New York: Random House, 1970.

Gordon, C. Wayne; Adler, Leta M.; and McNeil, John D. *Dimensions of Teacher Leadership in Classroom Social Systems.* Cooperative Research Project No. 1084. Los Angeles: University of California, 1963.

Gordon, Shirley B., and Whitfield, Raymond B. *A Formula for Teacher Preparation.* Washington, D.C.: American Association of Junior Colleges, 1967.

Gusfield, Joseph, and Riesman, David. "Faculty Culture and Academic Careers." In *The College Student and His Culture: An Analysis,* edited by K. Yamamoto. Boston: Houghton Mifflin, 1968.

Gustad, J. W. *Career Decisions of College Teachers.* Atlanta: Southern Regional Education Board, 1960.

————. "Policies and Practices in Faculty Evaluation." *The Educational Record* 42(1961):194–211.

Hakanson, Eugene Edward. "The College Professor: 1946–1965, as Revealed by an Analysis of Selected Magazine Articles." Doctoral dissertation, Indiana University, 1967.

Hall, Ray M., and Vincent, Antonio M. "Staff Selection and Appointment." In *Encyclopedia of Educational Research,* 3rd ed., edited by Chester Harris. New York: Macmillan, 1960.

Harris, Chester, and Liba, Marie, eds. *Encyclopedia of Educational Research,* 3rd ed. New York: Macmillan, 1960.

Havighurst, Robert J., and Neugarten, Bernice L. *Society and Education.* Boston: Allyn and Bacon, 1967.

Heath, Robert W. *The Ability of White Teachers to Relate to Black Students and to White Students.* Stanford, Calif.: Stanford Center for Research and Development in Teaching, Technical Report No. 10, 1970.

Heath, Roy. *The Reasonable Adventurer.* Pittsburgh: University of Pittsburgh Press, 1964.

Hechinger, Fred M. "A Call for More and Better Community Colleges." *New York Times,* 28 June 1970.

Heil, L. M. *Characteristics of Teacher Behavior and Competency Related to Achievement of Different Kinds of Children in Several Grades.* New York: Brooklyn College, 1960.

Heine, R. W. "A Comparison of Patients' Reports on Psychotherapeutic Experience with Psychoanalytic, Non-directive, and Alderian Therapists." Doctoral dissertation, University of Chicago, 1950.

Heist, Paul. "Professions and the Student." In *The College Student and His Culture: An Analysis,* edited by K. Yamamoto. Boston: Houghton Mifflin, 1968.

————; McConnell, T. R.; Matsler, F.; and Williams, Phoebe. "Personality and Scholarship." *Science* 133(1961):362–67.

————, and Wilson, Robert. "Curricular Experiences for the Creative." In *The Creative College Student, An Unmet Challenge,* edited by Paul Heist. San Francisco: Jossey-Bass, 1968.

————, et al. *Omnibus Personality Inventory: Research Manual.* Berkeley: Center for Research and Development in Higher Education, 1967.

Hendrix, Vernon L. "Relationship Between Personnel Policies and Faculty Life-Record Data in Public Junior Colleges." *California Journal of Educational Research* 15(1964):150–60. (ED 015 747)

Hilgard, Ernest R. *Theories of Learning.* New York: Appleton-Century-Crofts, 1956.

Hixson, Richard. "American Federation of Teachers." *Junior College Journal* 39(1968–69):10–13.

Holt, John. *How Children Learn.* New York: Pitman, 1967.

Holt, Robert R.; Luborsky, Lester B.; et al. *Personality Patterns of Psychiatrists.* New York: Basic Books, 1958.

Horney, Karen. *The Neurotic Personality of Our Time.* New York: Norton, 1937.

Howe, Harold, II. *The People Who Serve Education.* Washington, D.C.: U.S. Government Printing Office, 1969.

Hurlburt, Allen. *State Master Plans for Community Colleges.* ERIC Clearinghouse for Junior Colleges, monograph no. 8. Washington, D.C.: American Association of Junior Colleges, 1969. (ED 032 887)

Hutchins, Robert M. "A Constitutional Forum for Education." *The Center Magazine* 3(1970):83–85.

Illich, Ivan D. *Celebration of Awareness: A Call for Institutional Revolution.* New York: Doubleday, 1970.

Isaacson, Robert L.; McKeachie, Wilbert J.; and Milholland, John. "Correlations of Teacher Personality Variables and Student Ratings." *Journal of Educational Psychology* 54(1963):110–17.

Jacob, P. E. *Changing Values in College.* New York: Harper, 1957.

Janowitz, Morris. *Institution Building in Urban Education.* New York: Russell Sage Foundation, 1969.

Jencks, Christopher, and Riesman, David. *The Academic Revolution.* Garden City, N.Y.: Doubleday, 1968.

Jennings, Frank G. "The Two-Year Stretch." *Change* 2(1970):15–25.

Jerome, Judson. "The American Academy 1970." *Change* 1(1969):10–47.

Johnson, B. Lamar. "Footnotes on Junior College Standards." *California Journal of Secondary Education* 35(1960):277–83.

————. *Islands of Innovation Expanding: Changes in the Community College.* Beverly Hills, Calif.: Glencoe Press, 1969.

Jones, Richard M. *Fantasy and Feeling in Education.* New York: New York University Press, 1968.

Jung, C. G. *Psychological Types.* London: Routledge & Kegan Paul, 1923.

Justiz, Thomas D. "A Method for Identifying the Effective Teacher." Doctoral dissertation, University of California, Los Angeles, 1968.

Kaufman, Bel. *Up the Down Staircase.* Englewood Cliffs, N.J.: Prentice-Hall, 1964.

Keck, Donald J. "NFA Moves from Ideology to Action Program." *NFA Reports* 3(1970):4–5.

Kelley, Win, and Wilbur, Leslie. *Teaching in the Community Junior College.* New York: Appleton-Century-Crofts, 1970.

Kelly, George A. *A Theory of Personality.* New York: Norton, 1963.

Kelly, M. Frances. Unpublished manuscript, 1971.

————, and Connolly, John. *Orientation for Faculty in Junior Colleges.* ERIC Clearinghouse for Junior Colleges, monograph no. 10. Washington, D.C.: American Association for Junior Colleges, 1970. (ED 043 323)

Kelly, Robert L. "Great Teachers." *Bulletin of the Association of American Colleges* 15(1929):49–67.

Kinney, L. B. *Measure of a Good Teacher.* San Francisco: California Teachers Association, 1952.

Knapp, Robert H. "Changing Functions of the College Professor." In *The American College,* edited by N. Sanford. New York: John Wiley, 1962.

————, and Goodrich, H. B. *The Collegiate Origins of American Scientists.* Chicago: University of Chicago Press, 1952.

Kneller, George Frederick. *The Art and Science of Creativity.* New York: Holt, 1965.

Krathwohl, David R., et al. *Taxonomy of Educational Objectives II. Affective Domain.* New York: David McKay, 1964.

Kretschmer, Ernst. *Physique and Character: An Investigation of the Nature of Constitution and of the Theory of Temperament.* London: Kegan, 1945.

Kriegel, Leonard. "Great Books and Frozen Pizza." *Change* 2(1970):41–50.

Kris, E. *Psychoanalytic Explorations in Art.* New York: International Universities Press, 1952.

Lidz, Theodore. *The Person: His Development Throughout the Life Cycle.* New York: Basic Books, 1968.

Lieberman, Myron. *Education as a Profession.* Englewood Cliffs, N.J.: Prentice-Hall, 1956.

Lierheimer, Alvin P. "Changing the Palace Guard." *Phi Delta Kappan* 52 (1970):20–24.

Livingston, John C. "Faculty and Administrative Roles in Decision Making." In *Stress and Campus Response,* edited by G. Kerry Smith. San Francisco: Jossey-Bass, 1968.

Lombardi, John. *Student Activism in Junior Colleges: An Administrator's View.* ERIC Clearinghouse for Junior Colleges, monograph no. 6. Washington, D.C.: American Association of Junior Colleges, 1969. (ED 028 767)

Loomis, William George. "A Study of the Formal Preparation of Academic Teachers in Community Junior Colleges with Proposals for Oregon." Doctoral dissertation, Oregon State University, 1964.

Machetanz, Frederick A. "A Study of Student–Faculty Interaction in the Junior College." Doctoral dissertation, University of California, Los Angeles, 1969. (ED 031 230)

Malamud, Bernard. *The New Life.* New York: Farrar, Straus, and Cudahy, 1961.

Marking, Kasper. "An Analysis of the Relationship of Students and Instructor Attitude and Personality Similarities and Student Achievement in a Public Junior College." Doctoral dissertation, Washington State University, 1967.

Marland, Sidney P., Jr. "A Customer Counsels the Testers." In *Proceedings of the 1968 Invitational Conference on Testing Problems.* Princeton, N.J.: Educational Testing Service, 1969.

Mayhew, Lewis B. "Creative Responses to the Higher Education of the Future." *Nursing Outlook* 17(1969):28–33.

McClelland, D. C. *Personality.* New York: Welham Sloane Associates, 1951.

McKeachie, W. J. "Procedures and Techniques of Teaching: A Survey of Experimental Studies." In *The American College,* edited by N. Sanford. New York: John Wiley, 1962.

————. "Research on Teaching at the College and University Level." In *Handbook of Research on Teaching,* edited by N. Gage. Chicago: Rand McNally, 1963.

————. "Significant Student and Faculty Characteristics Relevant to Personalizing Higher Education." In *The Individual and the System,* edited by W. Minter, pp. 21–36. Boulder, Colorado: Western Interstate Commission for Higher Education, 1967.

————; Lin, Yi-Gwang; Milholland, John; and Isaacson, Robert. "Student Affiliation Motives, Teacher Warmth, and Academic Achievement." *Journal of Personality and Social Psychology* 4(1966).

McNeil, John D. "Antidote to a School Scandal," *Educational Forum* 31(1966): 69–77.

Medsker, Leland L. *The Junior College: Progress and Prospect.* New York: McGraw-Hill, 1960.

————, and Tillery, Dale. *Breaking the Access Barrier: A Profile of the American Junior College.* New York: McGraw-Hill, 1971.

————; Trent, James W., et al. *The Influence of Different Types of Public Higher Institutions on College Attendance from Varying Socio-economic and Ability Levels.* Berkeley, Calif.: Center for the Study of Higher Education, 1965.

Menninger, Karl. "Love Against Hate." In *Prologue to Teaching,* edited by M. Smiley and J. S. Diekhoff. New York: Oxford University Press, 1959.

Midwest Technical Educational Center. *Teaching Internships—Core Program.* Clayton, Mo.: St. Louis Junior College District; and Carbondale, Ill.: Southern Illinois University; 1967.

Miner, Robert W. "National Faculty Association of Community and Junior Colleges." *Junior College Journal* 39(1968–69):10–15.

Monroe, W. S. "Measuring Teacher Efficiency." *University of Illinois Bulletin.* Educational Research Circular no. 25. Urbana, Illinois: University of Illinois Press, 1924.

Mooney, W. T., Jr., and Brasted, R. C. *A Report on the Education and Training of Chemistry Teachers for Two-Year Colleges.* Stanford, Calif.: Department of Chemistry, Advisory Council on College Chemistry, Stanford University, 1969. (ED 034 523)

Moore, William. *Against the Odds.* San Francisco: Jossey-Bass, 1970.

Morse, William C.; Bloom, Richard; and Dunn, James. *A Study of School Class-*

room Behavior from Diverse Evaluative Frameworks: Mental Health, Substantive Learning, and Group Process. Cooperative Research Project No. 753. Ann Arbor, Mich.: University of Michigan, School of Education, 1961.

Morsh, Joseph E.; Burgess, George C.; and Smith, Paul N. *Student Achievement as a Measure of Instructor Effectiveness.* Project No. 7950, Task No. 77243. Lackland Air Force Base, Texas: Air Force Personnel and Training Research Center, 1955.

Munroe, Ruth L. *Prediction of the Adjustment and Academic Performance of College Students by a Modification of the Rorschach Method.* Applied Psychology monograph no. 7. Stanford, Calif.: Stanford University Press, 1945.

Murphy, G. *Personality: A Biosocial Approach to Origins and Structure.* New York: Harper, 1947.

Murray, H. A., et al. *Explorations in Personality.* New York: Oxford University Press, 1938.

Myers, I. B., and Briggs, K. C. *Myers–Briggs Type Indicator.* Princeton, N.J.: Educational Testing Service, 1962.

National Education Association. "The Teacher Looks at Personnel Administration." *Research Bulletin* 23(1945):93–147.

National Faculty Association. *Faculty Evaluation and Termination Procedures.* Washington, D.C.: National Faculty Association of Community and Junior Colleges, 1970.

National Science Foundation. *Junior College and Education in the Sciences.* Report to Subcommittee on Science, Research and Development of the Committee on Astronautics, U.S. House of Representatives, 90th Congress, 1st Session. Washington, D.C.: U.S. Government Printing Office, 1967.

Newcomb, T. M. *Social Psychology.* New York: Dryden, 1950.

_____. "Student Peer-Group Influence." In *The American College,* edited by N. Sanford. New York: John Wiley, 1962.

O'Connor, Edward F., and Justiz, Thomas. *Identifying the Effective Instructor.* ERIC Clearinghouse for Junior Colleges, Topical Paper No. 9. Los Angeles: University of California, 1970. (ED 035 416)

Oettinger, Anthony G. *Run, Computer, Run: The Mythology of Educational Innovation.* Cambridge, Mass.: Harvard University Press, 1969.

Orleans, Jacob S., et al. "Some Preliminary Thoughts on the Criteria of Teacher Effectiveness." *Journal of Educational Research* 45(1952):641–48.

Ort, Vergil K. "A Study of Some Techniques Used for Predicting the Success of Teachers." *Journal of Teacher Education* 15(1964):67–71.

Overturf, C. L., and Price, Edwin C. *Student Rating of Faculty at St. Johns River College.* Mimeographed. Palatka, Florida: St. Johns River Junior College, 1966. (ED 013 066)

Pace, C. Robert. Colloquium presentation, Graduate School of Education. Los Angeles: University of California, 1969.

_____. "Five College Environments." *College Board Review* 41(1960):24–28.

_____. "Implications of Differences in Campus Atmosphere." In *Personality Factors on the College Campus,* edited by R. L. Sutherland. Austin, Texas: The Hogg Foundation for Mental Health, 1962.

————, and Stern, G. G. "An Approach to the Measurement of Psychological Characteristics of College Environments." *Journal of Educational Psychology* 49(1958):269–77.

Palmer, Josephine S. "Role Concepts of Prospective Teachers of Young Children." Doctoral dissertation, Columbia University, 1954.

Park, Young. *Junior College Faculty: Their Values and Perceptions.* ERIC Clearinghouse for Junior Colleges, monograph no. 12. Washington, D.C.: American Association of Junior Colleges, 1971.

————. "The Junior College and University Teacher Training Programs." *Junior College Research Review* 5(1971).

Parsons, Talcott. *The Social System.* Glencoe, Illinois: The Free Press, 1951.

Peltier, Gary L. "Today's Salary Schedule." *The Educational Forum* 32(1968): 417–21.

Peterson, Richard E. "Reform in Higher Education—Demand of the Left and Right." *Liberal Education* 55(1969):60–77.

Phair, Tom S. *Third Year Survey Results: An Analysis of the Characteristics of New Full Time Faculty in California Community Colleges.* Mimeographed. Berkeley, Calif.: University of California, Office of Educational Career Services, 1969.

Phillippi, H. A., and Childress, J. R. "A Letter to Teachers." *The Educational Forum* 32(1968):403–9.

Popham, W. James. *Development of a Performance Test of Teaching Proficiency.* Final Report, U.S. Office of Education, Contract No. OE6–10– 254. Los Angeles: University of California, 1967.

Postman, Neil, and Weingartner, Charles. *Teaching as a Subversive Activity.* New York: Delacorte Press, 1969.

Pratt, George. "Flexibility of Personality as it Relates to the Hiring and Retention of Public Community College Faculty, New York State." Doctoral dissertation, New York University, 1966. (ED 023 382)

Prihoda, John J. *A Follow-up Study of Graduates of the University of California, Los Angeles Junior College Teacher Education Program.* Los Angeles: University of California, Los Angeles, forthcoming.

Reitz, Willard E.; Very, Phillip S.; and Guthrie, George M. "Experience, Expertness, and Ideal Teaching Relationships." *Educational and Psychological Measurement* 25(1965):1051–60.

Reynolds, James. *The Comprehensive Community College Curriculum.* Berkeley: McCutchan, 1969.

Richmond, W. K. *The Education Industry.* London: Methuen, 1969.

Riesman, David; Denney, Reuel; and Glazer, Nathan. *The Lonely Crowd.* New Haven: Yale University Press, 1950.

Riess, Louis. Article in *Preparing Two-Year College Teachers for the 70's.* Washington, D.C.: American Association of Junior Colleges, 1968.

Rio Hondo College. *Summary of Replies to Questionnaire on Criteria for Employment of Junior College Teachers.* Mimeographed. Whittier, Calif.: Rio Hondo Junior College, 1966.

Robinson, Lora H. "Improving College Teaching Through Faculty Selection and Evaluation: A Review." *Currents '70 from the ERIC Clearinghouse on Higher Education* 2(1970).

Roe, Anne. *The Psychology of Occupations.* New York: John Wiley, 1956.

Rogers, Carl. *Freedom to Learn.* Columbus, Ohio: Charles Merrill, 1969.

Rokeach, M. *The Open and Closed Mind: Investigations into the Nature of Belief and Personality Systems.* New York: Basic Books, 1960.

———. *Beliefs, Attitudes, and Values.* San Francisco: Jossey-Bass, 1968.

Rorschach, H. *Psychodiagnostics,* 5th ed. Berne, Switzerland: Hans Huber, 1922.

Rosenshine, Barak. *Teaching Behaviors and Student Achievement.* International Association for the Evaluation of Educational Achievement. In collaboration with Stanford Center for Research and Development in Teaching, Stanford University, and Teachers College, Columbia University, 1970.

Rossi, Nora, and Cole, Tom, trans. *Letter to a Teacher.* New York: Random House, 1970.

Roueche, John E. *Salvage, Redirection, or Custody?* ERIC Clearinghouse for Junior Colleges, monograph no. 1. Washington D.C.: American Association of Junior Colleges, 1968. (ED 019 077)

Ryan, Kevin, ed. *Don't Smile Until Christmas: Accounts of the First Year of Teaching.* Chicago: University of Chicago Press, 1970.

Sanford, Nevitt, ed. *The American College.* New York: John Wiley, 1962.

———. "The College Student in the World Today." In *The College Student and His Culture: An Analysis,* edited by K. Yamamoto. Boston: Houghton Mifflin, 1968.

———. *Issues in Personality Theory.* San Francisco: Jossey-Bass, 1970.

———. "Personality Development During the Academic Years." *Personnel and Guidance Journal* 35(1956):74–80.

———. *Self and Society.* New York: Atherton Press, 1966.

———. *Where Colleges Fail: A Study of the Student as a Person.* San Francisco: Jossey-Bass, 1967.

Sarbin, Theodore R. "Role Theory." In *Handbook of Social Psychology,* edited by G. Lindzey. Reading, Mass.: Addison-Wesley, 1954.

Schrag, Peter. "Memo to a Professor." *Change* 2(1970):5–7.

Schwab, Joseph J. *College Curriculum and Student Protest.* Chicago: University of Chicago Press, 1969.

Sheldon, W. H.; Stevens, S. S.; and Tucker, W. B. *The Varieties of Human Physique: An Introduction to Constitutional Psychology.* New York: Harper, 1940.

Siehr, Hugo. *Problems of New Faculty Members in Community Colleges.* Washington, D.C.: American Association of Junior Colleges, 1963.

Silberman, Charles E. *Crisis in the Classroom.* New York: Random House, 1970.

Simpson, Ray H., and Seidman, Jerome M. *Student Evaluation of Teaching and Learning.* Washington, D.C.: American Association of Colleges for Teacher Education, 1966.

Singer, Derek. "Do We Need a Community College Institute?" *Junior College Journal* 39(1968):36–41. (ED 024 388)

Smith, B. Othanel, and Meux, Milton. "Research in Teacher Education: Problems, Analysis, and Criticism." In *An Analysis and Projection of Research in Teacher Education,* edited by Frederick R. Cyphert. Columbus, Ohio: Ohio State University Research Foundation, 1964.

Smith, G. Kerry. "American Association for Higher Education." *Junior College Journal* 39 (1968–69) :11–17.

Sorenson, A. Garth; Husek, T. R.; and Yu, Constance. "Divergent Concepts of Teacher Role: An Approach to the Measurement of Teacher Effectiveness." *Journal of Educational Psychology* 54 (1963) :287–94.

Spock, Benjamin. *Decent and Indecent: Our Personal and Political Behavior.* New York: McCall, 1969.

Sprinthall, N. A.; Whitely, J. M.; and Mosher, R. L. "A Study of Teacher Effectiveness." *The Journal of Teacher Education* 17 (1966).

Sproul, Robert G. *Before and After the Junior College.* Los Angeles: The College Press, 1938.

Stern, George C.; Stein, Marvin J.; and Bloom, Benjamin S. *Methods in Personality Assessment,* rev. ed. Glencoe, Illinois: The Free Press, 1963.

Stratton, Alan G. "Needed: The Doctor of Arts in College Teaching." *Junior College Journal* 39 (1969) :19–23.

Summerskill, J. "Factors Associated with Student Attrition at Cornell University. Unpublished study, mimeographed. Ithaca, N.Y.: Cornell University, 1954.

Symonds, Percival. "Education and Psychotherapy." *Journal of Educational Psychology* 40 (1949) :1–32.

————. "Teaching as a Function of the Teacher's Personality." *Journal of Teacher Education* 5 (1954) :79–83.

Taylor, Harold. *Students Without Teachers.* Garden City, N.Y.: Doubleday, 1969.

Teilhet, Raul. "A Letter From Teachers." *The Educational Forum* 32 (1968) : 409–15.

Thomas, Caroline R.; Ross, Donald C.; and Freed, Ellen S. *An Index of Responses to the Group Rorschach Test.* Baltimore: Johns Hopkins Press, 1965.

Thornton, James W., Jr. *The Community Junior College,* 2nd ed. New York: John Wiley, 1966.

Tillery, Dale. *Differential Characteristics of Entering Freshmen at the University of California and their Peers at California Junior Colleges.* Berkeley, Calif.: University of California, School of Education, 1964. (ED 019 953)

Trabue, M. R. "Characteristics of College Instructors Desired by Liberal Arts College Presidents." Association of American Colleges, *Bulletin* 36 (1950) : 374–79.

Trent, James W., and Medsker, Leland L. *Beyond High School.* San Francisco: Jossey-Bass, 1968.

Trow, William. *Teacher and Technology.* New York: Appleton-Century-Crofts, 1963.

Tyler, Ralph W. "Changing Concepts of Educational Evaluation." In *Perspectives of Curriculum Evaluation,* edited by Tyler et al. Chicago: Rand McNally, 1967.

_____. "The Impact of Students on School and College." In *The College Student and His Culture: An Analysis,* edited by K. Yamamoto. Boston: Houghton Mifflin, 1968.

Von Hoffman, Nicholas. "Dropouts—Are They Just Tired?" *Chicago Sun Times,* section 3, p. 4, 11 January 1970.

Waks, Leonard J. "Philosophy, Education and the Doomsday Threat." *Review of Educational Research* 39(1969):607–21.

Wallen, N. E., and Travers, R. M. "Analysis and Investigation of Teaching Methods." In *Handbook of Research on Teaching,* edited by N. Gage. Chicago: Rand McNally, 1963.

Waller, Willard. *The Sociology of Teaching.* New York: John Wiley, 1932.

_____. "What Teaching Does to Teachers." In *Identity and Anxiety,* edited by M. Stein, A. Vidich, and D. White. New York: The Free Press, 1960.

Wallner, William. "Faculty–Student Relations and the Student Personnel Program of the Public Junior College." Doctoral dissertation, University of Illinois, 1966.

Warren, J. R. *Patterns of College Experience.* USOE Cooperative Research Project S–327. Claremont, California: College Student Personnel Institute and Claremont Graduate School and University Center, 1966.

Webster, H. *Research Manual: V.C. Attitude Inventory and V.C. Figure Preference Test.* Poughkeepsie, New York: Mellon Foundation, 1957.

White, William. *Psychosocial Principles Applied to Classroom Teaching.* New York: McGraw-Hill, 1969.

Wiegman, Robert. *General Education in Occupational Education Programs Offered by Junior Colleges.* Washington, D.C.: American Association of Junior Colleges, 1969. (ED 031 233)

Will, Richard Y. "The Education of a Teacher as a Person." *Journal of Teacher Education* 18(1967):471–75.

Williams, Cratis. "A Master's Degree Program for Junior College Teachers." Paper presented at the 6th annual meeting of the Council of Graduate Schools in the United States. Denver, Colorado, December 1966.

Wise, W. Max. *They Come for the Best of Reasons: College Students Today.* Washington, D.C.: American Council on Education, 1958.

Wittmer, Joe, and Webster, Gerald B. "The Relationship between Teaching Experience and Counselor Trainee Dogmatism." *Journal of Counseling Psychology* 16(1969):499–504.

Wortham, Mary. "The Case for a Doctor of Arts Degree: A View from Junior College Faculty." *AAUP Bulletin* 53(1967).

Wygal, Benjamin. "Personal Characteristics and Situational Perceptions of Junior College Instructors as Related to Innovativeness." Doctoral dissertation, University of Texas, 1966. (ED 019 964)

Yamamoto, K., ed. *The College Student and His Culture: An Analysis.* Boston: Houghton Mifflin, 1968.

_____. "Interprofessional Attitudes Among School Personnel: A Preliminary Exploration." *Journal of School Psychology* 3(1965):28–35.

Zamansky, H. S., and Goldman, A. E. "A Comparison of Two Methods of Analyzing Rorschach Data in Assessing Therapeutic Change." *Journal of Projective Techniques* 24(1960):75–82.

Index